CATASTROPHE SURVIVED

Catastrophe Survived

EURIPIDES' PLAYS
OF MIXED REVERSAL

ANNE PIPPIN BURNETT

CLARENDON PRESS · OXFORD

Oxford University Press, Walton Street, Oxford OX2 6DP

London New York Toronto
Delhi Bombay Calcutta Madras Karachi
Kuala Lumpur Singapore Hong Kong Tokyo
Nairobi Dar es Salaam Cape Town
Melbourne Auckland

and associated companies in
Beirut Berlin Ibadan Mexico City Nicosia

Oxford is a trade mark of Oxford University Press

Published in the United States
by Oxford University Press, New York

First published 1971
First issued in paperback 1985

British Library Cataloguing in Publication Data
Burnett, Anne Pippin
Catastrophe survived: Euripides' plays of
mixed reversal.
1. Euripides—Criticism and interpretation
882'.01   PA3978
ISBN 0-19-814038-X

Library of Congress Cataloging in Publication Data
Burnett, Anne Pippin, 1925–
Catastrophe survived.
Reprint. Originally published: Oxford: Clarendon Press, 1971.
Includes index.
1. Euripides—Criticism and interpretation.
2. Tragicomedy.   I. Title.
PA3978.B8   1985   882'.01   85-2935
ISBN 0-19-814038-X (pbk.)

Printed in Great Britain by
the Alden Press, Oxford

FOR
VIRGIL

PREFACE

I T is usually agreed that there can be no accurate discernment of an artist's intention apart from an understanding of the convention in which he worked. In the realm of Greek tragedy we know something of the physical modes, of the masks and buskins and long lateral entrances and withdrawals; we also know something of the verbal modes, though there is nothing left of the music or the dancing of this theatre. In the present study, however, I have concentrated upon another set of conventions that were in a sense looser, since they were not tied to the material facts of production. The conventions I refer to are those that directed the shaping of certain story-forms as they were borrowed from the single entertainer and recast for presentation by a singing chorus and a number of costumed and gesticulating players. Rooted as they were in the story-teller's mode, these conventions had a powerful constraint of their own, for they were known not only to the bard but to the audience as well, and were the source of the listener's conviction that an anecdote or a tale, a scene or a play, had been fully finished or curtailed, properly related or distorted in the narration.

The traditional tales of Greece had been told and retold; they had proliferated and stretched towards one another until in many places they had met, making a vast web of fiction wherein each part had its true proportion and its own ethical quality. Fragmented once again and displayed on the Attic stage, these stories brought with them their inner fictional imperatives and imposed upon the tragic genre a limited set of matrix-plots. Each of these developed characteristic scenes, tableaux and characters which could then be borrowed back and forth as the art of tragedy grew bolder and more complex. The return of a wanderer to his home, the display of a corpse, the attempt of a confidant to dissuade—elements of this sort, half-fictional and half-dramaturgical, were comparable for the tragic poet to the metrical elements that gave their cadence to the verse he wrote.

They were, that is to say, almost like his own heartbeat, their combinations and variations mixing in unconscious potentiality in his creating mind and dictating and censoring his play during its composition. The critic, like the metrician, appears after the fact to define what was for the poet indefinable; he tries to isolate and to classify in his attempt to make a vocabulary for his description of the indescribable. He may also be tempted to speculate about the history of the forms he is considering, hoping to surprise a poet in the timeless act of fitting his unique purpose to fixed and common mould.

The study of the typology of plot and scene is not new; as germinal to my own thinking I would mention, of many, two works, Richmond Lattimore's *Story Patterns in Attic Tragedy* and Eric Strohm's *Euripides*, in the last of which the idea of Euripides' conscious use of aberration is approached. I want to thank Miss Carrie Cowherd for help with the proofs, and my acknowledgements are due also to the American Council of Learned Societies, for this book was begun under one grant and finished under another from that generous source.

A.P.B.

Chicago,
March 1971

CONTENTS

I

MIXED AND MULTIPLE ACTION

THE essays of this book treat seven Euripidean examples of an unorthodox tragic form. Some of the seven, in slightly different company, have been called the 'happy ending plays', or again, the 'tyche plays', and all are usually classed as melodrama. They do not, however, all end quite happily; their plots do not reflect the power of mere accident, and their effects are not chiefly those of horror and sensationalism. On the other hand they are certainly all non-Aristotelian, as that term is usually understood, for these are dramas whose multiple plots revolve in both directions at once, mixing actions of catastrophe with others of favourable fortune. In them tragic reversal is shown simultaneously in its two contradictory forms, and though in the end one overturn upsets the other, each is made to evoke its own special set of emotions, so that the chief characteristic of these dramas is a meeting of conflicting moods. The heterogeneity of their action distinguishes them from other plays of multiple plot but constant overturn pattern like *Hecabe* or the *Phoenissae* and makes them seem instead, with their terrors and joys fulfilled and juxtaposed, closer kin to the satyr *Cyclops*.[1]

Aristotle described the best tragic praxis as the imitation of a single arc of overturn by means of one fictional event of major peripeteia, an event that would bring the central figure round preferably from good fortune into bad. He opposed the combination of several reversals in a single play, and he particularly opposed the mixing of the negative form of overturn with the opposite. Indeed, Aristotle almost seems to suggest that there would be a quality of aberration about any tragedy of multiple

---

[1] Technically both the *Heracleidae* and the *Supplices* might be said to belong to the category of mixed and multiple drama since each interrupts a sequence of positive actions with a single negative one of sacrifice. Both of these plays, however, seem to belong with the overt pageants like *Trojan Women* and *Phoenissae*, for in them each action is allowed to isolate itself as a discrete episode instead of being made an organic part of a truly compound plot.

and heterogeneous reversal,[2] but it is quite clear that the poets of the fifth century did not view the matter exactly as he did. The trilogies and tetralogies of the late sixth and early fifth centuries had, after all, been mixed sequences which found their true completion only when the final dramatic piece had come to its close. Presumably a trilogy could have been built upon the triple repetition of a single pattern of overturn, positive or negative, but judging from the evidence we have, this was not the poets' constant practice. The *Oresteia* begins with a tragedy of divine punishment; the negative pattern of its overturn is next repeated by a variant, the vengeance plot, and then upset by the positive reversal of a third, suppliant piece. The satyr play that followed was probably another positive action, this time one of escape, so that the total movement was from a redoubled negative to a redoubled positive form of the reversal of fortune. The Danaid trilogy apparently showed a sequence mixed in another order, its positive suppliant piece being followed by a negative vengeance play and then by a positive drama of vindication and escape from danger.[3] And likewise the Prometheus series, uncertain in so many details, did at least certainly juxtapose a negative punishment tragedy with a positive play of release and reconciliation. Evidently these older festival sequences had, like elegy and choral song, taken the repeated full circles of fortune's reversals for one of their favourite themes; the single, arrested, half-circle of overturn that Aristotle would have made canonical was typical only of their dismembered parts.

The discrete tragedy of single action that began to appear when the older sequences were abandoned must indeed have seemed a peculiarly artificial genre at first, a surviving fragment that had to pass for a whole. When a bit of human action was portrayed within this newly truncated praxis, that deed appeared

[2] *Poetics* 1453a30; here Aristotle posits a mixture of two plots that are impossible anyway, i.e., overturns of good fortune for the good and of bad fortune for the bad which would, by his own showing, owe their failure not simply to their heterogeneous combination but to their own flaws. Aristotle never discusses the true mixed and multiple plot, i.e., the combination of opposite overturns each in itself tragically satisfactory. He openly admires such a plot, in the *Iphigeneia amongst the Taurians*, but makes no attempt to find a place for it in his theoretical system.

[3] For the sequence of the Danaid trilogy, see A. F. Garvie, *Aeschylus' Supplices: Play and Trilogy* (Cambridge University Press, 1969), pp. 163–233.

to have stopped the surge of fortune, either at ebb or at flood, and thus the new form necessarily exaggerated the stature of men and simplified the character of heaven. Just for this reason, of course, the new disjunctive tragedy held out opportunities for the poet that were irresistible. With the discrete drama he could isolate a single human error, decision, or experience of pain or exaltation, and give it a new privacy and a new terror. He could force his principal into an artificial position of autonomy and so make him absorb within himself both the causes and the results of his actions. And in this way the dramatist could separate the moment of his play from the stream of time and, after the manner of the lyricist, make it both eternal and concrete.

The post-Aeschylean poet could hardly refuse the advantages of the dismantled trilogy, but the new tragic genre led him into certain risks. He had to give up the attempt to create dramas that might seem, like the *Oresteia*, to have neither beginning nor end, and in so doing he risked a loss of universality, for his alienated play, if it contained but a single change of fortune, magnified and frozen in its outcome, was apt to seem irrelevant to an audience that faced, in its own life, a manifold and shifting reality. Indeed Aristotle's rule, strictly, observed, would have forced the tragedian into a kind of irrelevance, for an autonomous arc of ascent or decline cannot be superimposed upon the incessant spiralling pattern of success and failure, rejoicing and despair, that marked the course of a man's life, according to ordinary Hellenic ideas.

Both Sophocles and Euripides responded brilliantly to the demands of the new genre,[4] but they showed, as they worked, a major preoccupation with devices that could introduce a covert multiplicity into the artificial tragedy of single reversal. Irony was used to uncover hidden contradictions in situations kept technically plain; choruses were made to consider tangential subjects or to experience unpredictable moods, that the play should not be crudely simplistic in its point of view, and in

[4] The *Philoctetes*, the two Oedipus plays, *Medea*, and the *Bacchae* are the only unequivocal examples outside trilogy of actions that are as single as Aristotle seems to demand. Both *Trachiniae* and *Hippolytus* nearly qualify, but both, like *Antigone*, come so close to organizing secondary actions about their secondary, destructive-agent figures that they are no longer truly single in effect.

addition the poets would from time to time dwell expressly on
the theme of the whirl of fate, as if to remind us that the rigid
finale to come was only an illusion. These, however, were all
merely verbal techniques for undermining the excessive unity
of the discrete tragedy. With peripeteia the dramatists found
that they could introduce heterogeneous truth into the action
itself, and so keep the grandeur of their pieces from swelling
into an over-smooth magniloquence.

Peripeteia is a specific scenic representation of an experience
of overturn; it is achieved within some lesser portion of the
entire staged action, usually in a single episode or scene. It is
present in most but not all tragedies, making them by the
Aristotelian distinction (1452a15) either simple or complex,
depending upon whether the principal is ever to be found at
one extreme of fortune at the beginning of a scene, and at the
opposite extreme at its end. Prometheus, for example, never
undergoes such a total rise or fall in any single section of his play,
and that tragedy is therefore a simple one.[5]

The examples of peripeteia that survive are of two general
sorts, here called major and minor, and it is with the second of
these that this argument is particularly concerned. Major
peripeteia occurs where a distillation of the tragedy's entire
praxis has become the matter of the stage action, as with Oedipus
and his discoveries, in the episode that follows the withdrawal of
Jocasta to her noose. The praxis overturn may be thus directly
pictured, or the scene may take a symbolic form, as it does when
Agamemnon submits to Clytemnestra in the matter of the
tapestries. It can also find a reflection in a bit of action that
employs a secondary character who suffers a revolution like to
that of the principal; it is to this last sub-type that Aristotle refers
with his example of the messenger in the *Oedipus Rex* (1452a25).
The second sort of peripeteia, the minor sort, is the representation
of an overturn that is opposite in its direction to that of the praxis.
Here, as in the major form, the actor may experience the
revolution with or without recognition, and he may be the
principal or a lesser figure. Thus Philoctetes, abandoned by
Neoptolemus (*Philoctetes*, 866 ff.), is suddenly brought from joy

---

[5] The recent discussion of D. W. Lucas, *Aristotle. Poetics* (Oxford, 1968), Appendix
III, pp. 291–8, exposes but does not resolve the difficulty of interpreting Aristotle
on this point.

to despair while he gains a new understanding of his situation, though the context is that of his positive reversal in a rescue plot. Old Oedipus can be cast down from hope to despair in the scene in which his daughters are taken from him (*Coloneus*, 720 ff.), though his play in its entirety is of the suppliant type that will move him from hopeless danger into confident security and beyond. And in the opposite sense Deianeira, a secondary figure, can be elevated to a peak of joyful expectation from her initial despondency, in the first episode of a play which is as a whole the imitation of Heracles' destruction.

Minor peripeteia is often spoken of as if it were merely a trick for heightening emotion by casting character and spectator up, just before casting them down (or vice versa), but this is an inadequate description of its purposes and effects. The poets of the single action tragedy soon discovered that an early scene displaying a reversal opposite to the ultimate one could establish a complexity of vision even though its illusory results were almost at once submerged in the dominant flow of the praxis. The brief emotional revolution that was created could not endure in its fictional host, but it did survive as a part of the total response of the watching audience. Deianeira's cry of joy (*Trachiniae*, 200) is the only such note struck in her play; its echo is soon lost, but the sound becomes an enduring dramaturgical fact. It is the brief imitation, in action, of the very different fates that women other than Deianeira have known. That cry, with its hint of what might have been, gives recognition to the existence of other truths and other terms upon which life may be lived, and so in a sense it verifies the impossibly narrow world of this particular tragedy. The cross-grained scenes of minor peripeteia are in fact vehicles by which a poet may philosophically qualify the assumptions that were aesthetically necessary to his play. Their use differs from the open admixture of opposing actions only in the realms of scale and permanence, and so an analysis of a few highly developed scenes of peripeteia may open the way to something Aristotle never quite achieved, a just appreciation of the compound tragic plot.[6]

---

[6] He very nearly does so, however, when he describes the plays which belong to what he calls the Complex Type (1455b34). In this passage he also distinguishes a Pathetic Type and an Ethical Type (and perhaps an Escape or Rescue Type), and it is plain that he is thinking not of form but of content when he says that there are

Best suited to the monolithic tragedy of single praxis was the sudden and impermanent change of direction based upon falsehood or incomprehension, and this kind of peripeteia can be seen in consummate realization in Oedipus' titanic 'Son of Tyche' speech and in the sprightly song that follows (*OR* 1076 ff.). These cap a scene that has cast Jocasta down in the play's true direction while it momentarily bore Oedipus up to his exultant crest of apparent success. The third episode of the *Oedipus Rex* is in fact a minuscule drama of mixed and multiple action, for in it Sophocles has drawn the perfect intersection of ascending and descending fortunes. The whole effect is only momentary of course, since Oedipus' sense of good fortune rests upon notions that are not only false but impious, but for its brief duration the scene is fully successful in arousing emotions of joyous release even in an audience that must also watch Jocasta and know the truth. Oedipus' moment of elation joins the play's system of references to his satyresque contest with the Sphinx to remind us that this is a man who has also known the sudden upward pitch of fortune's kindly favour, at another time.

Sophocles can be seen experimenting with another sort of peripeteia in the *Antigone*, and this time it is one that is built upon the actuality and not the mere illusion of co-existing, contradictory fates. The dramatist was engaged in this play in the dissection of an event, finding in the death of his heroine both her tragedy of willing sacrifice and Creon's of hubris destroyed. He showed these to be the bifurcated effect of a split cause found in a pair of linked decisions that emanated from the two contrasting natures of his principals. Sophocles had set himself the task of depicting this duality within the framework of the tragedy of single action, and so, having made his double analysis, his ultimate problem was to give primacy to the decision and the deed of his heroine. Her weight had finally to be greater than that of the character who ordered her death, for she was to

plays in which reversal and recognition are the very substance of the tragedy. This peripeteia that is no longer means but end is characteristic of the plays of interrupted catastrophe and constitute a third type of scenic reversal, one in which the apparent direction of praxis overturn is neither duplicated nor crossed but effectively upset. And this kind of peripeteia, as will be argued below, generally leads on to what is here called the compound plot, i.e., to one that contains multiple actions of more than one direction.

die as principal in her own drama, not merely as agent in a hubris tragedy. Her death, indeed, had to be made independent of the man who was responsible for it, if she was to have that tragic stature that Sophocles, above all others, instinctively understood.

The poet's solution to this problem was simply to destroy half of the causational system that he had established. And he did this by creating a situation that Aristotle was later to describe as the worst possible resolution for an intended crime (*Poetics* 1453b–54a).[7] He wrote a scene of peripeteia in which the temporary shift in the current of the overturn was based upon truth and reality rather than on falsehood and illusion; more important, this new direction of fortune was at once transformed into action. The tyrant's decision to prevent the burial had prepared the overt trap of catastrophe, and the girl's decision to honour her brother had made her enter it. The machine is about to spring when the author of the initial decision simply reconsiders it, and abandons it. Creon's change of mind is a practical fact, the genuine destruction of a genuine cause, and it means not only the abandonment of his action against the girl but the inauguration of a new action for her rescue. The scene with Tiresias is thus potentially the equal of Heracles' scene with the slave in *Alcestis*, for in each case a new purpose is discovered, a purpose that runs counter to the action of the play thus far and which will, when expressed in deeds, snatch the heroine from death. Unlike Heracles, Creon arrives too late, and thus Antigone takes neither justice nor mercy from the tyrant's hands, but the rescue action had for a few moments a fully-staged reality.

Antigone's suicide would have been technically sufficient to establish her independent relation to her fate, and the poet, had he made Creon's recognition of his error follow the news of her death, could almost have achieved that situation that Aristotle calls most deeply tragic amongst the plots of enacted crime (*Poetics* 1454a5). These possibilities were present, but Sophocles refused them, and chose instead to threaten the structure of his play by setting in motion a gratuitous counter-action that is kept from

[7] As an example of this mere abandonment of a course of action, Aristotle chooses another scene from the *Antigone*, the one in which Haemon simply gives up his attempt to kill his father.

interrupting the catastrophe only by a somewhat embarrassing manipulation of temporal chance. Clearly he expected great profit from this risk, and in fact the profit does accrue. Because a rescue action has been initiated, the audience is made to hear the account of Antigone's death against its own recently aroused fantasies of release, reconciliation and wedding festivities. It is obvious that the princess' fate gains pathos in this way, but far more important is its gain in authority. Creon's change of heart cannot reach Antigone because it is part of a world of ordinary reason and emotion, like the marriage she will never know. The late but sensible alteration in his decision helps to define the exaltation of her contrasted steadiness, but more than that it roots her choice in reality. She is not a doomed creature living in a hypothetical world of malignant forces, a figure irrelevant to human life as it is led outside the sacred confines of the theatre. She is not a moral exotic created by a playwright who seems to know of nothing beyond the tragic fictions of disaster. On the contrary, the play itself has admitted the possibility of a non-tragic truth—it has even imitated that truth in a portion of its action, and in so doing it has made its heroine, with her extra-ordinary strength and idealism, still a living imperative for the audience. The same impulse towards a simultaneous portrayal of the ideal and the real led, in the compound plays, to the development of opposing actions that were not artfully frustrated but were allowed instead to develop into full arcs of variant overturn.

The plays of reverse peripeteia thus offer a kind of parallel to those of mixed and multiple plot, but there is another and much older precedent in vengeance tragedy. Here the fiction determined that suffering and bloodshed would be dealt out by the principal; the play's praxis was the vengeance deed, and its central negative overturn was felt not by the doer but by the victim of the piece. The whole affair was, in its minimal form, curiously static because its central deed was retrospective and, from the hero's point of view, neutral in its effects. He, in the end, was simply returned to the state he had known before he had suffered wrong; he was quit of his debt to repay evil for evil, but otherwise his condition was quite unchanged. This meant that while it was easy enough to give ethical colour to the figure to be destroyed, it was extremely difficult in a simple vengeance action to endow the doer of the deed with any strong moral hue.[8]

The usual solution was simple but non-Aristotelian, for it lay in the introduction of a second, positive reversal to be felt by the principal. The effect of the *Choephoroi* is so powerful that it is hard to remember that Orestes' claim to the throne is there external to the simplest economy of the vengeance action and so constitutes a complication of the plot. The return of the exile was, however, an independent tale, a story that turned upon recognition and proof of identity (as vengeance properly did not) and that in no way required the shedding of blood. When this fiction is added to the vengeance action, as was almost constantly done in later plays, it means that the fulfilment of the negative praxis in the death of the enemy will bring new and positive results in the form of property, power and familial love for the principal. In Orestes' case these were postponed by the onslaught of the Furies, and came only in the subsequent play, but they are predicted, within the *Choephoroi*, by his own words and by the hearty vitality of the Nurse's scene.

When the act of vengeance was linked with the theme of the return of an exiled ruler it was no longer pragmatically neutral. It gained a permanent and institutionalized effect, and in becoming public it became more serious, as did the avenging hero. This is why post-Aeschylean playwrights continued in a frequent choice of vengeance stories that would allow them this added positive element. They also continued to exploit a second non-essential theme of the *Choephoroi* with a series of Electra figures. The presence of a second party, one who still suffered from the injustice of the victim-to-be, worked a thorough ethical rehabilitation upon the archaic vengeance hero, allowing him to raise and release a friend while he cut down an enemy. Without her, the principal could show only the single punitive profile of justice, but with her he could be drawn as a full and noble figure who recognized and responded to good as well as to evil. And so the sinister vengeance plot, compounded in this way, drew close to an opposite, happy action and began to

---

[8] The *Medea* is the only surviving example of a truly simple vengeance action outside trilogy; it demonstrates an extreme solution to the problem of making the unchanged agent more interesting than the victim, i.e. demonization of the principal, a solution also used in the final action of the *Hecuba*.

evoke emotions traditionally associated with romantic dramas in which an adventuring hero killed a monster and set a princess free.[9]

The simultaneous presence of both negative and positive overturn can be powerfully felt in the Sophoclean *Electra*, a vengeance play that finds its principal not in the avenging killer but in the secondary figure of the princess in distress. Here the poet so fully exploits the two opposite tendencies of the combined vengeance-rescue plot that, with a stage action still technically single, he creates an effect that is otherwise found only in dramas of multiple action, contriving the paradox of the fortunate catastrophe or, perhaps, of disastrous bliss.[10]

The arrival of Orestes at the beginning announces the vengeance action that is fulfilled in the final moments of the play, but the negative destruction of Clytemnestra and Aegisthus is here almost effaced by a major positive action, the rescue of Electra. In scenes that make brilliant use of brief and illusory peripeteia, the princess is forced from mere passive suffering into an active resolve. She takes to herself the unwanted role of vengeance killer, and then, in the late recognition scene, she experiences a permanent reversal of a new and saving sort. This scene constitutes the fulfilment of the inner action of the play, for it is so placed that it liberates Electra from what had come to seem a lonely and inevitable duty to kill. It liberates her from her fear and her isolation and her despair, from her whole unlovely crusade of hatred, just as the actual murders will liberate her finally from slavery in her father's house. This rescue casts her up in a triumphant rise that crosses the descent of her tormentors and complicates the pity and terror of their deaths with an emotion of the opposite sort. And the almost intolerable joy of the reunion of brother and sister is not a short-lived thing; it is not at once suffocated by a return of gloom, but becomes the continuing mood of the play. It is temporarily transformed into the joy of victory (which joy it softens and beautifies) and then, in our vision of the post-play world, it

---

[9] Except for *Medea*, surviving later vengeance plays are still Orestes plays, but conclusions may be drawn from the vengeance episodes of *Hecuba, Ion, IT* and *Orestes*, and from lost plays like *Antiope, Thyestes*, and *Cresphontes*.

[10] This is also the ultimate achievement of the *Bacchae*, where it has likewise been brought about by means of a subterranean action of rescue, the rescue of the Bacchantes.

grows tranquil in the pleasure of enthroned fraternal love. To protect this mood the poet has created a vague future free of the usual ominous threats. He suggests that these two royal heirs will move at once into the palace, and he is able to do this because he has forced the murder action into a subordinate position in his play. Electra's release has joined Orestes' return in such a vigorous assertion of positive overturn that the negative quality of the vengeance is effectively transcended.

Aristotle recognized the vengeance tragedy and saw peripeteia as the chief jewel in the tragic crown, in spite of the tendency of both to mix overturns of opposite sorts. In a third case, that of the interrupted catastrophe, he positively praised a plot that was openly diverse. In a passage that is as usual a little less than complete and clear (*Poetics* 1454a5) he specified a crime that was familial, intended, blind, and interrupted by a recognition as the ideal tragic event. Presumably he thought of the inter-rupted catastrophe as being still negative in spite of the quirk of its ending, and presumably he thought of it as still essentially a single action, since he had elsewhere stated that the best tragedy was single and negative in its overturn. A stage action entirely occupied by the imitation of the catastrophe to be frustrated would seem to be called for, but no example of such a play survives,[11] nor did Aristotle care to cite one, and a few moments' reflection tells us why. The interruption of a catas-trophe will almost inevitably bring a second action in its train, for if a tragic deed, carefully prepared and reasonable according to its own lights, is suddenly frustrated by a joyous scene, there is a danger that the spectator may simply choke on a crude superabundance of emotion. He needs help in consuming his exaggerated portion of pity and terror, and this means, in dramaturgical terms, that he needs a new action to absorb some of his contradictory response.

The play that Aristotle did cite perfectly illustrates the almost mechanical tendency of this plot towards the creation of a second action, for here an initial catastrophe is interrupted but replaced by another like it. The *Cresphontes* began with the return of a prince of the Orestes type, one who had been exiled by his

---

[11] The *Oedipus at Colonus* and the *Philoctetes* offer examples of a kind of mirror image—the last minute interruption of a positive overturn action, its success replaced by a success of an even higher sort.

father's murderer. The boy has been in touch with the palace through an old servant, but he has not seen his mother for many years, and she has long since been forced to become the usurper's queen. Cresphontes now means to kill the illegal ruler and to claim the throne, and he has formed a plan for gaining an audience with the king. Like Orestes, he announces his own death, and representing himself as the very man who killed the prince Cresphontes, he demands the reward that has been offered for that deed. His ruse succeeds and he is taken into the house, but before he can establish any liaison with his mother, she hears that her son's murderer is asleep in the guest quarters and she seizes an axe and runs to kill him in revenge. Her blind familial crime is interrupted only when the weapon is raised and ready to fall upon Cresphontes' sleeping head; somehow at this moment the old servant manages to convince her of the boy's true identity, and a recognition is effected. The fall of the axe is replaced by a maternal embrace, and the catastrophe is successfully averted.

This was the scene that caused Aristotle to cite the *Cresphontes* as an illustration of his optimum tragic event. It was a scene that Plutarch saw in performance, and he describes the effect upon an audience:

Remember Merope in the play, when she raised her axe against the son she thought had killed her son and said, 'I now deliver the blow you bought so dear'—what an uproar she caused in the theatre! The audience jumped to its feet in terror, fearing lest she should outrun the old man who tried to hold her back, and should give the boy a mortal wound.[12]

In the moments that followed the same spectators saw the blow arrested, the boy awakened, and a meeting of a mother and son who had for years been separated. With the axe still lying on the ground the embrace took place, and the watching heart, still constricted in panic, had to swell with love. This kind of scene was certainly high theatre, and it was also a vehicle for the telling of two opposing truths at once. The spectator was forced

---

[12] *Moralia* 998e; Ps.–Plutarch mentions the effect of a speech of Merope's from another part of the play (*Consol. ad Apoll.* c. 15, 110D). It is possible of course, that Plutarch had not actually seen the play, but even if his report is based only on hearsay it need not be discredited. On performances of *Cresphontes*, see A. Pertusi, *Dioniso*, xix (1956), 111–14.

to entertain simultaneously in his mind the contradictory conclusions that god is terrible in the dread fate he can provide,
and that he is wonderful in the bounty of his strange and merciful
releases. This was exactly the kind of profit Euripides knew how
to make from a true mixed and multiple action, but he also knew
better than to try to realize the whole of it in the last few moments
before his play was done. Instead, he drew off the blind horror
that had been made indigestible by the new and sudden joy
and transformed it, by means of a second vengeance action, into
the righteous terror that accompanies the witnessing of a just
and knowing act of blood. Merope followed the recognition with
an explanation in which she told how she had never ceased to
quarrel with her unwelcome spouse, and she and her son then
joined in an intrigue. They made a plan that seems to have
turned upon a trumped up reconciliation between husband and
wife and a parody of sacrifice, and they were successful in the
assassination of the king. This second, successful killing, the one
originally intended by Cresphontes, brought both mother and
son to a final peaceful residence in the royal palace.

In the case of the *Cresphontes* the two actions at least had a
constant overturn pattern, and the quality of heterogeneity
comes only from the rescue theme that attaches to the vengeance.
However, the second case of interruption hailed by the author
of the *Poetics* replaces its frustrated negative action not with a
second one of the same sort, but with a joyful rescue piece. The
play is the *Iphigeneia amongst the Taurians*, and Aristotle, in praising
it, praised one of the purest examples of Euripidean mixed
multiplicity. Evidently then a play that utilized compound and
heterogeneous action was not necessarily to be charged with
sensationalism; it might still count as a tragedy, even for the man
who made the strictest definition of that genre. It was in fact a
form with respectable precedents, moulded by serious purposes
and used by more than one of the classical dramatists. We know
at least that the two greatest poets of the discrete tragedy
experimented constantly with plays of more or less open multiplicity, creating dramas that mixed disparate elements in a
compressed imitation of the old three- and four-part productions.
There were real dangers in the attempt, for multiplication of
action does result in a dissipation of the powerful and simple
emotions of single tragedy which, once too often evoked, will

decline into philosophy. The spectator may begin to analyse and compare, to think and not to feel, but these of course may be the very responses the poet counts upon. Euripides, at any rate, seems to have felt that a multiplicity of contradictions in action could bring an enhanced sense of truth to the ancient art of tragedy, attaching its ballooning silken grandeurs more firmly to the earth.

The seven plays of this volume show a ceaseless formal experimentation but a steady poetic purpose. Some have only two actions, some have more; positive and negative plot elements mix in varying sequences and in varying combinations; satyr play motifs are strongly marked in some, in others almost undiscernible. Such variety might suggest that the plays belong together only by some quirk of definition, if their common heterogeneity of action did not house a common poetic statement. All seven plays in one way or another create a situation of catastrophe survived, and though they make differing dramatic analyses of that situation, all seven profit by it in the same way in the end. Each play shows human exertion to be blind and ineffective at best, sordid sometimes, and occasionally contemptible and cruel. And each play meanwhile depicts a divine pity and purpose that can, when it is ready, turn disaster into bliss.

This almost Hesiodic combination of cynicism and faith was not easily expressed by a fifth-century dramatist, for the conventions of the stage had been moulded by views that were at once prouder and more primitive. Old Comedy could show deeds that were incoherent and base, but it made them generally successful, and portrayed a contemptible world that was beneath the notice of the gods and got along quite well without them. Tragedy, on the other hand, usually depicted mortal exertions that were fully effective, for good or for bad—reified virtues or failings that provoked, in the negative cases at least, an exaggerated response from heaven. Only the heterogeneous plot allowed the poet to combine a comic view of man's efficacy with a tragic one of his responsibility.

The seven plays of catastrophe survived assert the possibility of virtue while showing it to be exceedingly rare; they insist upon its value but allow it no pragmatic use. The noble characters are finally as ineffective as the base, and yet all of them exist beneath a heaven that is the opposite of the indifferent sky of comedy, for every one of these compound tragedies has its interested, embodied, interfering divinity. Useless men and powerful gods meet together here much as they had on certain epic occasions, and like his epic predecessors, Euripides sometimes writes scenes for them that are sublimely funny. Here, as there, however, the effect is part of a serious purpose. The archaic notion of the sly foolishness of man could have a kind of protestant rigour about it, and so it does in Euripides' tragicomic plays, for virtue here is still demanded of beings who must watch that virtue robbed of every self-determined effect. These plays are, in their different ways, not a proud but a humiliating experience for the watching audience, and their unwelcome lesson in humility is made more inescapable than were the lessons of single tragedy.

Ordinarily tragedy did not deal with baseness or with foolishness, but it had made the blindness of men one of its principal tenets, and tragic irony, the device for conveying this blindness, had become the chief stylistic ornament of the classic stage. It was an elegant and indispensable tool, but irony had a major flaw as a teacher of humility, since it depended upon the creation of a knowing audience. The spectator who joined the poet in marvelling over the blindness of an Oedipus forgot to see himself in the blind man, for irony appreciated had made him feel as all-knowing as a god. Again and again the plays told of the dangers of misconstruing human strength and knowledge while their own inner symmetries were yet an encouragement to complacency. Euripides, who loved the effects of verbal irony, seems to have felt this paradox, and he developed in his mixed plays a set of counter-devices that would force the spectator from his omniscient throne. The multiplicity of their action allowed him to build terrifying structures of living contradictions, while the familiarity of each of their parts permitted a calculated disappointment of expectation. The known could be altered by mutation and distortion until the audience was forced to join the principals in their baffled groping.

What Euripides did in these plays was to exploit the conservatism of Attic tragedy for revolutionary purposes. He knew that the playwright who worked in the tragic genre had a tremendous power over his audience, because all of its responses had been educated by years of attendance at the festivals. The tragic plots were few, even the fictions were few, and the poet, in choosing among them, knew that each could evoke once more a unanimous, trained emotion and a wealth of predictable association. In a mood of conformity he would arouse the combined memories of all the other tragedies of his chosen type and then transcend them with variations that rendered the familiar motions of familar masks freshly awe-inspiring. If he were in a mildly experimental mood, the poet would still manipulate the same structural commonplaces, trying the effect, say, of suppressing a presumably indispensable scene, of filling an ordinarily masculine role with a woman, or of altering ethical valences while the action remained unchanged. A still more radical poet could combine these sophisticated practices with the creation of full-scale paradox as he juxtaposed one familiar action with another that was equally familiar, but contradictory in pattern. And when he did this, the result was far more deeply disturbing than any mere innovation could have been. The spectator found himself confronted with a stage world that had, moment by moment, all the appearance of banality but which jarred him as one may be jarred by the surrealist's confrontation of the teacup and the shoe.

Euripides' 'deviant' plays must thus be read against the 'norms' of tragic action that gave them their hallucinatory sense of safety betrayed, but those norms of course are never to be found in their pure form. Every written tragedy was a variant; the most memorable were apt to be those that varied to the widest extent, and these in turn were the ones most likely to be preserved. And yet for all this difficulty it is possible to deduce from surviving tragedy the general outlines of the six favourite hypothetical plots. These include three representations of negative overturn and three of positive overturn, so that each of the two major dramatic movements could be depicted in relation to a principal who was passive, active, or who acted upon himself. In negative overturn there were actions of punishment, divine or secular, in which the disastrous change of fortune was suffered by the central figure of the piece. There were actions of vengeance, in which destruction was wrought by the principal upon another figure, and there were actions of willing sacrifice, in which destruction was chosen by the principal for himself. In positive overturn there were plots of suppliants raised in which the change from wretchedness to good fortune was passively received by the principals; there were plots of rescue, in which it was wrought by one principal upon another, and there were actions of return, in which the central figure laid claim to a happiness rightly his own.

Each of these six actions might, in theory, supply a plot that was in Aristotle's terms simple or complex, depending upon the presence or absence of major peripeteia, and each could in theory exist in an interrupted as well as in a fulfilled form. In every case there was a wide range of possibilities for complication, nuance and shift of interest, but in every case too there were certain internal requirements and taboos that established patterns of ethical valence and dramaturgical procedure which seemed, at least, to be necessary. These traditional actions, with all their associations, their inhering moods and their pragmatic demands for certain situations and for certain human qualities, were the materials from which Euripides made his mixed and multiple plays. Least evident in his combinations are the plots that exalt humanity: divine punishment is subterranean to the *Andromache*, overt only in the *Madness of Heracles*, while sacrifice and return, the plots of noble self-sufficiency, appear only in *Alcestis*, *Helen* and the *Ion*. The suppliant plot, which normally praises god and the city, is used four times but with structure and ethos perverted in three instances, so that both the weak and the strong shall be touched by foolishness or error. On the other hand, vengeance interrupted, the natural plot of blindness and inefficacy, appears once in its most exalted form in the *Iphigeneia*, and twice more, each time in exaggerated and redoubled expression, in *Ion* and *Orestes*. Rescue is the final tragic-plot type, positive, primitive and usually secular, with an odour of the satyr play about it. In these mixed dramas rescue is sometimes muted, sometimes distorted, sometimes frankly maimed, and finally almost parodied in the *Orestes*, but it is present seven times in seven plays to provide the common symbolic action for catastrophe survived.

APPENDIX

CRESPHONTES

ANY reconstruction of *Cresphontes* must derive from Hyginus, *Fab.* 137 and 184, but we cannot be sure that all of the mythographer's details came from Euripides; his use of the alternative name for the prince proves that he knew other sources as well. The other secondary evidence is that of Plutarch on the scene of Merope's attempted murder, and this has stirred up a great deal of speculation as to how that event was staged. There are various possibilities. (1) The scene was merely reported by a messenger (Plutarch's description seems to rule this hypothesis out). (2) The scene was played on the *eccyclema*, which represented interior space (so Webster, *The Tragedies of Euripides* [London, 1967], p. 142, and Hourmouziades, *Production and Imagination* [Athens, 1965], pp. 105 ff.), but the scene was probably linked with an intrigue—was that also played on the *eccyclema*? If not, how do you step down off the *eccyclema*, from imaginary internal space to actual outdoor space, in mid scene? (3) A lateral area, perhaps one of the *paraskenia*, was used to represent the guest quarters (as may have been done in *Alcestis*), but when did the boy become visible there—would he sleep, visible to the audience but not to Merope and the old man, during their intrigue against him? (4) There may have been an attack upon a closed door, such as can be seen on one of the vases sometimes said to represent Clytemnestra (*Arch. Zeit.* [1854] tav. lxvi, a kylix from Berlin by Brygos), with the door opening and the Old Man catching Merope's hand at the same moment; this would not be unlike the penultimate scene of the *Helen*. (5) It may be that Hyginus has not reported the Euripidean scene— Plutarch after all says nothing about a *sleeping* boy—in which case a Merope who had gone in for her axe could rush out at a Cresphontes who had meanwhile come forth from a secondary door and been recognized by the Old Man. Fortunately, this problem does not have to be solved for the present purpose of considering the multiplicity of the action of the *Cresphontes*.

The major surviving fragment of the play, *Pap. Oxy.* 2458, Fr. I, comes from a gatekeeper scene. There is an unknown number of lines that look like monologue, then a gap in which the speaker evidently called someone out from the palace, identified himself to some degree, asked admission, and was refused. The scene then continues in stichomythia for something more than nineteen lines, and these make it plain that the stranger is Cresphontes, the prince, inquiring of a servant (of unknown sex, though the apparent display of sympathy with Merope at lines 32–5 suggests that it is a woman) about local affairs. It is to the point to compare the gatekeeper scene in *Helen*, where Menelaus, likewise seeking information and admittance, gains the first but not the last and learns to his surprise that Helen lives at this place. Here too it would make sense to suppose that the scene functions so that the stranger shall learn something that he did not know, i.e., that a reward has been offered for the killer of Cresphontes. The parallel statement in Euripides' *Electra* (χρυσὸν εἴφ' ὃς ἂν κτάνῃ, 32) shows how economically this fact could be stated, and makes it possible to suppose that this information was given by the gatekeeper in the missing lines at the bottom of col. 1, where the exiled prince is the subject of discussion. I think it likely that the boy recognized the reward as his opportunity, and bade the gatekeeper go in and tell the king that someone would speak to him on the subject of that reward.

Mette's suggestion (*Hermes* xcii [1964], 391–5) that this scene should be extended by the addition of Frag. 2, so that its two columns should represent the bottoms of cols. II and III of Frag. 1, is based on his reconstruction of line 54 (keeping the line nos. from the *Oxy. Pap.* publication). Here he recognizes frag. 1060 from the book fragments, and restores ἐχθροῖσιν εἴη πολεμίαν δάμαρτ' ἔχειν. He then concludes that such a remark should belong to the gatekeeper scene, where Cresphontes has presumably just been given some information about the queen. The identification of line 54 with frag. 1060 seems too good to give up (though Webster notes that *IT* 696 also ends with these same words), but there are strong reasons for rejecting Mette's order. If we add Frag. 2, col. I, to the stichomythia of Frag. 1, col. II, we get a confrontation between Cresphontes and an unknown person that ends with an invitation to enter (ἑστίας ἴθι, line 60) and yet is followed by a monologue that shows that Cresphontes did not enter. And in any case, who could invite a stranger to the hearth? It would have to be someone who was a master in the house, not an ordinary servant. (Clytemnestra can so invite Cassandra, or Orestes; the husband of Electra can ask strangers to his hearth; Admetus can do so, or Deianeira; whereas if the stranger finds himself dealing with a servant, he says something like 'let your masters know that I am here', as at *Cho.* 658 or *Helen* 447.) This line should belong to Polyphontes himself, and therefore the fragment should belong to a subsequent episode, when the king has come out. Does this mean we must give up Mette's restoration of line 54? The utterance of such a sentiment at first sight seems tactless in the presence of one who has such a wife, but the line might have been spoken

by the king himself .In explanation of the necessity for commanding
the murder of Cresphontes, Polyphontes might have made reference
to his wife's continued enmity to his regime. Such a reference might
also have been a part of his apology for having to doubt the stranger's
word and institute some sort of inquiry (as Hyginus reports he did)
since he fears plots against himself.

With the fragments left in Turner's order we have two separate
scenes, one a gatekeeper scene in which Cresphontes is refused
admission for the moment, the other a scene with the king which
ends with Cresphontes' entering the palace to await the results of
the king's inquiries. The first shows the major vengeance action in
formulation, the second shows it in the first stages of its success. It
seems almost certain that the first of these was a part of the prologue,
for Cresphontes' final exhortation to himself probably revealed to
the audience the newly determined detail of his plan to kill the king,
a speech (beginning at line 36, accepting Mette's τί δράσω;) that
could not have been delivered in the presence of the chorus. Thus
the prologue would have consisted of (a) introductory speech, (b)
gatekeeper scene, (c) brief monologue in which the prince prepared
himself for his interview with the man he meant to kill.

Since Cresphontes is left on stage, and since he cannot be allowed
to meet either Merope or the Old Man, it is reasonable to suppose
that the scene with Polyphontes followed at once. It need not have
occupied the whole of the next episode, however. After sending the
stranger indoors, Polyphontes might remain, and call Merope out
to question her about the status of her son. He would in turn tell
her of the stranger and his claim, and then go in. Merope would reasonably be left on stage to lament and then to try to revive her own
hopes, explaining to the chorus that she had recently sent the Old
Man for news of Cresphontes, and that she was expecting him at any
moment. (It is easy to imagine a monody, or a lyric exchange with
the chorus here, whose sex may be feminine, since the return to
Turner's order means that the masculine participle that seems to
appear at line 47 will not refer to them.) The next episode would be
the central one; the Old Man would arrive, tell the queen that the
boy was not to be found, and then be answered with her report of
the stranger come to claim the reward for his death. Together they
would agree, in a matter of minutes, to kill the murderer, and
would make the attack, which must have been arranged so that the
Old Man could get a good look at the victim just before the axe fell.
(Plutarch's words suggest a kind of race in which the Old Man tries
to catch the queen, which could be taken to support the fourth or
the fifth hypothesis above but not the second, since running would
seem to be impossible on the eccyclema.) The spectacle of the scene

seems to have duplicated that of another fictional scene that was perhaps staged in some lost play when Talthybius chased Clytemnestra and caught her axe just in time to keep her from killing Orestes and interrupting the murder of Aegisthus (best seen on a pelike by the Berlin painter, Vienna 3725; see E. Vermeule, *AJA* lxx [1966], fig. 12).

The argument for the continuation of the play is thus based upon Hyginus, whose report of the mock reconciliation and the mock sacrifice plainly reflects theatrical convention; it is also, however, based upon what is known of the opening of the play with its preparation for the vengeance murder of Polyphontes. And finally there are, among the book fragments, lines that seem of necessity to have come from the post-interruption scenes. Merope's 'manly' consolation (454 N² and 455 N²), which Ps.–Plutarch says the audience found affecting (*Consol. ad Apol.* c. 15, 110d) cannot have been uttered by the woman who was about to seize an axe and kill her son's murderer (likewise 458 N²); all these remarks belong to a time after the recognition. They are expressions of an assumed sentiment and so must belong to a scene of deceit, i.e., a second scene between Merope and Polyphontes though if this is the case, they were striking more for their conscious irony than for their consolatory effect. Merope's words about the murder of her first husband (451 N²) seem likewise far better suited to a woman who is engaged in intrigue than to one who has just received and half-believed the news of her son's death. The song to Eirene, Frag. 453 N², which Webster would make the parodos, seems badly out of place at the end of the dramatic prologue conjectured above, but it would follow nicely, as a note of artful pessimism, upon the extreme optimism of the recognition scene, or upon the false reconciliation scene between Merope and the king.

For all of these reasons it is necessary to posit a post-recognition intrigue between Merope and Cresphontes, then an episode in which the king is bamboozled and Merope offers to take part in sacrifices preliminary to giving the stranger his reward, and finally an appearance by Cresphontes and the queen, probably with the body of the vengeance victim.

II

ALCESTIS

THE oldest surviving play of Euripides is also the first of his experiments with the compound plot. The use of multiplicity in this little play is at once very simple and very bold, for the poet has not interrupted his first action, that he might introduce the second, nor has he placed a lesser action within the embrace of a greater. He has simply brought an action of death into blunt collision with an action of life, carrying the first to its fullest consummation—carrying the corpse to the tomb—and then allowing the second to undo all that had been done. Each of the plots belongs to one of the familiar types, and in this play the conventions, within each of the actions, are handled with unusual respect. There is little of that wilful distortion of normal character and situation that marks the later plays of mixed multiplicity; it is the juxtaposition itself that has excited the poet's inventiveness.

The first half of the *Alcestis* is a tragedy of willing sacrifice. It is a plot that we know in a number of instances, and one whose inner necessities can be quite simply stated.[1] The action in a sacrifice play is, like the action in a play of divine punishment, openly identified with the concerned will of god, and this means that except under extraordinary circumstances (as with the miracle at the end of the *Iphigeneia at Aulis*) this plot will not exist in an interrupted form. Its causal beginning lies normally in an express divine command, and often the announcement of this command makes up part of the stage action. This is not the

---

[1] Sacrifice actions in trilogy: *Seven against Thebes*; in tragedy of single action: *Antigone, Iphigeneia at Aulis*; as part of multiple plot: Macaria's action in *Children of Heracles*; Polyxena's action in *Hecuba*; Menoeceus' action in *Phoenissae*. (Evadne's episode in the Euripidean *Suppliants* is not really developed; the attempted sacrifice in the *Iphigeneia Amongst the Taurians* has nothing to do with this plot type but belongs rather to the vengeance category.) In fragmentary tragedy: *Erechtheus* (C. Austin, *Nova Fragmenta Euripidea* [Kleine Texte 187, Berlin, 1968], pp. 22–40); probably also the Sophoclean *Andromeda*, though this cannot be proved. On the constant elements in these plots, see J. Schmitt, 'Freiwilliger Opfertod bei Euripides', *Religionsgesch. Versuche u. Vorarbeiten* xvii (1921), 1–103.

case in the *Seven*, where the 'command' takes the form of Oedipus' curse, nor in *Antigone*, where it comes not from a single god but from the whole heavenly organization and is announced not publicly but by the private whispered voice of the heart that understands *nomos*. In the *Phoenissae*, however, Tiresias announces the need for a sacrifice on stage (911); in the *Hecuba* the demand is announced by the ghost of Polydorus, by Hecuba's dream, and by the chorus, who report the appearance of the demonic power itself, the ghost of Achilles in his splendid armour (40; 92 ff.; 108 ff.); in the *Children of Heracles* the command, which comes in a conjunction of oracles and signs, but refers itself to Kore, is reported by Demophon (408–9). In the *Iphigeneia at Aulis* the actual command belongs to the recent past, but it is reported by Agamemnon (89), and again by Menelaus (358), both times in direct relation to the interested divinity.

A sacrifice tragedy describes the death of an appropriate victim, a perfect individual, and in its primitive form it will not make justice any part of its subject, since it has nothing to do with punishment. There is no question of hamartia because this act of divine destruction, unlike that of a punishment plot, has not a negative but a positive, ritual purpose: it alleviates some evil abroad in the world. A sense of inevitability comes not from the notion of Dike, but from the divine command, and the death is made acceptable from a human point of view, not by a free past action of *dyssebeia* on the part of the principal, but by a free present action of willing piety.

The sacrifice death is given its highest dramatic value by being made to serve a particular purpose which can be imitated in the tragic action. The more unequivocally serious that purpose, the more serious the tragedy. Sacrifice fictions told of deaths that saved a threatened crop or man or house or army or city, but tragedy preferred the grandest of these objects. Family and city profit by Macaria's death, while it is the city that is threatened, then revived by a death, in the *Phoenissae*, and by multiple deaths in the *Seven* and the *Erechtheus*. Antigone's case is special because her death has been demanded in the first instance by Creon, and only ultimately by heaven's immutable laws, and so the question of justice has been introduced. Yet in the end Antigone, by her own choice, saves Thebes from polluted altars and from Creon's unregenerate tyranny, healing a city that was sick; her play finally becomes one that praises the ideal city, the city the heroine has taught the ruler to recognize, and this element of affirmation is necessary to the classic sacrifice plot. If such a play is to come to a comfortable close, it must celebrate not only the sacrificial victim but the object of salvation as well, for only thus will its defiance of our secular notions of justice be forgotten.

If the occasion of the sacrifice is diminished, the action itself necessarily loses seriousness, as can be seen in the case of Polyxena's death. Euripides, in the *Hecuba*, writes a full sacrifice tragedy compressed into a pair of episodes. It begins with the announcement of the supernatural command, then shows the despair of the kin companion, the resolve of the principal tested by an attempt to dissuade, the suggestion of a substitution, the reassertion of the victim's determination to die, the farewell scene, the departure, the messenger's account of the death, and finally the formal lamentation and description of funeral honours. The little plot is whole, the women are beautifully drawn, and Polyxena is both firm and maidenly in the decorum of her choice and her death. The whole event, however, is given a terrible hollowness by the fact that this chosen death is, from Polyxena's point of view, not a sacrifice at all, but simply a suicide. No god that she recognizes has asked for her blood, and her death will not serve any purpose that she has an interest in. On the contrary, she dies to gratify the tomb and the ghost of her city's conqueror, to allow his companions a favourable voyage home as they carry with them their spoils, her mother and her companions as slaves. Polyxena dies only for her own honour, and not a little out of a justified distaste for life, and so her death affirms nothing, but becomes a bitter, incidental, discoordinate event, as Euripides meant it to be.

A subtler distortion of the conventional value of sacrifice is made in the *Iphigeneia at Aulis*, for here the girl decides that she dies for Hellas, and teaches herself to put aside her eagerness for life, wealth, and a bridegroom, in order that Greece may be saved. The audience, however, has meanwhile been taught to feel that Greece was never in danger, and that Iphigeneia's death in fact is serving only the plans of Ulysses, the battle-rage of the army, and the ambition of Agamemnon. The playwright takes advantage of the fact that sacrifice is so often associated with the rescue of a besieged city and the ending of a war, so that this one, which sets a war in motion and inaugurates the siege of a foreign city, shall seem especially dubious.

Sacrifice actions in their normal forms had no place for the portrayal of foolishness or of villainy, though they did provide a potential role for a coward or the man who honoured his own survival over that of the city in its piety. There is always a dissuader, for otherwise the decision of the principal cannot be depicted in action, but if this character is seriously debased his true function is undermined, since there is no special glory in resisting the temptations of the craven. Thus Antigone benefits ethically from her confrontation with Ismene, who is still worthy to be her sister, far more than does Menoeceus in the *Phoenissae*, from his firmness in the face of Creon's selfishness. The principal's willingness may be set off directly against the unwillingness of another, however, if the divine command has been general and not specific. This motif of unwillingness appears in the *Children of Heracles*, where Demophon had refused his own daughters and those of his nobles as sacrificial victims; these, however, are figures never seen on stage, and the same can be said of the more appropriate victims that occur to Iphigeneia's fancy as she contemplates her death. The idea of taking vengeance upon a defaulter is expressed only once, and dimly, in Hecuba's passionate wish that she might see Helen suffer as Polyxena will (*Hec.* 441–3).[2]

The chorus of a sacrifice tragedy will ordinarily represent the community to be saved, and the economy of the stage figures must also provide a messenger, for this death, like that of a tragedy of divine punishment (and unlike that of a vengeance play) is pleasing to god and is thus to be dwelt upon. The sacrifice plot lends itself easily to simplicity; it may be permanently interrupted by a new dispensation from heaven, but it is hardly open to lesser contradictions in its action since its characters act knowingly and in accordance with a supernatural command. The principal must be willing, and thus resistance can come only from someone near to him or, very briefly, as with poor Iphigeneia, from himself. The minimal sacrifice plot

---

[2] One might more remotely compare Orestes' words to Menelaus at *Or.* 658 ff., where he suggests that Hermione should have died instead of Iphigeneia and that she might yet be held accountable for her cousin's death.

thus moves steadily on towards the ritual shedding of blood, undisturbed by problems of *hamartia* or of divine justice, and its final effect is paradoxically one of revival. The social organism has sickened, but has found its cure; the victim has suffered and is gone, but the city returns to health, and has a new subject now for its songs of *arete*.

The Alcestis myths told of a type of sacrifice slightly different from the tragic sacrifices discussed, for hers was a love-sacrifice.[3] She does not, with her life, buy back a city from plague or conquest; she buys back her husband from Death. She has, however, had her command from heaven, and it has come from a god who is responsible for the fruitfulness of her husband's land. In herself she conforms perfectly to the established standard: she is, like all the other sacrificial victims, young; she is willing, and like many of her fellow victims, she has had a choice. She might, like Macaria, have survived, and she has no more scruple than the other against talking realistically of alternatives (*Alc.* 284 ff.; cf. *Hcld.* 523; 579–80; 591; in the same general class are Antigone's lament for the marriage she might have had, at 876, Polyxena's at *Hec.* 416, and Iphigeneia's rueful reference to marriage and children at *IA* 1398–9). It is, after all, this reluctance to leave life (*Alc.* 289) that gives a positive value to their choice of death, rescuing their decisions from the private despair that marked Polyxena's anti-tragic death. Like Praxithea, Alcestis has made her calculations (*Alc.* 284 ff.; *Erechtheus*, fr. 50, 5 ff. [Austin, p. 25]); she expects a profit for those who will survive (cf. Macaria, *Hcld.* 581), in that children who would else have been orphans (288) are yet to have both a mother and a father (377; cf. Macaria and Iphigeneia, who likewise recommend children to the care of those they leave, *Hcld.* 574; *IA* 1450). For herself, Alcestis expects fair fame, as Iphigeneia did, and Praxithea for her daughters (*Alc.* 324; *IA* 1376; 1383; *Erechth.* fr. 50, 34–5 [Austin, p. 27]), but she is like Iphigeneia (*IA* 1437) in her lack of interest in funeral honours; she asks an honour of another sort, that of not being replaced in the house (305). Alcestis reiterates the care that Polyxena and Macaria felt for the seemliness of their deaths (*Alc.* 159–61; *Hec.* 432–4; *Hcld.* 561), even though she believes, as Iphigeneia seems to have done,

---

[3] The fairy-tale type is discussed by A. Lesky, 'Alkestis, der Mythus u. das Drama', *S.B. Akad. Wien* (Ph. Hist. Kl.), cciii:2 (1925), 1–86.

that there are others who might better have been slain (*Alc.* 291; cf. the hint at *IA* 1417). Alcestis laments her own death, but more moderately than any of the other victims except Macaria and Menoeceus (*Alc.* 264–5; *Antig.* 806 ff.; *Hec.* 416; 418; 420; *IA* 1279 ff.); like them she sadly salutes the light of her final day (*Alc.* 244; *Hec.* 411; cf. 435; *Antig.* 879–80; *IA* 1281–2), believing like them, that only by her death can she avoid betraying others (*Alc.* 180–1; *Hcld.* 522; *Phoen.* 1003; *Supp.* 1024; *Antig.* 46).

Alcestis' role is thus given a strong outward conformity to that of her prototype, and the same can be said of the role of Admetus. He takes the part of an Iolaus or a Hecuba or a Clytemnestra and is the one who tries to keep the sacrifice from taking place (cf. his 357 with *IA* 1211). Like Iolaus, he cannot quarrel with a god's command (*Alc.* 420–1; *Hcld.* 600), but like Hecuba and Clytemnestra he bewails his own fate, since he must lose a loved one, complaining that he is destroyed and begging the victim not to abandon him (*Alc.* 380; 386; 388; 391; *Hec.* 438 ff.; cf. 431; *IA* 1465–6). Like Polyxena's mother, he would cling to the sacrifice and die with her, and he must be told by others that this cannot be (*Alc.* 382–3; cf. 897–8; *Hec.* 396–400, reproved by Polyxena at 402 ff.; cf. *IA* 1469). Like Iolaus he hails the virtue of this female saviour and promises honour to her (*Alc.* 366 ff. and 328; *Hcld.* 597 ff. and 567); like him he is reluctant, later, to admit to an outsider that a victim has been sacrificed (*Alc.* 513 etc.; *Hcld.* 634).

Alcestis' sacrifice tragedy is thus apparently in perfect ethical agreement with other plays of its type, and the same can be said of its structure, with two interesting exceptions. Naturally there is compression, since this is a drama in miniature, but all the usual elements can be recognized. The announcement of the supernatural command and the contest over its fulfilment, which would normally provide the opening episodes, have in this case taken place many years ago, but they are described in the prologue. There remain a messenger speech, a scene of farewell and lamentation, and a scene of honours to the corpse, but it is notable that the messenger speech has been shifted from its normal position. This speech ordinarily occurs late and describes the death itself, but here is has been moved forward in the action and used to describe the victim in her decision. It thus supplies some of the ethical colour that would otherwise have been added in the missing scene of contest.

The messenger figure can be used here in this unconventional way because in this play, and only in this play, the sacrificial death actually takes place on stage. This indeed is where Alcestis is radically different from tragedy's other willing sacrifices, for she does not die in an off-stage ritual magnified by the report of its crowds and its public pomp. Her death is a private affair quietly imitated by the action itself, an event at once more civilized and more primitive than the other sacrificial deaths. There is no priest here, with his sacrificial knife, but neither is there any altar, and Alcestis' apparently natural demise is tantamount to being handed over to a ravening monster. She sees Thanatos in her visions, grotesque and horrible, as the audience had seen him in the prologue when he was on his way to cut the sacrificial lock of hair.

Alcestis' funeral, like her death, is seen where other such honours are only described. Hecuba closes Polyxena's drama by asking to be allowed to prepare her daughter's corpse with her own hands, Macaria is promised vaguer but continuing attentions at her tomb, and Athena gives directions for the burial of the daughters of Erechtheus and for their further honours as lesser divinities (Fr. 65, 67–70 [Austin, pp. 37–8]). In Antigone's case there is not even this verbal imitation of the funeral, whereas Alcestis' corpse is ritually carried out as a part of the staged action of her play. Alcestis' sacrifice tragedy thus in a sense makes up for its lost initial scenes by the unusual completeness of its finale, and the overt effect of this emphasis is to make her life seem to be more than ever irrevocably at an end.

The extraordinarily concrete death with its unusual privacy and its suggestion of magic and demonism is the first and most obvious innovation in this conventional piece. The second innovation is a more radical one, for it is the expansion of an otherwise dimly expressed motif into a major scene—the scene of recrimination between Admetus and his father. Lesky has shown that the two who refuse before the third, the lover, accepts the role of the sacrifice, is a standard motif in the fairy tales[4] that

---

[4] For a late representation of the scene of the testing of Admetus' family at his deathbed, see A. Ferrua, *Le pitture della nuova catacomba di via Latina* (Vatican, 1960), tav. lxxvi. 2.

tell of lengthened lives purchased in this way, but refusal, as noted above, had not become a structural part of the sacrifice tragedy.[5] Its fictions, unlike those of folk-tale, were usually chosen from a religious context, where refusal might inaugurate a separate action of divine punishment against the defaulter, and would in addition undermine the necessary sense of inevitability in the action. The refusals of Pheres and his wife, in the *Alcestis*, are placed well back in the past, that they should not interfere with the necessity of this day's death, but as soon as Alcestis is gone, they are disinterred with peculiar violence and allowed to interrupt the funeral in a shocking way. Pheres reenacts his earlier refusal to die for his son in a scene whose only strained parallel is Creon's in the *Phoenissae*. There, however, a man refused to let his son die for the city, and went off to organize the boy's escape muttering 'Let Thebes collapse!' which is, after all, a very different thing from this old man's refusal to die, himself, for his son. Thus the near conformity of Alcestis' drama to the type of the sacrifice plot has brought the two innovations and with them the two unexpected, gratuitous figures of Thanatos and Pheres into extreme prominence. Both old, ugly, grotesque, and technically unwanted in this action, these figures must between them carry the weight of the poet's special intention as he wrote this part of his play.

Heracles' action, the second of the play, begins just before Alcestis' is finished, but the two are cleanly discriminated. When the first is over, all the persons connected with it leave the playing area and go in a formal procession to Alcestis' tomb, marking the chiasmus in the play by leaving the newly arrived Heracles and a single servant in sole possession of the stage. His ensuing drama inherits a very specific situation, but for all its peculiarities, it is clearly a rescue piece.

The best known rescue fictions attach to figures like Ariadne or Semele, heroines rescued from exile or from monsters by heroes magical or divine, and transported to become goddesses, queens, or brides. Tragic rescues, however, were not necessarily

[5] Note E. Petersen, 'Andromeda', *JHS* xxiv (1904), 99–112, who thought he had found vase-painting evidence for a scene in the Sophoclean *Andromeda* in which the girl's fiancé, a 'degenerate prince', refused to act as the monster's victim. Unfortunately the figure he read as an effete male was in fact Andromeda in her Oriental costume; see K. M. Phillips, Jr., 'Perseus and Andromeda', *AJA* lxxii (1968), 6–7.

so limited either in character or situation.[6] Enough survives of the Euripidean *Andromeda* to allow certain general assumptions,[7] and to encourage a reconstruction by analogy of the satyr play *Hesione* whose preparations are shown on the Promonos vase; in addition we can recognize the rescue action in its masculine form in the *Philoctetes* and the satyr *Cyclops*, and can use it perhaps as an hypothesis for the *Prometheus Luomenos*.

A rescue action presupposes a victim immobilized and in danger from a threatening creature; often he is an unwilling sacrifice to a power that has something monstrous or pre-Olympian about it. After a prologue of lament, the normal stage action begins with the arrival (properly accidental) of the hero; the simplest plot economy does not call for recognition (though this became popular when the plot was taken over by mothers and sons) but for a kind of love scene in which the champion decides to risk his life to save the helpless victim. Since the true *agon*, the struggle with the monster, must occur off-stage in tragedy, it may be replaced in the staged action with a second encounter between the champion and someone more ordinary who does not wish to release the victim, even when the danger is past. The proper ending of the play is some form of physical translation, for only the removal of the victim from the place of exposure will embody the praxis of the piece in a visible stage event. Often the removal is associated with marriage, even when the particular fiction makes the marriage of the two principals an impossibility.

According to these terms Andromeda was saved from her monster by Perseus who had seen her, 'like a statue' (fr. 125 N[2]), on her rock, and who had fallen in love with her; he took her away as his bride, but only after a long argument with her father that seems to have ended in threats. Hesione was rescued from another sort of serpent by Heracles, and then had to be wrested from her ungrateful family before she could be given as a prize to the hero's closest friend. Likewise Semele was rescued from Hades by Dionysus (as Perithoos was by Heracles, in a satyr play)

---

[6] Rescue actions in trilogy: [*Prometheus Luomenos*]; in tragedy of single action: *Philoctetes*; Euripides' *Andromeda*; as part of multiple plot best represented by *Iphigeneia amongst the Taurians* and *Helen*

[7] For painted evidence, see K. M. Phillips, Jr., op cit., plates 1-20.

and taken to Olympus as a queen, and Prometheus was rescued from the eagle by a champion who still had to deal with Zeus. In the *Cyclops* the princess in distress is the satyr chorus, which has been captured by a monster; Odysseus, like Perseus, happens by in the course of his adventures and the champion and Silenus play a 'love scene' in terms of hospitality, pledging themseves in food and wine. Because this is satyr play, the monster may appear on stage and so there is no need for a second source of resistance to the rescue action. And since wine and a parody of love are the weapons used in the initial phase of the conquest of the Cyclops, the central *agon* is played out almost in its entirety for all to see; only the final moments when the beast is blinded must be conveyed, like a vengeance death, by shouts from behind the scenes. The monster is not killed but maimed, the 'princess' is liberated, and in the end the fat old satyr and all his band are carried off, for all the world like a plural Ariadne, to Dionysus and a place of 'endless pleasure, endless love', as Dryden would have had it. The marriage motif is clearly expressed, for the satyrs have had occasion to speak of the deprivations they have suffered for lack of available nymphs.

This is obviously the genre to which the second portion of the *Alcestis* belongs. To a Silenus–Laomedon–Admetus a Heracles comes, as he likewise comes to Troy in the *Hesione* and as Odysseus comes to the Cyclops' cave, asking hospitality. His love for Admetus is of long standing and his fresh receipt of food and drink binds him to repayment. When the present situation is finally explained to him, and he learns that Alcestis is the prey of the monster Thanatos, he goes off to challenge him, and soon reappears with the rescued victim who has been taken from the place of death and is now conferred in marriage upon an Admetus–Telamon. The parallel with the *Hesione* is the closest, and so it is not surprising to find strong satyr-play elements in this rescue play. The opening motif of hospitality suggests a satyresque quality that is confirmed in the scene which is, for this discrete drama, the crucial one of discovery and decision. It is Heracles' inability to see that a tragedy has just been played on these boards that provides the only complication in the piece; he does not know that the local princess has been sacrificed to a monster. His ignorance is a nice reflection of the gap between the two plots, but it must be destroyed if his own action is to continue, and the poet has arranged that his initiation to the truth shall be by means of wine. It is thus technically wine that, in true satyr drama fashion, both oils the plot and saves the girl.

Heracles' drama is, like that of Alcestis, very much compressed but unlike hers, instead of adding a scene, it subtracts one, and a very important one, from the proper rescue sequence. Many scholars have suspected that an overt physical conflict supplied the original matter of the satyr play and there is some reason to think that Heracles and Thanatos may have struggled visibly in Phrynichus' *Alcestis*.[8] The victory over the monster is at any rate the central deed in any rescue action, and its description will provide the major portion of tragic emotion served up by such a play. It is the *pathos* of the monster that measures the danger of the heroine, the strength of the hero, and the marvel of the escape, but this *pathos* is, in the *Alcestis* version, almost wholly absent. It is true that Heracles does, before the event, describe the wrestling match he expects, and his words are precise and full of the anticipated joy of battle (846–9). Afterwards, however, he is involved in the fooling of Admetus, and the few lines he spends on his confrontation with the enemy are couched in playfully athletic terms (1026–33).[9] We assume that he found Thanatos by the tomb and pounced on him according to plan, but we are never given the anticipated pleasure of a full account. Worst of all, we never learn what became of the monstrous demon figure—did he skulk away, is he waiting still, did he injure Heracles, or is he perhaps a coward who dropped his prey and ran?

A rescue action that has neither messenger speech nor scene of confrontation between hero and monster should be wholly unsatisfactory, and yet there is no sense, at the end of the *Alcestis*, of anything but completeness. The palace has been restored and is a place that can once again offer unstinted hospitality to its friends; Thanatos does not appear to lurk, he seems to have

[8] See A. Dieterich, *Pulcinella* (Leipzig,1 897), 64 ff.; L. Weber, 'ΦΡΥΝΙΧΟΥ ΑΛΚΗΣΤΙΣ' *Rh. Mus.* lxxix (1930), 35 ff. There is evidence at least of long and technical descriptions of such struggles in satyr plays; see Schol. Ar. *Ran.* 688: ὁ τραγικὸς Φρύνιχος ἐν 'Ανταίῳ δράματι περὶ παλαισμάτων πολλὰ διεξῆλθεν.

[9] The winning of a girl as a prize in a contest is the theme of at least one other satyr play, the mysterious *Phineus/Oineus* of *Pap. Oxy.* viii (1911), No. 1083.

been banished, though the audience has neither seen nor heard of his depature. How has the plot so easily survived the omission of its core scene? The answer is that the scene has not been left out, but has been played by proxies in a substitute scene of conflict. There is in the second half of the play (after the entrance of Heracles) a hard-fought contest that ends in the rout of an enemy, and it is no mere messenger-speech affair, but a rough spectacle. The Admetus–Pheres scene that belongs to the fiction but not to the structure of Alcestis' drama was postponed, that it might be played after the heroine has been handed over to Thanatos. It was thrust into the satyr portion of the entertainment that it might replace, in the emotional economy of that action, the struggle with the monster. It is thus structurally parallel to the scene of Perseus' dispute with the father of Andromeda.

The major innovation of the sacrifice drama is now explained. Its unprecedented scene of hatred and recrimination, aimed at the victim who refused, is a double of the satyr-drama's wrestling match, and in its transposed position it serves to lock the tragedy into the succeeding satyr play. This artificial joining of two structures, each one of which would seem to make the other impossible, has been effected with an almost magical technical skill, and yet in theory the double and contradictory action of the *Alcestis* seems to remain a defiance of probability, of nature, and of the rules for play-making. Its true success can only be measured against the artist's reasons for attempting such a structural perversity, and these must be sought in the content of the play.

We have noticed that Alcestis does not die offstage at an altar, surrounded by officiating priests, but rather here on her own couch, surrounded by her lamenting family. There has been a divine command, but it came long ago; there was a threatening public disaster—the imminent death of the king—but it too was alleviated long ago. And so, with Alcestis as with Antigone, it is important to ask exactly what purpose the victim herself saw her death as serving. We need to know how she evaluated the continuing organism that her small drama formally praises, and we need to know something of its actual quality. Sophocles has made us believe that the Thebes Antigone left would be a city that honoured the changeless laws of its earth and the justice sworn on god's name. The question here is what Euripides has asked us to believe about Alcestis' parallel achievement.

The prologue explains the bare reason for Alcestis' death: she contracted long ago to die in exchange for her husband, and today is the day appointed for the fulfilment of her engagement. Her sacrifice is viewed here simply as an event in the history of the House of Admetus, one incident in a sequence of benefactions and their repayment that has accompanied Apollo's fruitful association with the place. As the citizens mourn their queen in the parodos and the servant describes her preparations for death, the emphasis is upon the woman, the victim in her perfection, and not upon the function of the death. When Alcestis appears, however, she makes a plain statement of the reasons which led her to choose this death and of the results she wishes it to have. The lucid economy of her explanation has shocked some moderns,[10] but her secret is that she sees her problem as simple. She begins with the fact that her promise to die was freely made, not forced upon her. She knows that her action will bring *kleos*, and she is not uninterested in fame, but her idea is to confer it upon her husband and her children. There are, however, more precise results that she has in mind, and she insists upon success in these. Life is good, and therefore self-sacrifice has no value of itself; it must bring results that continued life could not, results that are more valuable than life. She has bought a prolongation of her husband's life but she does not see this as a mere extension of the physical processes of Admetus' flesh. It is Admetus as husband and father, master of a hearth, lord of a household and ruler of a land that she would preserve.

Alcestis chose to die rather than to live as Admetus' widow (the two existing possibilities, once Pheres and his wife had declined) because she saw that in these circumstances her death would best serve that to which her life was dedicated, her marriage in this house. She states this with cool precision, but Euripides makes her reveal as well her passionate idealism. She would not betray her marriage bed and her husband (180–1); she honoured her husband's life more than her own, though she loved life well (282 ff.); her children can be despots in their father's house, though she is dead, as they could not be in the

---

[10] But in its defence, A. Lesky, *Die griechische Tragödie* (Stuttgart, 1964), p. 178.

house of a stepfather (280 ff.). In Alcestis' cosmos Marriage is a pure element to be named with Sun, Air, and Earth (244–9). Her husband and bed are one, as are husband and hearth;[11] she confides her children to Hestia (163 ff.) and to Admetus (375), for the two are inseparable in her thought. Husband, children, house, and marriage make up a single ideal concept which her death will save. It is more valuable to her than her sharp delight in life, and having seen what was best she felt that to choose any course but death would have been shameful (180; cf. Plato *Apol.* 28B).

Alcestis' farewells are made to her marriage bed, the symbol of temporal union; her recommendations for the future are made to the goddess of the eternal foyer, from whose altar nothing can be taken away.[12] Nothing that she does has any reference to romantic love, for this concept is unknown to her. She is ruled by *philia* (279), the feeling proper among friends and members of the same family.[13] She expects to be forgotten (381, 387) and assumes that another will sleep in her bed (181–2), but these things do not interest her. The success she demands is that her marriage should continue after she is gone; it must not be imitated or replaced, for her death is to make it immortal.

Alcestis dies only when the results she wants have been promised her. What she asks is specific; she says in effect: 'I refused to give our children a stepfather; I ask in return that you shall not give them a stepmother.' This finely calculated return of like for like which takes no account of the quality of the initial benefaction and which has nothing to do with gratitude or love, this repayment which cannot pretend to be worthy of Alcestis' deed, she labels 'just' (302). Admetus agrees as a

---

[11] Cf. Eurip., Frag. 318 Nauck[2]: γυνὴ γὰρ ἐξελθοῦσα πατρῴων δόμων οὐ τῶν τεκόντων ἐστίν, ἀλλὰ τοῦ λέχους.

[12] M. P. Nilsson, *Geschichte der griechischen Religion* (Munich, 1955–61), i, 337.

[13] See Bruno Snell, *Poetry and Society* (Bloomington, Ind., 1961), pp. 83 ff. on *philia* in marriage. Some moderns, recognizing that Alcestis is not acting 'for love', conclude that she is either a calculating or a disenchanted woman; others, confusing her salute to her bed with a romantic gesture, believe that she *is* acting 'for love', and that Admetus is a brute for not returning her feeling. She, however, tells the audience and Admetus that reason, not passion, moved her (had her motive been passion it would have been less to her credit; cf. *Medea*, 526–31). Phaedrus, in the *Symposium*, tried to make Alcestis a figure for the power of *eros* (179C), but he is corrected at 208D, where Alcestis is said to have acted ὑπὲρ ἀρετῆς ἀθανάτου.

matter of course (note how his reference to Thessalian brides, l. 331, echoes hers to Thessalian grooms, l. 285; they make exactly paired renunciations), but he is no more satisfied than an Apollo would have been by this mean return of like for like. Hastily he adds extensions and embellishments to his covenant in the attempt to respond to her *philia*: he will not only not marry a new wife, he will grieve for this one forever, sacrificing not only the joy of future sons, but all joys. He will not only close his house to the potential enemy stepmother, he will drive away the actual enemy, the father who has behaved like a stepfather (636 ff.). A comparison of his parents' action with that of Alcestis has proved to him that they deserve not love but hatred from him (338–41; cf. her accusation of them at 290 ff.). From this day on he will be a stranger to the pleasures of music and masculine company, nor will he have any female companion to solace him.

Had he simply proposed never to install the concubine Alcestis took for granted, the effect could only have been crude. Admetus instead makes a promise that is positive, delicately stated, and filled with a powerful meaning:

> A master's hand will counterfeit your form,
> an idol share my bed, and I will kneel and touch,
> call out your name, in semblance holding one
> I shall not hold again.
> A pleasure cold as ice will lift
> the weight upon my soul and then perhaps your ghost
> will enter as I dream, bringing to my heart
> some cheer, for it is always sweet
> to glimpse a friend in sleep,
> however short his stay. (348–56) [14]

[14] A great deal of nonsense has been written about this passage, proving only that scholars take their Krafft-Ebing too seriously. The ideas of death, simulacra, resurrection, and marriage had a strong association, since every year at the Anthesteria the dead Dionysus was imaged by a mask fixed to a post, then brought to life to enjoy the ritual of his marriage (see Nilsson, op. cit., i, 583; 587; G. van Hoorn. *Choes and Anthesteria* [Leyden, 1957], pp. 24–5; and for use of a Dionysus herm in the *hieros gamos*, see Hetty Goldman, 'The Origin of the Greek Herm', *AJA* xlvi [1942], 58–68, esp. 66 and Fig. 9). The statue motif occurs also in the story of Laodameia (Hyg. *Fab.* 103, 104), about whom Euripides wrote a tragedy (see U. von Wilamo-witz-Moellendorff, 'Sepulcri Portuensis Imagines' [1929], *Kl. Schr.*, V:1 [1937], 524–7, where it is argued that Admetus' speech proves that Laodameia's love was impious and perverse!). Here the wife who would not betray her husband though he was dead (Frag. 655 Nauck²), and who kept him alive as best she could with a

Since he is not Orpheus (357) this will be his way of bringing his wife back from Hades. He will live in the dream he hopes to induce with the *eidolon*, himself a sleeping image of her death, host to her phantom imitation of life. She has asked that her marriage be kept alive; Admetus determines as far as possible to keep his wife alive too, as statue and as ghost (cf. 328). At the same time he arranges to die with her; his life will be like death (288, 242-3, 278, 666, 802, 1082, 1084), its goal that moment when his corpse will lie beside death's image of her while his soul seeks her shade in the house she is to prepare below (363-8).

Thus when Alcestis has died we know what she meant to preserve, but we are not sure of her success. She did not, as far as we can tell, want a life that was like a death for Admetus, a house without music, or a land where a perpetual funeral was celebrated. The later scene of Admetus' homecoming after her entombment gives a further measure of what her death has wrought. Formally, this scene functions as a ritual lamentation and so as a final tribute of praise for the heroine of the sacrifice action, but it also describes the state of the house whose health she had presumably ensured, and that state is unsatisfactory. The *philia* that had bound husband and wife together has indeed been preserved, as Alcestis wished it to be, but *philia* means living with two souls instead of one (900; cf. 1054, 1103) and the full experience of what this can mean, when one of those is dead, reaches Admetus on his return from the tomb. In spite of his fictions[15] he is to suffer life, not death, and he realizes that here at last he has outstripped his wife in unhappiness (935-6). The scene (861-961) in which he greets the humiliating actuality of an unwanted life is the reverse image of her farewell to a richly desirable world. She, before, with face unstained by any tear, had moved serenely through a much-loved house where linen lay in orderly chests. Admetus now loathes the very walls of the building and cannot enter where she is not; he cries out and longs for death, as he imagines the sordid minutiae of the life

---

statue in her bed, was rewarded with his miraculous brief return to life. One of the effects of Euripides' use of the statue motif in the *Alcestis* is that her resurrection is understood poetically as the breathing of life into a statue, a process which may have been dramatized in Sophocles' satyr play *Pandora* (see F. Brommer, *Satyrspiele*[2] [Berlin, 1959], p. 52).

[15] These fictions are reinforced now by the chorus: Alcestis' tomb is to be no tomb but a shrine (999; note *sebas* and its echoes from Admetus at 279 and 1060).

that awaits him in this ill-kept house filled only with emptiness. Her tears fell only once, in farewell to the bed she would not betray; in the service of that same bed, now deserted (925), he must waste his spirit in a struggle with each day's petty lusts (950–3). She willed the joy of her good fame to those she left behind, but Admetus looks forward to the agony of knowing himself slandered by enemy tongues (954–60).

At this point the magical and the natural results of Alcestis' death have had their full description. The sacrifice is a success, as far as mortal endeavour can make it so, for Admetus is alive, his promises are given and the hearth is preserved, but the real has not become the ideal. The immortal marriage will be a grievous phantom thing at best, and the continuing house will be shadowed by grief and by slurs on its master's reputation. And so Alcestis' sacrifice, for all its beauty, comes to its formal close without a proper sense of fulfilment. Admetus is literally unable to re-enter his house, and though the Moirae are satisfied, we are not.

The play is so put together, however, that the initial scenes of the second action have by this time already been performed and have already begun to exert their reviving influence. When Alcestis' body is carried into the house, Admetus accompanies it to close the first episode, with the play almost half finished. The next personage to appear is someone from another world. Heracles comes geographically from afar, and he comes also from another genre, for his stage appearances up to this time had been almost exclusively made in comedy and satyr play (the one exception being, as far as we know, the *Luomenos*.) Admetus and Alcestis have been living a life of almost Edwardian security and civilization, but Heracles comes directly from frontiers not yet safely drawn between men and the beasts and monsters of an older savagery. Like Odysseus in the *Cyclops* he is perfectly confident, however; his life is hard, but if it is simply a ceaseless journey from one trial to the next, so it is also a journey from one victory to the next. When he learns that his present opponent is the third son of Ares, his response is a hearty 'Well, I've already taken care of the other two!' (499 ff.).

Unlike Odysseus, however, Heracles has come not by accident and in dire need, but on purpose to visit his friend and to be feasted and entertained as was his due. His demand is not for the minimum, but for the maximum of hospitality. When he learns that there is grief in the house he turns away in propriety, and so allows his friend to make the fullest gesture of graciousness with perfect freedom, as he presses his guest to enter the house. To Heracles' proposal that he find shelter somewhere else, Admetus answers, 'That is impossible. May no such evil visit me!' (539) and 'You shall sit at no other hearth but mine' (545), reaffirming, even in this hour of desolation, the honour and the health of his house.

As soon as Admetus has sent his friend indoors the audience is reminded of that other, gratuitous act which stands with Alcestis' decision as one of the two mortal causes of everything seen on this stage. The reception of Heracles is the double of Admetus' original reception of Apollo and will have the same sort of consequence; this much is made explicit in the ode which follows (605; cf. Apollo at 68–9). Thus Admetus, making the first move of his new life, is shown to re-enact the past. He faces a second test of hospitality, more difficult than the first, since Heracles' arrival is apparently so untimely. However, his new duty to Alcestis (his promise to mourn and yet to live as if his wife were still alive) coincides with his continuing duty as a nobleman. His simple impulse to deny Alcestis' death shows him the way, and he has soon fulfilled Apollo's requirement by offering the hospitality of his house to Heracles. When the traveller's fateful entrance into the guest quarters has been accomplished, Admetus explains his reasons (553–60). He could not have turned his friend away, for to do so would have threatened the reputation of his house and the future reception of its members elsewhere. Whereas Alcestis saw the house from within, an enclosed space with the marriage bed as its centre, Admetus honours its outward aspect. For him the house includes the city (533), a city which has obligations toward other cities. The house where Alcestis' children are to rule is also the *polis*, and he values its good name more than his own sharp need to grieve alone for his wife. Even the servant, whose views are much more limited than his master's, recognizes that Admetus was governed by *aidos*, the sense of proper reverence felt toward one's family and the gods (823).

Once, before the play began, Admetus had taken in a guest without realizing the full meaning of his action, and he will do so again, before the play has ended. The three actions are given such heavy echoes that they stand each as a type of the other two. Apollo was presumably unrecognized; Heracles is recognized only as a friend, not as a saviour; Alcestis will be veiled. In every case Admetus acts out of respect for his house: the desire to give it its due and to preserve in this way its ideal existence in men's opinion. The first reception resulted in *philia* (42); the second has friendship as its partial cause (1037); in the final case, the desire that a friend shall not become an enemy causes the reception (1106) which has the return of Alcestis' *philia* as its effect.

In the scene that follows, this central act of friendship and welcome is matched by an act of enmity, as Pheres is abused and driven away. The primary fairy-tale identification of Pheres is not as father but as one who refused to do what Alcestis did, and Euripides has done his best to preserve this single character for the old man. When he arrives on the scene one fact and only one is known about him, but it has been stated four times over: Pheres, though ripe for death, refused to exchange his life for his son's (16, Apollo; 290-2, Alcestis; 338-9, Admetus; 468-70, Chorus). The woman who chose to die has given her reasons; now, in the presence of her corpse, the audience hears the explanation of the man who refused the same deed.

Pheres begins with a fair speech in praise of Alcestis. If there was a convention for portraying the hypocrite, the actor probably followed it here, for Euripides has made Pheres' own words prove him disingenuous. He begins by saying that he would sympathize and share in his son's misfortunes (614), but soon he admits that whether Admetus be wretched or joyful is no concern of his (685-6). Alcestis he calls wise (615) when he thinks he has benefited from her action (625), an idiot (728), when it is suggested that he might have done as she did. The noble deed (623) becomes a stupid error when he imagines himself performing it (710). He congratulates Alcestis on her most glorious life in his first speech (623), but reveals in his next that he does not believe in glory (726). He wishes her well in Hades (627), then states his own conviction that the time below is long but never sweet (692-3). With each self-contradiction he proves what Admetus had earlier said (339)—he is a friend only in words.

When his trumpery offering of praise has been rejected, Pheres states his reasons for refusing to save his son, beginning at the same point that Alcestis had chosen. No debt bound him to die for Admetus, and he loved life. *Dike* was enough for him, and *dike* meant holding on to the same tangible things that Alcestis had decided to relinquish. The house, for him, was a complex of lands and flocks (687) to be counted and consumed, not a complex of ideals to be preserved. He values only the sweets of this earth (693) and thus the best life is the longest one. Pheres does not care for reputation and he admits that he knows nothing of sympathy; it is his own fate a man cares about, not that of anyone else (712). And in so denying *philia* he isolates himself from every other being in the play save Death alone; all the rest, from god to slave, experience what it is to live with two souls instead of one (Admetus, 883–4; cf. Apollo, 42; the household, 192–3 and 825; the chorus, 210–12; Alcestis, 313–19; Heracles, 1010). Thus the old problem posed by Apollo was even simpler for Pheres than it had been for Alcestis, since self-sacrifice is inconceivable to a man who stands outside society, recognizing nothing but material goods. Such a man could easily allow his own kin to be protected by one who was not of their blood, though he thus betrayed his house as well as his son.

Pheres freely admits that his present good fortune is owed to Alcestis (620–1, 625), and he comes with a token repayment. She, however, had not intended to be his benefactor, and so his gift is refused. Admetus then proceeds to withdraw the advantages which had come to the old people through Alcestis' sacrifice, and as he explains himself he repeats words that she had spoken (651–2; cf. 295–6). He charges Pheres with responsibility for Alcestis' death, and honouring the symmachy of marriage makes her enemy his and that of his house. Pheres is forbidden access to the hearth where her spirit resides, and is driven away from the halls that belong now to her children. The old parents will have, however, exactly what they bargained for (662–6, 735–6). Pheres had chosen, not honourable death for himself and survival for his son, but continued life for himself and death for his son. Burial at the hands of his son had not then seemed important to him. Now Admetus says in effect: 'You have the continuing life that you wanted; you will have also the rest of your choice, the dead son and a burial by strangers.'

He renders his father the sort of justice the old man had proclaimed, the calculated *dike* of Thanatos, and could say now in
his father's words, 'How do I wrong you? What do I deprive
you of?' (689). Admetus casts off his father, not by doing any
violence to the man, but by announcing his own symbolic
death (666).[16] At the same time he declares that he will substitute Alcestis, although she is dead and an outsider, for his living
father and mother; she will receive the honour and care due by
tradition to Pheres and his wife (646–7). He has pretended to
doubt that Pheres really was his father (636 ff.) and in the end
he threatens to disown him publicly, choosing with fine bitterness
the word by which, ordinarily, a father would disown a child
whose paternity he denied (ἀπειπεῖν 737; 738).[17]

In receiving Heracles, Admetus repeated his original reception of Apollo; in refusing Pheres he seems to repeat Apollo's
confrontation with Death. As in the earlier scene, a young and
powerful figure comes out of the house, meets an old man[18]
who has entered from the parodos, and a dispute about Alcestis
ensues. Admetus, like Apollo, argues that the old are meetest
for death, while Pheres, like Thanatos, denies it. Pheres accuses
Admetus of having too little respect for established custom, as
Death had reproached Apollo. Apollo asked a favour; Thanatos
refused; Apollo answered, 'It will happen anyway, by another
agency, and you will get no thanks but become my enemy.'
Admetus had long ago asked a favour and Pheres had refused;
now Admetus says, 'It has happened anyway, by another
agency, and you will get no thanks but be my enemy.' The
visual and verbal parallelism suggests that the Pheres scene has
been constructed with a special intention. This scene is the play's
agon in the technical sense, and it is made to seem almost a life
and death struggle.

[16] His father in a sense casts him off in return by charging him with murder; the
term *phoneus* (730) is precisely as accurate as the *haima* of 733 is real, but Pheres can
thus revenge himself. The mention of Acastus creates a dim echo of the story of
Aegisthus' daughter who charged Orestes with the murder of her father.

[17] This is also the word which describes an adoptive parent's ending of his relationship with an adopted child; see M. Broadbent, *Studies in Greek Genealogy* (Leiden,
1968), p. 230.

[18] For death as an old man, bald, ugly, and almost naked, see C. Smith, 'A Vase
with a Representation of Heracles and Geras', *JHS* iv (1883), 100 ff. And for further
analysis of the motifs of the prologue, see A. P. Burnett, 'The Virtues of Admetus',
CP lx (1965), 242–3.

Admetus is like Apollo in this scene, and he is also like a Heracles, for he duplicates one of the hero's famous exploits. As Hebe's husband, Heracles stood for youth, which meant that he stood for the conquest of old age. He did not promise a second youth, such as the old men of the *Madness of Heracles* chorus asked, but he did offer protection against the pains and the diseases of the old. This power of his became, in mythic terms, another contest, one in which he defeated the demon Old Age, a figure scarcely distinguishable from a Ker or from death himself. In certain figurative representations he can be seen attacking an ugly little old man who is Geras,[19] much as he will soon attack Thanatos and much as Admetus here attacks his father, Pheres. The association strengthens the impression that Admetus has here pre-empted the function of the hero and has entered into the same contest that Heracles will soon engage in by the tomb, for the spectator is left with the subrational sense that the ugly figure whom Apollo allowed to enter the house has now been driven off by its master.

In the paired scenes upon which the compound plot of the *Alcestis* turns, the spectator watches Admetus join his wife in an action to save his house. He repays a friend of that house with a benefaction and its enemy with enmity; the one who has threatened the hearth is driven away and the one who will save it is taken in. Since Heracles is young and jolly, a banqueter and a bringer of life, while Pheres is old and mean and associated with death, the king has shown himself truly king by driving out old Hunger and bringing in Wealth and Health.[20] Like a celebrant at the Anthesteria he has said to Pheres, θύραζε κῆρ;[21] like the citizens of Thasos in their house inscriptions he has said

---

[19] P. Hartwig, 'Heracles und Geras', *Philol,.* l (1891), 185 ff. For a good reproduction of the Louvre pelike, see R. Flacelière and P. Devambez, *Héraclès. Images et Récits* (Paris, 1966), pl. xix.

[20] See O. Kern, (βουλίμου ἐξέλασις), *Arch. f. Religionwiss.*, xv (1912), 642, for an argument that a public ritual of this sort existed at Athens in the early 4th cent. F. Cornford, *The Origin of Attic Comedy* (London, 1914), p. 78, compares the Pheres scene with the final *agon* of the *Clouds* and its preceding whipping scene, viewing it as an example of the conflict of the Young King and the Old King. The Impostor scenes of Old Comedy would seem to offer a closer parallel (esp. the gift-bearing impostors of the *Birds*); these figures are often stripped of their clothing or attributes, as Pheres is stripped of his fatherhood and his share in Admetus' house.

[21] Van Hoorn, op. cit., p. 20.; Nilsson, op. cit., i, 597.

to Heracles, ἐνθάδε κατοικεῖ (1151).²² These actions strengthen his house and likewise strengthen his immortal alliance with Alcestis as he makes her friends his friends, her enemies his.²³

Alcestis' action was a miniature tragedy, Heracles' a miniature satyr play. The two are linked and interlocked by a series of structural tricks of great subtlety, but also by the perfect unity of the poet's dramatic intention. Thanatos, a satyr play figure, has been made to cross over into the tragedy, where he magically transformed an action that ordinarily cannot be interrupted into one that can be undone. His presence converted the sacrifice heroine who had to die into a rescue heroine who had to be saved from a threatening monster. Meanwhile Admetus, a tragic figure, was made to cross over into the satyr play, usurping the functions of its central role. Heracles brought with him the vine-leaves and the brutishness of the second genre, reminding us that in a sense this whole affair had been begun in the same mood when Apollo made the Moirae drunk. He of course did literally meet the monster; he wrestled with Death and took Alcestis from him, but her return to the palace was possible only because Admetus had independently fulfilled her dying purposes in a way that her mere death could not.

Like a single member of a trilogy, the sacrifice tragedy was brought to formal completion but left, as, for example, the *Choephoroi* is, with brooding questions still abroad. These were only answered in the scenes that immediately followed upon the victim's death, the scenes in which Admetus began the restoration of his house. Only his welcome of Heracles and his rejection of Pheres could finally arrange a stable situation in which a tragic sequence could come to a serene close. The history that began with the divine command and the search for a sacrificial victim, that continued with Alcestis' drama of death, could have ended with Admetus' re-enactment of his first deed of entertaining a god, but Euripides has meant all along that

---

²² For apotropaic door inscriptions naming Heracles, see *BCH* lxxxvi:2 (1962), 608–9; for a general description of Heracles as protector of door and hearth, see Ch. Picard, 'Hercule, héros malheureux et bénéfique', *Hommages à Jean Bayet* (Brussels, 1964), pp. 561 ff.

²³ He thus makes his city like the prosperous, god-loved city described at *Eumen.* 984–6, where citizens would χάρματα δ' ἀντιδιδοῖεν κοινοφιλεῖ διανοίᾳ καὶ στυγεῖν μιᾷ φρενί.

his play should contain everything proper to the celebration of Dionysus' festival. He can dare to bring back Alcestis, as Semele was brought back, from death, because such an action will frustrate a mere demon, not a god. Thanatos can be over-borne, as the Moirae were before, since Apollo is willing, and the audience can bear the dissolution of Alcestis' achievement in dying, because her true achievement has been made secure. The full expression of the satyresque in the final scene thus has a happy propriety, bringing as it does a gratuitous salvation after the pity and terror have been felt and then have ebbed away. The disguise, the trick, the girl won at the games as a prize, the imputations of lustfulness to Admetus all come from satyr play and serve to convert this shortest of trilogies into a tetralogy. The motifs of marriage and of banqueting are here, but the finale, for all its boisterousness, has been carefully built so as to be worthy of what has gone before.

The trick being played on Admetus creates the peculiar, happy tension of this scene. It makes this third test of friendship, hospitality, and faith by far the most difficult one of all. Admetus must close the door to betrayal of his wife, and yet open it to the gift of his friend and the gods (1071). He must reject what he takes to be a False Alcestis without depriving himself and his house of the true presence of his wife. The audience watches Admetus' nobility guide him once again in a situation he does not wholly understand. The entertainment of this woman will, he believes, bring him a grief more bitter than any he has felt (1069), but rather than damage his friendship with Heracles (1106) he will accept this further suffering. Heracles' ironical offer of a joyful reward does not tempt him (1101); his resistance breaks only when his friend urgently begs the favour (1107). His plain statements that he can have nothing to do with the girl (1056, 1090) have served to separate the threat to Alcestis from the threat to himself, and thus he agrees to receive the property of Heracles (at the cost of pain to himself), while he refuses to accept a substitute for his wife. In so acting he completes the salvation of Alcestis (1020, 1119) and bears out the chorus's prediction that his aristocratic piety, incomprehensible to themselves, will find a reward at last (600–5, the close of the House of Admetus Ode). And in fact Admetus crosses his threshold not with his friend's property but with his own wife restored, for Heracles sees to it that he shall receive the recognition token, the touch of Alcestis, before the eyes of the audience. Husband and wife step back into their restored house each in his own character and each aware of his new felicity. Their alliance has been strengthened, the false friendship of Pheres is at an end, the true friendship of Heracles is firmer than before (1152, he will return), and the reputations of king, queen, and house have been fixed forever by the miracle. Admetus and Alcestis are harboured now in a better life than any they had known before (1157), and at last by Apollo's will the ideal has been made real.

III

IPHIGENEIA AMONGST THE TAURIANS

THE *Iphigeneia amongst the Taurians* is, like the *Alcestis*, a play of rescue deserved. Again like *Alcestis*, it was a favourite with Goethe and it is easy to see why, for this is the most humane and good-tempered of the classical tragedies. Its central event is the permanent interruption of that ancient catastrophe, human sacrifice, and this interruption is seen as a form of divine rescue for mortals. The gods, as usual, can here be read in more than one way, but no one will deny that the raw subject of the *Iphigeneia* is salvation. The verbal surface of the play is heavy with *soteiria* words,[1] and the poet has amused himself by wringing from his fiction no less than ten examples of the rescue of human beings.

Both of the principals of this play owe their present existence to moments in the past when they were snatched from particularly unpleasant fates by the hand (28–30) or, in Orestes' case, by the wit (965) of god. Both are nevertheless still in need of saving, and their two rescues mingle to make the positive overturn action of the play. Orestes' new rescue from the Furies, however, has been made contingent upon a third major act of salvation, his rescue of the cult statue of Artemis from the Taurians, and his attempt to do this leads to his capture by the power he meant to liberate. Consequently Orestes must be rescued afresh and twice over, from the priestess of Artemis and from her patron king, before the action can come to a successful close. And when these five present rescues have to all appearances

---

1 The curious thing is that Euripides does not allow a single σωτήρ word to appear until he has begun the second episode, while from that point on their relative frequency is roughly three times that of *OC*, another tragedy that especially favours the 'saving' words. Among the plays of Euripides the most nearly comparable density is found in *Orestes* (28 in a play of 1693 lines). Here, 27 of the 34 usages (in 1499 lines) are in the second episode; one in the deception scene with Thoas; three in the speech of the second messenger, and three in Athena's speech. This kind of verbal control need not be quite conscious, but it is typical of Euripides; cf. *HF*, where *elpis* words completely disappear, after heavy use, when the suppliant section of the play is done.

been effected and all the beneficiaries are on board ship, the ship is driven back by a storm and everyone must be rescued again, *en masse*, by Athena in person. This sweeping divine act of rescue, finally, so influences Thoas, the Taurian king, that he is rescued from his barbarity and decides to play the saviour himself. At the close of the *Iphigeneia* he first arranges for the rescue of the chorus of Greek girls whom the heroine had had to abandon, and then by abrogating the bloody Taurian cult he works the salvation of all those future Greeks who may visit the Taurian shores.

This magnificent salvo of rescues marks a play of festive complexity in which we are clearly meant to enjoy the feats of technical prowess that are on display at the same time that we experience the true emotions of tragedy. The poet was peculiarly free in this play, for he had found his fiction in one of the empty pockets that mythology occasionally leaves.[2] He could manipulate his plot quite as he chose, and the first thing that is evident is that he was interested here in formal symmetries. He tells a story of two fraternal pairs, one divine and one mortal, a group of four who have so assorted themselves that the brother god, Apollo, is the patron of the mortal brother, Orestes, while his sister, Artemis, stands in the same relation to the mortal sister, Iphigeneia.[3] The final achievement of the play is double, as each brother rescues his sister in a mirroring pair of actions that are simultaneous and interdependent, yet markedly different in significance. Apollo's rescue of Artemis is achieved through the agency of the mortal Orestes, but it is willed by the god and so is sure of success. Orestes' resue of Iphigeneia, on the other hand, is an improvised affair; it seems to be an example of a gratuitous human action, but it too is marked by the poet's ingenious formalism, for this mortal rescue is achieved through the agency of Artemis' cult statue.

The linked fraternal rescues, each the reverse image of the

---

[2] It is quite probable that Euripides was the inventor of this story of Iphigeneia's return, along with the Tauric journey of Orestes; see D. J. Conacher, *Euripidean Drama* (Toronto, 1967), pp. 304–5 and the Appendix on the myth below. It should be noted however that Grégoire strongly asserts the opposite in his introduction to the play (*Euripide*, IV [Assoc. Guillaume Budé, Paris, 1925], p. 97): 'La tradition orale, l'*hieros logos* des temples de Braurôn et d'Halae ont dû lui fournir la donnée essentielle de son drame.'

[3] This system of relationships is always present, but most strongly dwelt upon at 1401–2.

other, are crossed by an action of another sort, a tragedy of blind kin-murder that is interrupted in its catastrophe, and it is here that the poet has been most inventive. He has made this negative action, technically one of vengeance, into a complete inner drama, and has set it, unbroken, in the centre of his play like the blazon in a tapestry. Its theme is freedom, and it imitates an action in which mortals themselves interrupt their own crime and liberate themselves from blindness, chance, and their own past histories.

When the inner playlet opens, the mortal pair have taken up attitudes that directly defy both their own desires and the will of the gods. Every element in the double rescue situation has gone wrong, for the mortal sister is preparing to kill her rescuing brother, while the divine sister is demanding the blood of the man her Delphic brother has sent for her salvation. Orestes' purpose—the rescue of the goddess—is one Iphigeneia could feel sympathy with, but she knows nothing of it, and her identity is equally unknown to him. Thanks to their ignorance and their blindness, the barbaric Taurian cult is ready, like some earth-bred monster, to devour the Olympian agent who has been sent to challenge it.

Artemis and Iphigeneia are engaged in a version of the blind vengeance plot, but they happen to have set themselves against a divinely authored rescue action. Such a situation would seem to call for heavenly interference,[4] but Euripides has arranged affairs so that, here among the Taurians, it is the free interplay of human ethos that undoes this counterplot and brings the play back to its providential praxis. The brother and sister arrive at their recognition unaided, and when each has taught the other his identity, Orestes recognizes both the ordained necessity of rescuing the goddess and also the free possibility of releasing his sister as well. Of his own free will he embraces the two rescues in a new and single purpose and in so doing he unwittingly discovers the mechanism of escape for himself and his friend. His eagerness joins with Iphigeneia's wit and together they carry off the cult statue that saves them, even as they rescue it.

---

[4] Compare the similar situation in the *Ion*, where the divinely willed return action (like Orestes' rescue of Artemis here) and its parallel release for Creusa (like Orestes' rescue of Iphigeneia) are crossed by Creusa's threat to Ion (like the attempted sacrifice of Orestes). There the threat has to be dealt with directly by the god.

This counter-plot about the priestess who almost takes her own brother as a sacrificial victim is played out in its minimal form entirely within the second episode of the *Iphigeneia*. Its catastrophe is close and truly fearful, but the drama begins with a happy augury and ends with a confident prayer to its own cheated divinity. Its opening is signalled, indeed, by a prophetic tableau reminiscent of the symbolic prologue of the *Alcestis*, as the idea of liberation is imitated in a brief stage action. Iphigeneia, before anything else is said or done, orders the guards who have brought the victims to release them, and the audience watches while Orestes and Pylades are unbound, enjoying a vision that will serve them well.[5] These bonds will be assumed once more and cast off once more before the same two find themselves, unbound and free, in command of the vessel of escape. The largest meaning of the tableau and its fulfilment is stated while it is being staged, for the priestess announces solemnly that those who belong to the gods shall not be in chains (468–9).

Like the whole play, this central episode of catastrophe undone has been constructed with an almost mathematical symmetry, and the single recognition word that marks the interruption of its pathos has been placed precisely at its centre. The name 'Orestes' sounds out at line 769, just half-way through the great unbroken second act that stretches from line 467 to line 1088.[6] It occurs in the second of three balanced and plainly divided scenes which are arranged so as to produce a crescendo of discoveries as the principals rise beyond the literal recognition of friendly faces to the ultimate recognition of the powers that have shaped their present situation.

In the first of these three scenes (467–642) Iphigeneia discovers that her brother is not dead, and this discovery leads directly to her decision to put an old scheme of escape in motion. It moves her away from the idea of her victims' death and towards that of her own salvation, a spiritual turn that is made physical when she ends the scene by putting down the instruments of her office and going inside the temple to get the letter she has prepared—her plea for help. In the brief time since the captives

---

[5] For the magical significance of this tableau, see Nilsson, op. cit., i. 114.

[6] This section of the play is sometimes reported as two episodes, but its action is perfectly continuous and the chorus' lines at 644–65, short, without responsion, and wholly dramatic, in no way function as a stasimon would.

were brought to her she has experienced a full peripeteia from despair to hope and she is already much less the priestess and much more the princess than she was at the opening of her play. The threat of catastrophe has not grown, it has diminished, for when this scene began two men were to be killed, whereas now, at its close, only one is to die and the other is to be sent back to Greece alive. The letter which will in a sense save them all has already begun its work, but it could not come into play until Iphigeneia had been told that Orestes was alive. This scene's discovery, then, is the first of a saving train of circumstances and so it is of absolute importance to determine how the poet has brought it about.

The situation, when Iphigeneia and Orestes first confront one another, is formally like that of the first scene between the nurse and Phaedra in the *Hippolytus*, for the action demands that the one shall learn what the other is determined not to tell. Orestes' first break from his stubborn refusal to give any information is as important, for good, as Phaedra's is for evil, and curiously enough the reasons for the two lapses are not dissimilar. Iphigeneia has been struck, the moment she glimpsed her victims, by admiration, pity and an instinctive sense of kinship. Since she is not to be physically guilty of their deaths, she can express these feelings with the immediate candor of her innocence, but her simple curiosity is at first rebuffed, just as her pity is, by an adamant Orestes. He is almost rude, but the poet has made him a true match for his sister in his inbred quality. He is unable to be taciturn when she asks about his relationship to Pylades and he grants her a fragment of personal information (498). This first lapse, provoked by *philia*, is soon followed by a second which is dictated by another prime element in the noble character. Honour means that a prince of Argos cannot refuse a demand made upon him in the name of *charis* (507; cf. 547, where she must get him past the name of Agamemnon with another plea for a favour), and when the friendly priestess frankly asks a favour she is rewarded with the name of her captive's fatherland. From this moment Orestes' anonymity is doomed, and so is the vengeance plot.

Orestes' 'weak' points are like Phaedra's, love and honour, and through them the decisive breach is made. His partner in the scene is, however, not like the nurse, and the fineness of her nature is displayed in the series of questions that now follow, demands artfully arranged by the poet to demonstrate the conflicting emotions that the inquirer feels. Iphigeneia begins in bitterness, and asks first after those she holds responsible for her present friendless fate: Helen, Calchas, Odysseus, Achilles, and finally Agamemnon. She hopes to hear that they have suffered, but all her trumped-up desire for vengeance dissolves when she hears of her father's death and the murder of Clytemnestra. Her bitterness is laid to rest permanently when she includes Agamemnon in her pity for herself at Aulis: 'Wretched she was, and wretched the father who killed her' (565; cf. her later statement at 992). Orestes, in the line that follows, gives her a chance to curse Helen once more, but she passes it by, and turning from those she had tried to hate to the thought of one she loved, she asks at last for news of Agamemnon's son.

With her vengeance thus renounced, the climax of the scene arrives. Orestes' answer is not meant to be encouraging ('He lives, poor wretch, everywhere and nowhere' 568), but it bursts upon Iphigeneia as the bright waking from a protracted nightmare. 'Farewell, you lying dreams!' she cries, 'you were but nothingness' (569). One part of the truth has been discovered, and with it comes an unconscious grasp of the whole, for Iphigeneia at once finds the man before her transformed. She had looked upon him as a victim for the goddess, but now she sees him, more rightly than she knows, as a saviour for herself. This effect is obscured, almost as soon as it is produced, by Orestes' refusal to take the rescuer's role. He presses it upon Pylades, but the audience knows that he will soon accept his proper function, and meanwhile his insistence upon playing the victim allows the poet to exploit the expected ironies as Iphigeneia promises to do all a sister would in the tending of his tomb (627–35). The dramatist can afford to play, for the work of the scene is done and the recognition stands prepared. When Iphigeneia goes into the temple for her letter, she takes the first mechanical step towards her own and her brother's salvation. The plot is safe and its ethical colour has been firmly set, for the scene has shown how innocence, pity, and love have led the captive priestess to ask exactly those things which the nobility of her victim could not refuse.

The letter itself, the key to the recognition scene (643–900) that follows, is a charming curiosity. Technically superfluous, it has that multiplicity of right effects that marks the truly ingenious poetic idea. Euripides had set himself the task of inventing a recognition that should be as nearly as possible simultaneous in its effects; he evidently meant it to depend neither upon physical tokens nor upon outside interference but to emanate from the parties concerned, and he clearly wished it to involve all three of his actors. The fictional situation is one in which two people insist upon withholding their names. Since the reason for silence is in both cases pride, persuasion cannot be used, and since each is consciously protracting the ignorance of the other, most of the usual revelatory accidents are likewise ruled out as solutions to this deadlock. One or the other of the characters must be tricked by the dramatist into an unwitting disclosure and under these conditions the most obvious mechanism is the overheard soliloquy.[7] This is the device that Euripides has chosen, but Iphigeneia's self-betrayal is no ordinary contrived affair of unlikely musings overheard by auditors who are hidden in the arras. Her private words are contained instead in a letter that she wrote long ago, and they are overheard by Orestes as she reads them out to his friend. From the letter Orestes learns the priestess' identity, or rather, by a typical Euripidean trick, he learns his own, finding himself to be identical with the brother she at last specifies by name ('Say to Orestes . . .' 769).

Iphigeneia's recitation is prepared with inordinate cleverness—her doubts of Pylades' perfect faith, their reciprocal oaths, his lawyer-like insistence upon stopping up an apparent loophole in their agreement—and in the end this expenditure of poetic skill betrays one central fact: that the letter is not the mechanism of recognition but is on the contrary a looming obstacle. Only when the tablets have been in fancy left at the bottom of the sea can the situation shape itself as it should, for it is speech that must be obtained, if this scene is to succeed. Why then, when Iphigeneia could so easily have given her message orally in the first place, has this troublesome letter been forced upon the recognition scene?

[7] It is likewise in essence the device of the Sophoclean *Electra*, where the heroine's lamentation over the urn is addressed to no one but herself, though others are present.

As soon as we ask what the letter brings to the scene, its justification becomes plain. Without a physical message, the pantomime of delivery would be impossible, and it is that brief moment of inspired 'play-acting' that gives the whole scene its extraordinary brightness. There is a comic gaiety in the little trick that is played on Iphigeneia, and it works a minor miracle. The exhausted and hopeless captives are rejuvenated in an instant and the august priestess seems almost to be in short skirts again as Orestes and Pylades mime the delivery and receipt of the letter for all the world like a pair of schoolboys teasing a favourite sister (788–94). They have known her through the last fifteen lines,[8] and their joy has been wordlessly communicated, but they have chosen to keep their faces straight in order that Pylades might formally take custody of the precious letter, turn, and with mock solemnity present it to his friend. Orestes as solemnly receives it, then throws it to the ground and pounces on his sister in what seems to her a most disrespectful embrace. This evocation of a joy at once spirited and pure is the effect for which so much ingenuity has been expended. It is a theatrical moment that has never been rivalled and it gives to the *Iphigeneia* an uncloying sweetness that is to be savoured still.

But why a letter prepared long ago, and kept for years in the temple? Granted that it would be awkward for the priestess to sit down on stage and prepare her tablets, could she not have been sent within to write her message (as Phaedra is, in other circumstances)? Of course she could, but Euripides, once he had determined upon a physical letter, saw that it might serve as an external confirmation of his portrait of his heroine. The letter written and kept is a material witness to a principal quality of Iphigeneia's spirit, her faithful confidence, reminding

---

[8] Some unnecessary problems have been created over lines 777 ff. I would follow Hermann in assigning 777 to Orestes, 778–9 to Iphigeneia, the ὦ θεοί of 780 to Orestes, the rest to Iphigeneia, then 781–2 to Orestes. These last two lines are called 'puzzling' by Platnauer and have been agonized over by many, but this is largely because of their wrong ascription to Pylades. In Orestes' mouth they make perfect sense. Iphigeneia says, 'Why do you interrupt and call upon the gods?' and her brother, who has begun to see the truth, answers, 'It is nothing. Go ahead. My thoughts have strayed, and were I to question you I would probably have to give up a thing I long to believe in.' ἐξέβην ἄλλοσε means 'I was thinking of something else, i.e., not of your letter but of the incredible notion that you might be my lost sister, Iphigeneia.'

us that she had never quite ceased to hope for rescue and return. The letter is also evidence of the heroine's chief negative virtue, her refusal to see her priestly office as an opportunity for revenge. The notion of vengeance has been urged upon her (cf. the messenger, at 337–9), and it is inherent in her situation, but she has evidently always been as incapable of hatred as she shows herself this day. The letter testifies to this, for it is the work of an earlier Greek captive who found the priestess so sympathetic that he was willing to do her a favour, though he was to die a victim of her cult.[9]

Surely, however, this letter which is so much a part of herself might have been carried with adequate probability in the priestess' robes? Why did the dramatist arrange the unprecedented quick exit and re-entrance of one of his characters during the course of an episode? Here the answer must lie in what transpires during the absence so awkwardly purchased, and with this we come to the last of the letter's effects. To get her letter Iphigeneia hurries into the temple and while she is gone a little scene is played between Orestes and Pylades, a scene that is both isolated and intensified by the temporary removal of the priestess (644–724; note how its end is marked by Orestes' 'But hush . . . she is returning!'). The subject is established at once by the chorus, who sing a few phrases to mark the articulation of the scene, and find themselves unable to decide whether the victim or the friend who will survive him is the more pitiable (655–6). Orestes wants to speculate about the origins of the priestess, but Pylades insists on speaking of their relative fortunes. He cannot endure to live on and seem to profit from Orestes' death, and, careless of Iphigeneia's escape, he asks to be allowed to die with his friend, as he has lived with him (674–86). This speech allows Orestes to repeat the gesture that he had already made in insisting that he, and not Pylades, should be the Taurians' victim. He means to be a love-sacrifice as well as a sacrifice to Artemis, and his argument is that of Alcestis, reduced to its smallest scale. Anything that he could do with an extended life, Pylades could do far better; he would like, however, a token repayment in the form of care for his tomb, and the continuation of his name. Pylades, like Admetus, can only accept nobly and

---

[9] Paley, who was gentler than the ancients, would have this earlier Greek repaid, like Pylades, with salvation; see his note at 593.

promise all that is asked; he has offered his own love-sacrifice and it has been refused.

Twice more before the episode is over a love-sacrifice will be made, in spirit though not in flesh, and the whole sequence takes on a heavy significance through this repetition. As soon as Iphigeneia realizes that Apollo intends Orestes to escape, she considers the possibility that this might be brought about only at the cost of her life. Before the recognition, when she had first learned that Orestes was alive, she had seen her problem as, 'How can I get my brother to save me?' but now she asks herself, 'How can I save my brother?' and she answers, 'With my life, if need be.' Like Alcestis she says, 'The best thing would be if we could all survive—you, me and the goddess—but if that cannot be, then my life is the cheapest price we can pay for a partial salvation since it is, after all, only a female life' (999 ff.). Orestes refuses his sister's sacrifice, but the plan of escape that they make together demands the sacrifice of the entire chorus to the three who are to return to Greece. This favour Iphigeneia has the courage to ask (1056 ff.), promising, as indeed her play does, the paradoxical reward of salvation for those who lay down their lives (1067–8; cf. Helen's vaguer promise, *Helen* 1389). The Greek women have no reason to expect that her promise can be kept, but they agree to the risk of death, if it can serve the princess's escape.

The events of this long episode culminate in a decision to cheat the Tauric cult of its ritual sacrifice, but every one of the mortals present has meanwhile shown himself ready to serve a friend as a love-sacrifice. This theme is stated most boldly in the little scene between Orestes and Pylades, and it is there coupled with the apparently complementary theme of criticism of the gods. Earlier, Orestes had suggested that there was a disorderly uproar in heaven that might destroy a perfectly sane man (572–5), but here his doubt hardens into a kind of blasphemy, for he finds not disorder but a self-seeking cruelty in god. Having himself insisted upon this death, he counts it against Apollo as a divine crime[10] and concludes that he has been shamefully tricked in the matter of this trip to the Taurians:

[10] Compare the like spiritual sophistry that leads Amphitryon into blasphemy at *HF* 339–47; see below, pp. 163 ff.

Phoebus made a lie of prophecy
and used his oracle to drive me out of Greece,
ashamed of his own mantic words that once
had found my reverent ear and made of me
my mother's doom—a man who wished to die.

(711–15)

In the last moment before the recognition the dramatist thus uses the private exchange between Orestes and his friend to sound the spiritual state of his hero. Orestes' willingness to die is a measure of his love for Pylades, but it is also seen to be a measure of his conviction that Apollo is his enemy. So much can be said of him before. As soon as the duet of recognition is finished the poet takes another sounding, and this time he gets a very different result, for he finds a new Orestes who is ready to offer to Apollo far more than he had earlier offered to his friend. Orestes had been eager to die before out of a distaste for both heaven and earth, but now he is eager to live, though ready to die if he must, in the service of Apollo or in the interest of Iphigeneia (1009 ff.).

Pylades' first words, when the recognition music is over, announce the beginning of a new action that aims at salvation (905), and Orestes responds at once with phrases that betray a total revolution in his views of heaven and its relation to the affairs of men. Pylades has said that they face a moment of *kairos*, and Orestes answers:

You are right, and I think that fortune
will support us, for when a man is earnest
heaven likes to show its strength in his behalf.

(909–11)

This speech is separated from his bitter conclusion that 'Phoebus' oracles are of little use to me' (723) only by the one hundred and seventy-five line recognition scene, but the new tone is no mere brief rush of optimism. It affects Orestes' view of the present and the future, and it also causes him to revise his version of the past, for as he speaks a new Apollo and a new Delphi begin to appear.

Iphigeneia's apparently unseasonable questions about affairs at home provoke Orestes' tale of the linked promise and command that have brought him from Delphi to the Tauric shores.

There is no hint of dissatisfaction with heaven now, as he tells how Apollo had saved him once and has promised to save him again, and he ends with a simple exhortation. 'Let's work this salvation that Apollo has defined. If we can take the statue, my madness will release me and I can take you away in my many-oared ship, back to Mycenae at last!' (979–82). He will hear nothing of his sister's talk of buying his life with hers, arguing now that there is harmony in heaven, and that Apollo's command is therefore a promise of success (1012–16). In him the recognition has wrought a physical and a spiritual transformation, for he is bold where before he was afraid, his resentment of the god has turned to gratitude, and his escape from the Furies seems already to have begun.

Orestes has recognized his sister and, through her, the true nature of Apollo. Iphigeneia likewise moves from the discovery of her brother to a fuller discovery of the goddess whose creature she is. The bloody rites that she herself takes part in have long disturbed her, for she could not reconcile them with her own experience of Artemis at Aulis, or with her conception of what divinity must be (380 ff.). She had hesitantly reached the conclusion that she was serving only man, not god, when she offered human sacrifices, and that Artemis' thirst for blood was merely a fiction of the Taurians (389–90). These thoughts find perfect confirmation now in the revelation that Orestes makes to her of Apollo's will. If Artemis is to be separated from the barbarities of the Taurians, it must be because she wishes to leave them (so Orestes, at 1012–13). And this means that she is, in truth, the pure goddess her priestess had yearned for (391) and had once known. With this new understanding, Iphigeneia sees her way at once to an apparent betrayal of her patron god.[11] No scruple troubles her promise that she will not sacrifice the appointed victim (994), for she knows that the goddess never wanted an honour such as this. The scene at Aulis has been repeated, and she has herself acted the hated part of Agamemnon, but she is allowed now to imitate the saving miracle as well. And when Orestes explains his designs upon the cult-statue of the Taurians, Iphigeneia easily sees the appropriateness of stealing the goddess who once stole her (28). She closes the episode with a prayer that

---

[11] Compare Theonoe's decision to 'betray' her prophetic calling at *Helen*, 1017; see below, pp. 93 ff.

remembers, in good hymn form, that former time when Artemis had cheated herself of a human sacrifice:[12]

> Lady who saved me in the vale of Aulis,
> who stole me from my father's hand,
> save me now once more, and save my friends!
> Do not betray the tongue of Loxias,
> but leave this barbarous land and come
> graciously to Attica. This is no seemly home
> for you, and now a blessed city calls.
>
> (1082–8)

The inner play is over, its catastrophe not only interrupted but quite undone by the decision to escape and by the sense of divine favour that now fills principals who had seemed abandoned to themselves and dead to one another. There is a new danger now, and a new action, for the recognition has paradoxically altered the physical situation for the worse. Where first two, then one, were condemned to die, there are now three who are threatened with death in the service of Apollo's rescue plan, yet all are now perfectly confident. The risk is plain, but Iphigeneia, in the scene of Thoas' deception (episode three, 1152–233) is jubilant to the point of exaltation. Perhaps this is because she is actually holding the cult statue in her arms; her coolness and her wit, at any rate, can only be called inspired. The audience too has meanwhile been drawn into this new mood of confidence, for it has been taught to approve these three who have, unaided, fought free from an ambush of chance and returned to heaven's campaign.

In perfect contrast to Helen (to whom she is so often compared) Iphigeneia takes a single central truth and uses it to deceive her oppressor, the king of the Taurians. In her escape intrigue, true reference to the actual guilt of the past functions almost like a magic password, opening the temple doors to the xoanon and clearing a free path to the water. She argues that Artemis' statue has been soiled with blood (and so it has been, by the Tauric cult, as long as anyone can remember) and must now be

---

[12] Notice the Taurian messenger's perfect misunderstanding when he accuses an Iphigeneia he believes to have forgotten her just vengeance of 'forgetting the bloodshed of Aulis and betraying the goddess' (1418–19). What Iphigeneia does is remember the bloodshed of Aulis, i.e., remember that it was a deer's blood and not her own that was shed.

purified and re-established in a place that is pure (Attica); she explains that the source of the contamination is in the victims who have been dedicated to the goddess, since the present victims are touched with a peculiar form of blood guilt and are in need of a special lustration which she means to give to them. All of these statements are true; they need only to be tricked out with a certain artful vagueness and the miasma of Clytemnestra's blood becomes a positive element in the happy outcome of this play.

In what Thoas calls her 'prooimion' Iphigeneia describes what has been happening in the temple as an ill-omened thing which must be exorcised, and then she adds, 'I dedicate the tale (*epos*) I tell to Sanctity' (1161), announcing to those who can understand her that a pious fiction will be told. Her one real invention is a brilliant example of how she can lie and yet, by the saving grace of the goddess's presence, be truthful still. The pressing necessity of everything she urges is proved to the king by a report of what he takes to be a temple miracle, though it is actually no more than the physical fact he is at the moment witnessing. How does Iphigeneia know that the sacrifice is unclean? Because, says the priestess who has come out of the temple with the cult statue in her arms, the goddess has abandoned her accustomed place! (1165; the phrase can even mean 'has left her temporary quarters and turned towards home'). And when Thoas asks whether Artemis moved of her own free will or was toppled by an earthquake, Iphigeneia answers in full faith, 'Of her own will', for she is sure now that she understands the goddess's will (1167).[13]

As she uses her brother's actual guilt in the fabrication of their salvation, so Iphigeneia also uses the desire for vengeance that she once briefly felt but now has put aside. Thoas must trust her absolutely, or he will see how foolish he is to let this Greek priestess take two Greek captives off to the seashore in undisturbed secrecy. She therefore takes a piece of truth ('the strangers have told her that her brother lives') and adds a piece of falsehood ('and that her father lives as well') and allows Thoas to draw the conclusion of his own desires. 'You were not interested,

---

[13] She also says that the statue closed its eyes, a detail which suggests that the image at Brauron may have been reported to have closed eyes; cf. the tale about the Trojan Athena image, Strabo 6.1.14.

of course, but thought only of the service of the goddess', he
says, and she responds, 'Yes, I hate all of Greece, for she was my
destruction' (1186–7). If she is indifferent even to her father
and brother, simply because they are Greeks, how little has he
to fear from these two captive strangers! So thinks Thoas, and
he accedes to all her demands.

The king is a courtly, and, in his own sense, a pious man,
and so it is easy to bend him to purposes that have been described
with such skilful duplicity. In the end he can only admire
Iphigeneia more than he had before, saying with unconscious
appropriateness, 'How just your piety and your foresight are!'
and, 'The city will marvel at you, and with good cause!' (1202
and 1214). She meanwhile has reached a pitch of something
dangerously near levity, for when all is settled she risks a final
sally. 'And if I should seem long', she counsels ('How long should
I wait?' he asks) . . . 'do not be surprised!' (1220). One final
prayer to Artemis and she departs with her brother and his
friend, never to be seen again in these parts. Her last words are
consummate in their deceptive truth:

> Oh virgin child of Leto and of Zeus,
> I will rinse away these victims' gore
> and sacrifice, where sacrifice is due!
> You will have a dwelling that is pure
> and we shall be content. I say no more
> but make my meaning clear
> to gods who understand all things
> and clear to you, my Queen!
>
> (1230–3)

The exit of the three principals is marked by a light-hearted
ode and then followed by a messenger scene which must be
considered with its corresponding architectural partner, the
messenger scene of the first episode. Euripides has here paired
two speeches in a fashion that is prophetic of the two reports
from the mountain that enclose the central action of the *Bacchae*,
for here too the second unseen event is played in the same locale
as the first, and here too the second is so constructed that it
repeats the movements of the first, and brings a new meaning to
them.

Early in this day a group of cowherds who were at the shore
received a report of the arrival of stranger gods; they debated

among themselves and decided to investigate; they saw two young men, one in a fit of madness, and they heard the name 'Pylades' spoken. The cowherds attacked the two young men but were beaten back; they found that the rocks they threw would not strike the strangers, but they did at last knock the swords from their hands and so exhaust the two that they sank down helpless to the ground and were taken captive by the crowd. Such was the First Messenger's tale. Now the Second Messenger comes, and he tells of citizens in the king's service who are at the same shore; they are struck with the idea that the same strangers may be escaping; they debate among themselves and decide to investigate; they see the two young men in the act of getting their ship under weigh, and they hear the name 'Orestes' spoken. The guards attack, but are beaten back and the ship gets off, but in the last possible moment it is struck by an inshore wind and driven back helpless to the beach where it is captured by the crowd. The upshot of the first capture was that two were to die, victims of the local cult; the upshot of the second is that the same two, and with them the priestess of the cult, are to die as secular criminals, either thrown from a cliff or impaled upon sharpened stakes.

We seem to be confronted with a solecism, the only example in tragedy of an interrupted catastrophe in its positive version, an interrupted felicity! All that the day and the drama have accomplished has been swept away by the great wave that drove the Greek ship back upon the Taurian shore, and the accomplishment thus engulfed has been a magnificent one. The perfect congruency between the two messenger scenes has marked once more the fact that these were no ordinary escapes. Orestes' departure from these shores was his departure from madness, while Iphigeneia's was her flight from complicity in the impious Tauric rites. This double liberation had been threatened by a chance; this seems to be the instruction of the echoes between the two speeches, for it was apparently only chance that kept Orestes' name from being sounded at the beginning, as it was at the end, and so it was chance that allowed Iphigeneia to attempt her sacrifice. The mortals had defeated that chance, however, and had turned and begun to fight for their own freedom with irreproachable strategy. Iphigeneia had used truth and her goddess, and Orestes and Pylades had fought unarmed (notice the point that is made of this, 1367–8) against enormous odds in an encounter almost literally bloodless. (Line 1374 does record a few minor bumps and scratches but this is the extent of the damage.) All that they were attempting was in strict accordance with the proclaimed will of Apollo, and it had been ironically pronounced an example of 'just piety and foresight' by their helpless opponent (1202).

By this time, indeed, these principals have come to seem not only ordinarily pious but ritually spotless as well. Iphigeneia has given the cult image and the two erstwhile victims a lustral Black Sea bath and as she herself says, the sea washes away all mortal corruption (1193). The two young men had previously entered a door set round with human skulls,[14] where a death-demanding goddess dwelt; they had made a gesture of placation to her by putting on her bonds, and then they had been led out of the place of blood, back into new life and freedom, by that same divinity. And from their 'katabasis' they had brought back a hostage, Iphigeneia (their Theseus), and a word—'salvation's renowned name' (905; cf. the conceit built on the idea of secret doctrine at 1092 and the messenger's unconscious δεῖ γὰρ αὐτὸν εἰδέναι τὰ δρώμενα of the uninitiate barbarian king at 1295).

This symbolic action of initiation is strengthened in its effect by the poet, who has arranged a verbal release from criminality for the whole House of Atreus. He could not remove the blood from the history of that notorious house, and he would not have wanted to, for only with principals chosen from such a context could he have arranged his peculiar overturn, from extremest guilt to perfect innocence. What he has done is to leave the old crimes as they were but to obscure them whenever possible by a crowd of fine images. Thus the chorus never recognizes the criminality of Orestes, but sees him as a hero on a quest, likening him to one of the Argonauts and inaugurating a system of allusions that reminds the audience that this is a man who has passed through the Symplegades (especially in the first stasimon; 422, cf. 241; 260; 355; 746; 890; 1398). They excise the blackest names from the family history, never speaking of Atreidae, but rather of Tantalids or Pelopids, while Iphigeneia clears Tantalus

---

[14] A. M. Dale, *WS* lxix (1956), p. 101, denies that this was a visible Hades décor, but there is no reason to doubt the existence of elaborate painted sets, and this one is explicitly described.

with her explicit repudiation of his banquet (386 ff.).[15] The family crime is thus pushed well back into the past and is reduced from dining on children's flesh to the mere removal of a lower-class accomplice. The quarrel between the famous brothers so artfully left nameless by the chorus is referred to by means of a pair of images that bathe the whole sinister affair in an argent glow, for the golden ram and the sun that stood still are used to draw the eye away from the slaughter and to fix it instead upon the wealth of the house, its nobility, and its kinship with the gods (191 ff., cf. 813).

This poetic redemption of the House of Atreus is carried one step further in the recognition scene, for there the old Atreid crimes are actually made to contribute to the happy recognition, just as Orestes' blood-guilt is made to contribute to the later escape. Orestes begins, following the chorus's example, by muffling his father's and his grandfather's names in that of Pelops (807), but the poet has here prepared a better trick. He makes the boy call up, among the unseen recognition tokens, the memory of a childish piece of tapestry that his sister had made, one that depicted the quarrel of Thyestes and Atreus (812), and with this single stroke he assigns the whole history to the realm of fiction, making it the sort of thing that is recited or put into an embroidery. (This, incidentally, is the play's only mention of Thyestes; Atreus is named here and at 3.) In this guise the old outrage, once again imaged not by dismembered bodies but by the golden lamb (813), takes its part in the hopeful resolution of the play. The spear of Pelops, symbol of the family's first crime, is even more thoroughly tamed, for it turns up like some beribboned Heracles among the princess's gowns in the Argive gynaeceum (823 ff). The antique murder weapon becomes the final memory token that proves to Iphigeneia that her brother is found and, thus utilized, it joins the Thyestes tapestry to represent a pair of ancient misdeeds that almost seem to be examples of the fortunate fall.

By means such as these the spectator has been led to admire the young Atreids and to think of them as cleansed initiates whose

---

[15] On Iphigeneia's glossing over of the evils of her house in the prologue, see Max Treu, 'Wohl dem, der seiner Väter gern gedenkt', *Gymnasium*, lxxv. 5 (1968), 435–52, where her attitude is seen as an expression of her longing for home. Her opening should be contrasted with that of Electra in *Orestes*, with its quick triple repetition of Atreus' name and its direct reference to Thyestes' feast (*Or.* 15).

salvation is assured. Yet having seen them succeed in a free rescue of themselves from death and crime, he now seems to see them fail in the foreordained rescue of Artemis, a failure that would frustrate heaven and condemn the humans to a peculiarly barbaric death. The messenger ends his tale and Thoas prepares to recapture the Greeks while the audience sits restless and perplexed by this apparent defeat not only of virtue and piety but of the most mysterious promises that Greek faith had to offer.

With the storm the poet places an unexpected obstacle in the way of fortune's upturning wheel, but in the next moment he provides an Athena who announces from her machine that she has already undone this contradiction, interrupting the interruption of the felicity. Evidently the sea was roused only that it might be calmed, and we are clearly meant to draw instruction from this sequence of events. The report of the wave seems to testify to the existence of an unidentified force at large in creation, a force strong enough to destroy with ease the noblest of human achievements, but weak enough to be set aside by god with an even greater ease. This force, so gratuitously brought to our attention, has not been named by the poet, who evidently thought that the source and significance of the wave would be immediately plain to his audience. The modern reader, however, finds this sudden near disaster hard to comprehend and must search his text for some illumination, before he can be satisfied that it is not a blatant case of sensation for its own sake.

The messenger, in the body of his report, describes what seems to be a perfectly natural though unusual event (1390-7). He speaks of an initial ferocious wave and a fearful gust of wind which together strike the ship as soon as it passes out of the protected harbour. Then a second wave comes, and this one drives the Greeks relentlessly back to the enemy shore. There is no mysterious voice, no monstrous appearance or other indication of the supernatural,[16] but nonetheless the messenger, at the end

---

[16] The passage (1390-6) is corrupt, but Murray's and Mekler's ἐστί' (1395) turn it into sense. I cannot agree with Morrison's objections to the mention of sail here (CR lxiv [1950], 4-5), for the crew would not wait to raise sail until the ship was in open sea, but would do so just before they passed out of the harbour mouth. Thus we can translate: 'The crew roared out a happy shout and struck the sea with their oars. The ship, while it was within the harbour, moved along with the bit in its teeth, but when it passed into the open sea it fell upon a violent wave and

of his speech, interprets his tale almost as an epiphany. He confidently reports that it is Poseidon who has thus robbed the three Greeks of all hope of salvation; he has handed them over to Thoas because he continues to be angry with the Pelopidae over the siege of Troy (1414–17).[17] Meanwhile, the messenger has also reported Iphigeneia's response to the disaster, and it turns out that she has read the event differently, taking the wave as an omen sent by Artemis to express her opposition to the rape of her cult statue (1398–402). Had one or the other of these gods alone been named, we might have felt fairly certain that the supernatural interpretation was correct, but with both Poseidon and Artemis put forward as authors of the wave the case for divine interference is a far less compelling one.

The messenger speech thus suggests either natural chance or one of two divinities as the cause of the inimical wave, and we look to Athena for guidance in an ambiguous situation. She seems to rule out Iphigeneia's reading of the reverse, for she represents the transportation of the statue as a necessary and neutral event (1453 ff.). She does not, however, make any explicit choice between the remaining two possibilities, nature and Poseidon, for she does not specify what the power was that she, Apollo, Artemis, and Poseidon have just rallied to defeat. She reports only that the latter god has smoothed the sea now for Orestes' escaping oar. Whether he was called in as the god who had caused the turbulence in the first place, or simply as the god with marine jurisdiction Athena does not say.

The goddess in the machine will not name the force that the Olympian group has just conquered, but she does at least tell us how she procured Poseidon's aid, and in so doing she allows for the final identification of the author of the wave. Like Iphigeneia with her brother, so Athena with her father's brother simply asked a favour (*charis*, 1444) and everything came right. The god was bound as the mortal was, by an aristocratic code of honour, and this fact gives the clue to the poet's intent. He has chosen to depict the residents of heaven as members of a noble

was driven hard, for a fearful wind, coming upon them suddenly, blew the ship's sail clean back over the stern. The oarsmen struggled and kicked (in vain) against the sea, but an inrolling billow bore them back upon the land.'

[17] Note however Page, *Actors' Interpolations* (Oxford, 1934), p. 78, where it is urged that these lines are not genuine. The objection rests principally on the use of παρέχειν, and does not seem strong enough to warrant excision.

and well regulated family, respectful of law, interested in mortality and cognizant of one another's plans. This means that if the unfortunate wave was first created and then stilled by the god Poseidon, the dramatist is saying that heaven conquers its own anarchistic impulses by an appeal to a fixed and positive custom—a statement that suffers from internal contradiction.[18] If, on the other hand, the wave took its origin in one of nature's random tendencies, the dramatist has said that heaven controls idle chances such as this through its own loving internal order—an assertion that does at least make sense.

This play takes the role of accident in human life more seriously than any other Euripidean tragedy does.[19] Whether this is or is not a chance-dominated world is one of the subjects upon which its characters speculate, and the theme is introduced in the opening lines of the first stasimon. There the chorus wonders at the unexpected arrival of a pair of strangers, assuming that these men (known to the audience as Apollo's emissaries) have struck this shore by accident while in pursuit of gain. In a passage reminiscent of Hesiod on going to sea or of Solon on ambition, the women reflect upon the foolish and avid courage that they believe has now betrayed the young men to a chancy death. Orestes has reason to know that something other than chance has shaped his destiny, but Iphigeneia, while she is under the spell of her dream, seems to share the chorus's vision of a tyche-governed universe (475 ff.; 489; 501). She never sees chance and heaven as being at cross purposes, however, and in the recognition duet, when she once more feels the force of providence, her phrases suggest that even if she had actually presided at the death of her brother this would have been but one more example of a chance that is guided by god (867, in its manuscript position). Orestes likewise after the recognition sees *tyche* as a subordinate aspect of a divine intention (τὸ θεῖον) that is powerful and benignant as it touches men's affairs (909–11). And

[18] This is not the same as the statement of the *Hippolytus*, where it is said that the anarchy of heaven answers to a kind of negative regulation by which spheres of interest are respected. The divine order is there viewed much as 'healthy free enterprise' once was among economists.

[19] Ever since the publication of Solmsen's influential article, 'Euripides' Ion im Vergleich mit anderen Tragödien', *Hermes*, lxix (1934), 390–419, plays that do not really concern themselves with chance at all have come to be called 'Tyche plays', a most unfortunate appellation.

finally Athena corrects the initial misapprehension of the chorus, stating absolutely that Orestes came here at the behest of Apollo, whose commands carry the weight of destiny (1438–9). Thus the verbal teaching of the play seems to be that the autonomous power of *tyche* is merely an appearance, while the power of heaven is reality.

The teaching of the plot is the same, though the action, in order to assert this truth, has to give a prominent place to chance; it offers a demonstration first of the power of that force, and then of the ease with which it can be subdued by god. The opening capture of Orestes and Pylades was due to an outrageous chance, for what business had the cowherds to be at the shore? (Note Iphigeneia's astonished question at 254.) The failure or Orestes and Iphigeneia to recognize each other at the outset was likewise dictated by the chance that kept Orestes' name from sounding in the cowherd's ear. His anonymity makes the prince the puppet of chance and the poet ensures our understanding of this fact by causing the victim to respond, when the priestess asks for the name his father has given him, with: 'You might with justice call me Dystyches!' (500). Brute accident has cast Orestes as the enemy in a plot of blind vengeance when he was meant to play the hero of a providential rescue piece, and when he is about to submit to the death demanded by this counter-plot Orestes sums his situation up: 'One must let *tyche* have its way' (489).

All of this emphasis upon *tyche* means that it was chance over which the mortals were victorious when they managed their recognition and so their interruption of the vengeance action. Their victory indeed was so marked that it made the wave a moral necessity, for if chance is to be thought of as separate from but under the power of providence, then mortals, however admirable and pious they be, cannot be allowed an easy triumph over it. Euripides has indulged in this play in an almost Pelagian celebration of the virtue and wit of man, but he has found, in the gigantic wave, a remedy for his near-heresy. This final accident allows him to maintain the scale of his portrait of humanity almost undiminished, while he yet concludes his piece with a demonstration of the power of the gods. Everything these mortals had won from chance is destroyed by a resurgence of that force and those who were strong and confident are swiftly made hopeless and weak. At once, however, Athena restores what chance had taken away. The escape is renewed, but transformed so that it is no longer merely a vulgar example of success; it is now a reward of virtue. The ship sets out again for the open sea, and in this departure there will be none of the rough disorder of the second messenger's tale. In fulfilment of the cowherd's initial vision, the three mortals will go off at last like journeying demi-gods, their voyage sped by Apollo's lyre and the pipes of Pan, as it was in the chorus's prophetic song (1123 ff.).[20] This triumph, though deserved, is not the fruit of a worldly eagerness; it is a gift from god, and the story thus becomes one that a Solon or a Pindar might have heard with full approval.

Chance's single wave was as good as a deluge for the mortals on the ship, but viewed from heaven it was the merest ripple in a sea that was easily calmed. This chance that is strong enough to provoke gods as well as men, yet so weak that it disappears within an instant has, in this play, a curious, semi-demonic power. Iphigeneia knows it as one of three essences in a universe that contains the divine, the mortal, and the unexpected (895); it plays upon ignorance and leads men deeper into blindness (ἡ γὰρ τύχη παρήγαγ' ἐς τὸ δυσμαθές 478), and it is imaged not only by the wave but by Iphigeneia's dream.

The dream was the motive force in the counter-plot that rose against the gods' rescue plans—the plot that represents the accidental in this play. By convincing Iphigeneia that her brother was dead, it blocked the recognition and at the same time turned Iphigeneia's ordinary reluctance to sacrifice into her best imitation of a wish to spill Greek blood (348 ff.). If this same dream had visited a baser priestess, the sacrifice would have been hurried forward with no questions asked, the catastrophe would have been completed, and Iphigeneia would have been the principal in an exotic vengeance killing. And since *tyche* as well as providence knows how to play with irony, this is exactly what the dream predicted. Its vision of the priestess-sister preparing the victim-brother for his ritual death was a prophecy of accident triumphant.

The dream was probably first invented merely as a double dramaturgical trick. It allowed the poet to create a seeming resurrection for his hero, on his first appearance, and it also allowed him to mark an over-all reversal for his heroine, from

<hr/>

[20] For kidnapping and carrying off as symbolic of transport to another life, see Ch. Picard, *Les Religions préhelléniques* (Paris, 1948), pp. 171 ff.

the depths of a Hades-oriented despair to an ultimate, godlike transportation across a magical sea. Once created, however, the dream offered a difficult problem, for its tremendous influence had to be dispelled before Iphigeneia could produce her cherished letter and get the recognition under way.

The dream overshadowed the first third of the play. Iphigeneia wept, she poured libations, and she resolved upon a new vengefulness, all under its spell. Then, at the briefest word from a stranger, she is seen to bid her dream good-bye and to act at once in the confident assumption that her brother lives. Only the rapidity of the continuing action saves her from seeming frivolous as she so easily throws off the weight of her obsession. The spectator is for the moment distracted, but the sudden dissolution of the dream leaves the mechanism of the funeral parodos sadly revealed, and before long he is sure to wonder why a dream that could be so lightly dismissed was ever taken seriously.

Euripides knew that this question would arise, and he chose to meet it directly. He did not try to distract us permanently from this specious and deceptive dream, but returned to it instead and made it central to the imagery and instruction of his play. In the final choral ode he treats the dream, its error, and what has superseded it, explaining how a vision could be so hallucinating, so nearly prophetic, and so quickly repudiated. Dreams, his chorus announces, are the false rivals of revelation, manufactured by Apollo's old enemy, Earth. It is she who gives them power and verisimilitude but, being herself alienated from the authors of men's fortunes, she cannot give them truth. Dreams are thus like chance events; they belong among the random things of the world which, this myth suggests, are the vestigial evidences of a pre-Olympian time. A true understanding of the past, the present or the future can come only from the power that is superior to both time and chance, and so is to be got only at the oracular shrines of the Olympian gods, by their aid and favour.

Thus paraphrased, the content of the ode sounds solemn enough. The mythic context is the subjection of the chthonian to the Olympian powers, and the event related is the same one the Pythia describes in the prologue of the *Eumenides*. But how the characters have changed! Euripides has equipped his Delphic aetiology with a fiction at once funny and grotesque, making his song the descendant of the Homeric hymns to Hermes and

Apollo²¹ and a companion piece in small to Sophocles' satyr play, the *Ichneutae*. His story is of an overgrown baby god who slays a great snake and sets himself up in full pomp at the oracular shrine of an elder relative. When she retaliates, and takes away his business with her invention of prophetic dreams, the indignant infant turns to papa, and Zeus is so enchanted by his son's precocious greed that he laughs aloud (1274). To please his boy he diverts the truth from dreams and grants to Apollo a monopoly of true prophecy.

Euripides has elsewhere been at pains to remind his audience that this is a sequel to the *Eumenides* (most plainly at 940 ff.), and this final ode suggests that he meant it to be an alternate for the Aeschylean *Proteus*. Next to nothing is known about the fourth member of the *Oresteia* tetralogy but we can recognize, in this rewritten finale to the drama of the House of Atreus, a standard satyr play motif cleverly used as comment on the older poet's work. That bitter learning through suffering which was the gift of the Aeschylean Zeus here finds its complement in another sort of learning granted by another sort of god. The old knowledge was necessarily made of remorse, but the new gift of Apolline prophecy brings, in this play, a general liberation from grief (κακῶν ἔκλυσις 899; λῆξις μανιῶν 981; μετάστασις πόνων 991-2) even though the mortal who profits by it most is at first scornful of its value (711-15). Zeus' laughing gift to Apollo and to mankind is thus like the gifts of wine and fire and music that appear in satyr plays, and it is surely no accident that in describing it the poet makes his single reference to Dionysus

---

²¹ In the Hymn to Hermes it is the outraged baby Hermes who stands beside Zeus, still holding his little blanket, and boldly lies about the stolen cattle so that Zeus laughs out loud at his son's audacity and his dishonesty (387-90; cf. *IT* 1274-5). Apollo in the same hymn is somewhat older; it is he who takes the case to Zeus, with a curious reference to a reputation of his own for greed (*h. Herm.* 334-5). He finally gives up his cattle to Hermes, in exchange for the lyre, but refuses to share his control of prophecy, except for the ancient and fallible divination of the bee-women which he scornfully grants to Hermes if he wants it (*h. Herm.* 550 ff.). In the more serious Hymn to Apollo a second version of the rival to Delphi appears; Telphusa there plays the part that Earth does in the Euripidean lyric, but being a minor power she is simply dispossessed and pinned beneath a cliff. The story of the rival form of prophecy existed also in a third version, reflected by Zenobius, *Proverbiorum centuria* v. 75; here it is Athena who invents the too popular second form of prophecy, divination by lot, which Zeus, because he loves his son, makes false.

The infancy of gods and heroes is one of the set themes of satyr play, witness *Ichneutae, Dionysiscus, Heracleiscus, Dictyulci*; the gods' gifts and inventions provide another, witness *Pyrkaeus, Ichneutae, Dionysiscus, Pandora, Triptolemus* (if it was satyr), etc. For this ode, Euripides has combined the two motifs.

(1234). The wine god has nothing to do with the myth of Apollo and his establishment at Delphi, nothing to do with the story of Iphigeneia, but he is, above all, the god of liberation, and the release that is effected at the end of this tragedy is as genial and as general as anything wrought by a satyr play.[22]

The Argive prince who left the stage almost unnoticed in the middle of the *Eumenides* had gone off like the obscure guest of honour from a party invaded by swells, from which fact Euripides chose to conclude that his release had not been truly procured. His Orestes is still pursued by a splinter group of Erinyes who refused to become Eumenides and remained at large even after the Aeschylean judgement (970–1). Athena suffers, perhaps, by the innovation, but it allows the poet to create a new Apolline salvation, cast in the form of healing prophecy. The oracle that sent Orestes to the Taurians is thus finally made to raise the House of Atreus (845–9) by reviving an Orestes who was as good as dead and sending him home in a burst of bliss, his madness and the Furies all forgotten. And so the *Iphigeneia* becomes a kind of parable, as satyr drama also sometimes did, in which providence and prophecy overcome chance and dreams, and Apollo slays a new dragon in the form of the Tauric cult.[23]

---

[22] The whole satyr chorus is often released from some form of servitude at the end of the satyr play and sent home to Dionysus. The promised transportation of the chorus of the *Iphigeneia* is, however, the only tragic example of an action that thus permanently liberates and removes the chorus, though close parallels are offered by the *Bacchae* and by *Philoctetes*. Other satyr touches in the *Iphigeneia* are most notable in the first messenger's speech, where the setting is pastoral, a cave is mentioned, and the cowherds are described as indecisive and cowardly; they even set up a call for help like the call that goes out at the beginning of the *Dictyulci*. The presence of Pan in the chorus's vision of the voyage of escape also adds a strong and unexpected Dionysiac note (1125–6). The satyr who appeared on an Apulian Iphigeneia vase (now lost; see Reinach, *Répertoire des vases peints grecs et étrusques* [Paris, 1922], ii, 133) may have reflected the painter's appreciation of this quality in the present drama; it is curious to note also that Pearson thought that the Sophoclean *Chryses* was a satyr play (see his *Fragments*, ii, 328).

[23] The *Iphigeneia* is always compared to the *Helen*, but the play it most closely resembles in structure is the *Cyclops*. Iphigeneia and the chorus, like Silenus and the satyrs, are prisoners, their temple as bloody as the Cyclops' cave. To them come Orestes and Pylades, like Odysseus and his crew; Iphigeneia, like Silenus, is at first loyal to her master and she nearly causes the destruction of the rescuers, who are taken into the temple as the Greek sailors were into the cave. However, kinship persuades her to co-operate with the champion, as wine persuades Silenus, and she deceives Thoas in a scene that is parallel to Silenus' seduction of the Cyclops. In the end of both plays all Greeks escape leaving behind, in the one case an incapacitated monster, in the other a discontinued death rite.

APPENDIX

THE MYTH

In some pre-Hesiodic time a gratified epic audience first learned that Agamemnon had been the victim of an illusion and that Iphigeneia did not die at Aulis but was made immortal. The variant was repeated in the *Cypria*, where the girl became Hecate (Proclus, 142, ed. Severyns), and a fragment of Hesiod gives us the scene in which Agamemnon's daughter, here called Iphimede, is made into an *eidolon*, much to the confusion of the Greeks. She is to become Hecate, and the poet gives the event of her transformation a strong magical flavour by having Artemis pour ambrosia over the princess, 'from head to foot', to make her immortal and invulnerable to the knife (fr. 23, Merkelbach-West).

If a poet wished to minimize not only the cruelty of Artemis but also the guilt of Agamemnon he could, like Stesichorus, choose the further variant which made the sacrificed girl not the king's daughter but a daughter of Helen and Theseus (Page, *PMG*, 215). Only the substitution of the hind, however, will really let both Artemis and Agamemnon off; it leaves the sacrifice fully intended by the king, but blessedly unfulfilled, and it seems to make the whole event a didactic one, pointing the way to a substitution of animal for human sacrifice.

With Iphigeneia translated to heaven and the blood of humans repudiated by Artemis, the reputation of the goddess was saved and nothing further needed to be said. A good story, however, resists coming to an end, and a way was soon found to continue this one, since apotheosis was obviously not the only way for an inventive goddess to save a favourite. The princess could just as well be whisked away, unchanged, and transplanted in another part of the world; stories just as strange, after all, were told of Pythagoras and of Abaris. A suitable place for the girl would be one where she could serve the goddess who had saved her, and her story, if it was to go on, had a kind of obligation to tell of how she got vengeance for the outrage she had suffered. Proclus reports a Taurian translation, as well as an apotheosis, as figuring in the *Cypria*, but these are properly alternative, not complementary, solutions, and one suspects that the epitomizer was influenced, like the corrector of this passage, by a Euripidean detail (see Severyns, *Recherches sur la Chrestomathie*, iii, 151). However, since there is no way to date the invention of this alternative fate for Iphigeneia, and since there is no compelling reason why it must have been later than the invention of the rescue by

apotheosis, it is admittedly possible that both versions were known
to the author of the *Cypria*. At any rate the tale of the miraculously
rescued priestess who directed the sacrifice of her sacrificers was
being told in the sixth century, and was given Taurus as its scene. The
further shores of the Black Sea were almost as far as the realms of
Hecate, and they were especially appropriate to the new fiction since
they were associated with reports of mass immolations at royal
burials (Herod. iv. 71–2).[24] The Taurians in particular were reputed
to have a goddess to whom strangers were sometimes sacrificed, and
by the time of Herodotus she had come to be called by Iphigeneia's
name (iv. 103).

The story of Iphigeneia the Taurian priestess had its own internal
rightness, but it did not satisfy the original bowdlerizing impulse of
those who had first altered the tale of the sacrifice at Aulis. Artemis,
in order to provide vengeance for her creature, had once more to
become bloodthirsty, and so the defence of her cult and character
was undone. There was a human problem, too, for whereas the
goddess Iphigeneia had a reward, the priestess Iphigeneia, though
she rejoiced in honour and revenge, still was left by her fiction as an
exile and in a sense a slave. Yet another chapter to the story was
required, and a new innovator, faced with someone far away who
needed to be set free and brought home again, saw the relevance of
the Andromeda pattern. He solved his problem neatly by treating
the erstwhile sacrifical victim as a damsel in distress.

The best saviour in the tale of the rescued maiden is a husband,
actual or potential, or a son, but in Iphigeneia's case there was only
one male member of her family left, her brother Orestes.[25] He would
have to rescue this elder sister from the Taurians, just as he had
rescued Electra from Aegisthus and his persecutions. Clytemnestra's
blood had set him wandering, so he could easily be made to arrive
on this new scene by accident, as Heracles had arrived among the
Trojans, or Perseus in Ethiopia. On the other hand, since he would
inevitably bring his own history with him into this new tale, a
tighter causation could be supplied if his trip to the Black Sea were

---

[24] At Kertch in the Caucasus there seems to have been a continuation of such
burials from the early bronze age to imperial times and perhaps even until the time
of the Crusades; see A. Baschmakoff, 'Origine tauridienne du mythe d'Iphigenie',
Bull. de l'Assoc. Guillaume Budé, No. 64 (July, 1939), 3–21.

[25] There were variants that made Neoptolemus the son of Iphigeneia and Achilles,
or that allowed Achilles to leave Aulis and spend years in searching for his lost bride,
or that gave him at least a happy eternity with her on the island of Leuke where the
two were a pair of minor deities, but there is no knowing when or where these stories
came into being or how current they were. Euripides, in the *Iphigeneia amongst the
Taurians*, makes a strong use of the bride-of-Achilles motif (25; 216; 364–5; 537–9;
819; 856), but his Iphigeneia seems still to class that hero among her enemies.

commanded by Apollo. And since the story was to have a happy ending for Iphigeneia, his own fate could be made to mingle with his sister's if this journey became for him one of those fairy-tale trials of endurance by which a hero wins a throne. Since he was Orestes, his return to political life would be the mark of his final purgation from blood guilt, and so the reward of his successful quest would be liberation and purity as well as rule. The rescue hero is properly rewarded with the princess's hand, but in this case the marriage motif had to be transferred to the secondary hero, Pylades, who is to marry the sister of the rescued lady.

The tale of Iphigeneia reached its consummate human form when it was thus rounded out with a return to Greece for the surviving victim of Aulis, and the return of her brother to their father's throne. The problem of Artemis and her reputation, however, was potentially exacerbated, for there would be, in this new story pattern, an inevitable tendency to assign to the goddess the traditional role of the monster who held the princess captive. Someone saw that the solution here was to rescue the goddess as well as her priestess, and saw too that if Apollo sent Orestes for this purpose, the gods in general could benefit from Artemis' exoneration. Someone saw that this doubling of Orestes' mission meant that the hero could reasonably arrive among the Taurians, sent by Apollo but ignorant of his sister's residence there, and that the story could thus encompass the delights of a complicated recognition scene. Whoever the others were (if indeed it was not a single poet who worked out this whole final rescue phase of the Iphigeneia tale) this ultimate innovator was obviously a man of the theatre, for recognition means little in narrative, everything on stage.

When had this story been adapted for the theatre? We know of no other tragedian who treated it (though Sophocles used an episode from the journey home and wrote a *Chryses* which was evidently a kind of sequel to the *Iphigeneia*),[26] and the most efficient conclusion is that it was Euripides himself who first dramatized the tale. It seems almost certain that he invented the blind arrival and the recognition problem; it seems very probable that he invented the motif of the captured statue, and it is perfectly possible that he was responsible for the whole idea of Orestes' quest and Iphigeneia's return by these means.

[26] Grégoire (op. cit., pp. 97–8) reports the *Chryses* as prior to the *IT*, but he arrives at this sequence by dating *Chryses* to 416 when all we know is that it is presumably pre-414; and by dating *IT* to 414 on the assumption that it must post-date *Electra* (or be simultaneous with it) and that *Electra* is correctly dated by Parmentier at 413. Since many would date *Electra* in the '20s, and since *IT* can as easily go back to 416, while nothing fixes *Chryses* to a date so close to the *Birds*, the whole structure falls. The chronological situation here is far too obscure for dogmatism.

IV

HELEN

OR his *Alcestis* Euripides joined two equal, opposite actions, each complete. The *Helen*, a much later play which is like the *Alcestis* because of its satyresque tone, is just as daring, though less arbitrary, in its form. Here there is an accomplished mingling of two like actions, two traditional plots of positive overturn, and then, when these have been brought to a successful conclusion, there is a sudden glimpse of their obverse. For a few moments a new tragedy intrudes, and it is one of idealism and self-sacrifice in which a second heroine faces destruction. Beneath the smiling surface of the suppliant-rescue play, a negative reversal, a miniature *Antigone* drama, has been taking shape, to be revealed only for an instant, when the first heroine is already safe. It is then miraculously interrupted by a voice from the machine, and Theonoe joins the rest in safety.

The prologue of the *Helen*, like that of *Alcestis*, summarizes the whole action, but not this time by means of a miniature morality play. Here instead there is a scene built upon a figure apparently unrelated to the fiction, a figure whose function is something like that of the 'mythic example' in choral poetry. Teucer's arrival doubles that of Menelaus, but his true double is Helen herself. He, like Helen, has suffered, through no fault of his own, in men's eyes. He has been wholly rejected by Telamon, as Helen will be temporarily by Menelaus, and he has been driven from Salamis, as Helen fears she will be from Sparta, should she ever find her way home again. And yet Teucer knows, as Helen does, that he is under a god's special care. Guided by Apollo he is at this very moment almost safe in his haven, his new fatherland, and Helen too, when her play begins, is on the eve of her divinely organized salvation and return. Menelaus will offer a third example of salvation, and his rescue of Helen will create a threat and then the occasion for a fourth divine salvation for Theonoe. The Teucer episode thus sets the pattern and points to a consanguinity in the cases of Helen, Menelaus and Theonoe. It puts each escape into a context of like escapes, so that each is felt to have solemn precedents and to carry a promise of future repetitions. The fantastic fiction of the *Helen* is thus, by its prologue, rendered general and so, potentially at least, moral and didactic.

Teucer leaves the stage with a prayer that fixes the outcome of the Helen story; it also strikes the note of comic irony characteristic of this play. He curses the Helen who was at Troy and prays that she shall never reach Sparta; then he turns to the Helen before him and wishes her good fortune forever. Unknown to him, that other Helen is to be destroyed in a very short time, though not in any way he could have imagined, while the true Helen is to be assured of eternal bliss before the play is done. Teucer's prologue prayer joins with the promises of the Dioscuri at the very end to round off the formal composition of the play. The device is as old as poetry, and tragedians regularly used it to suggest that there was order in the cosmos as well as in festival drama. This particular system of encircling echoes, however, is built upon the unwitting revelation of a joyous truth, and it announces that the cosmos of the *Helen* is principally organized not for despair and destruction but for ecstatic survival.

Another announcement about the special nature of the *Helen* is made early in the play. From Teucer Helen has heard a great many grievous things, some false and some true, and so, as soon as he is gone, she begins a lament. She is mourning her lost mother, brothers, and husband; she feels that all her hope is gone, but she does not, for all that, fling herself into her dirge. Instead she steps forward, like some noted epinician performer, to begin with a stylized *prooimion* in which she calls upon the sirens and upon Persephone for help in composing her melody.[1] Euripides has chosen to make the art of singing the first subject of her song, borrowing an old device from epic and choral poetry to use for purposes of his own. By this means he takes the first opportunity the tragic form will allow him to speak of art itself and to warn

---

[1] Note that when the chorus later (1107 ff.) decides to lament Helen's misfortunes they repeat the same graceful formality, calling upon the nightingale to come and teach them the proper strain. Euripides often makes his choruses specify the kind of song they are singing (e.g., *IT* 179), but that is not the same thing as this apostrophe to a private, almost symbolic muse.

his audience that he expects of them, not an emotional response, but an almost Japanese finesse. They are to be aware of every level of this performance, as conscious of production details as they would have been at Hieron's court, and they are invited to think about the poet and the process of composition that lies behind the danced and costumed play.

With the opening of the first episode the action proper is expected to begin. When her song is finished and the chorus has come, Helen resumes her original posture at the base of a tomb and the stage has for a moment the look of a conventional suppliant drama. At once, however, anomalies appear. The pursued is, as is so frequently the case, female, and the violence from which she flees is sexual, making Helen seem to conform to the Danaid type. Her refuge, however, is not an altar but a grave, that of an outlandish king, doubtless represented with Egyptian motifs in its decoration. The central visual element then, the one that embodied and enforced the religious nature of the ordinary suppliant situation, has been transmuted here, and this means that the ethical coloration will likewise have suffered a change. Because the refuge in this suppliant situation is both secular and exotic, the problems that attach to it will be, for an Athenian audience, less solemn, the heroine less august, than is usually the case in a fiction of this sort.

The tomb of Proteus is in fact indicative of some very curious truths about this particular refugee. The drama of the suppliant situation arises, like most drama, from uncertainty. The only thing to be taken for granted is that the pursuer is impious and willing to violate the *nomoi* of the gods. But will he arrive before or after the protector? How pious will the protector be, and how strong? Will the suppliant be driven to suicide, or left to starve in his other-worldly accommodations? All of these questions arise in the normal suppliant situation which is, as a result, a test of faith and nerve first of all for the one who must rest motionless at the altar. He displays his ethical quality and the strength of his resolve in a situation of known and unknown threats. He has the opportunity to act out his recognition of something worse than death and therefore of something better than life, and so he is a fully tragic figure, though his conventional plot moves him only from the altar to safety in the *polis* as it runs its course.

Helen, however, has not been cut to this pattern of faith in uncertainty. She has been told directly by a god—for she and Hermes conversed, apparently, as they flew down to Egypt over the Cretan Sea—that Menelaus will rescue her. Only Teucer's misinformation gives her any claim to the ordinary suppliant's opposite suspicion that human help may never come. Even more destructive of a truly tragic posture for Helen is the fact that it does not matter in life and death terms whether he comes or not, for Helen is perfectly safe. The pursuer is, in respect to this particular refuge, the most pious of men, and he has no intention of violating the heroine's sanctuary. Theoclymenus will honour his father's tomb forever (note his first words, at 1165 ff.) and he has already done so for such a long time that the whole affair has taken on a quality of absurdity and ennui. The usual suppliant cannot long survive in sanctuary; his fate must be settled within the time it takes to starve, but Helen is not afflicted by the ordinary taboos. She seems to have turned the base of Proteus' tomb into a kind of outdoor boudoir (though some of her clothes are kept inside the palace) and trays have evidently been sent out to her regularly. Theoclymenus is exasperated at being made to wait for his bride, but he feels no other inconvenience at finding this perpetual camper before the palace gate. In sum, then, the refugee knows no discomfort, the pursuer respects the asylum, and the local tyrant (in this case also the pursuer) is not being blackmailed by a threat to the purity of his shrines. There is a general air of lassitude where there should be one of urgency, for all the elements that ordinarily force a resolution upon a suppliant situation have here atrophied or decayed. Even time has forgotten its usual occupations, and Helen remains young and beautiful, as intact as some bright insect, in this amber Egyptian air.

The first episode of a suppliant play ordinarily brings the pursued to sanctuary and provides a meeting either with villain or protector (or with agents of theirs). The essential movement of the scene is towards the altar, in discovery or rediscovery of its protective power, and to that altar the suppliant must cling. The first episode of the *Helen*, however, introduces neither villain nor protector, but a figure and a concept wholly foreign to suppliant drama. And it makes its principal move not towards but away from sanctuary. There is within this palace someone who is not the local ruler, someone who cannot resolve the physical threat with force but who can wholly eliminate the ethical problems that arise from Helen's new uncertainty. This is Theonoe the prophetess, who can tell Helen whether Menelaus lives or not, and whether he will rescue her. Faith and resolve are no longer in demand when one is certain of the future, and as if to demonstrate the fact that knowledge is incompatible with the suppliant situation, Helen, in her first episode, lightly breaks her tenure at the tomb as soon as she is reminded of the prophetess within. She gets up and moves into the palace almost casually, demolishing her own tragic role as she goes.

When Helen leaves her sanctuary and the stage, the chorus leaves with her, breaking with their tragic conventions as sharply as Helen does with hers. Doubtless the poet thought of this as a mechanism for marking his own departure from the usual paths of tragedy, but he would hardly have allowed himself such an innovation unless it could serve the overt ends of his dramatic purpose.[2] He will treat the traditional tragic form as if it were some giant Sebastian set up as his target but, in the case of the *Helen* at least, each arrow he aims will be of the highest polish.

By moving the chorus Euripides has arranged that his next scene shall be played without the normal internal audience of tragedy. Under these circumstances Menelaus' arrival marks a kind of fresh start, for it comes as a second prologue, and the figure of the prince is given a startling prominence. His first speech, like Euripidean prologue speeches generally, is a long unbroken piece in which he addresses the audience more directly than he ever will again. He does not *say* anything that he could not have said to the chorus, but he says it all more pompously and at far greater length. More important is the altered visual effect. Had he entered among the chorus, Menelaus would have been like a host of other figures, messengers and secondary personnages; his tattered clothes and his melodramatic escape would have been reflected and absorbed by the response of a sympathetic crowd. This Menelaus, however, must walk nakedly from the parodos entrance to the centre of the playing area with nothing to cover his long approach. Once there he must stand, quite alone, like some adolescent in a

---

[2] Compare the removal of the chorus at *Ajax* 814, a necessity if the stage suicide was to be arranged.

nightmare, and deliver a set speech to an audience that has plenty of time to snigger at his rags.

Arriving from afar, Menelaus invites comparison with the adventurer heroes, the rescue and vengeance men whose types are made by Heracles and the Sophoclean Orestes, but his costume and his account of his recent history almost transform the stage. His ship has wrecked and he has come, like Odysseus in the *Cyclops*, in search of food for himself and the men left behind on the beach. All this brings the shore very near and suggests that the visible Egyptian palace belongs to no city but stands somewhere in wilderness, like that other 'underworld' spot, the Sicilian cave. The scenic conventions of tragedy are mixed, in the mind's eye, with those of satyr play, and the absence of the chorus will allow for a moment the fantastic suspicion that it might on its return sport shaggy ears and phalluses.

From Menelaus' own point of view the absence of the chorus means that he need not dissimulate before the gatekeeper. He is free to display an abject spinelessness that has only one parallel in tragedy (in the Phrygian of the *Orestes*), though it is a chief ingredient in the standard satyr character. His exchange with the old woman is, tragically speaking, so outrageous that it must be taken very seriously by the critic of the play. This is the audience's first view of its hero in action and it affords a dreadful contrast to his pompous verbal presentation of himself. Menelaus is measured against his unworthy antagonist on an empty stage that makes his moral and physical defeat less evident to himself but grotesquely plain to the spectator.

Gatekeeper scenes had been written many times over. Aeschylus' Orestes plays such a scene (*Choeph.* 652–67), as did Cresphontes and Hypsipyle's sons and doubtless others of the rescue and vengeance men. Odysseus parodies the scene in *Cyclops*, and Dionysus, in the *Frogs*, turns it into farce (cf. also *Clouds* 126 ff.). Taken seriously it is a scene for a man who has already seized his own destiny and made his own plans—for the slightly sinister hero of vengeance tragedy or for the buoyantly bold adventurer. It is a scene for an active man bent upon success. When Odysseus hears from Silenus of a blood-thirsty master in the neighbourhood, he still firmly orders a meal for all (*Cycl.* 133), and he speaks as coolly when faced with the Cyclops himself. Menelaus, on the other hand, seems almost stunned when he receives like news. Soon indeed he is immobilized by metaphysical speculation—are there more Helens and more Zeuses in heaven and earth than he had formerly supposed?—but even before this dizzying proposition occurs to him he behaves as no tragic creature can. In his very first response to the old servant he bends like a waiter before a crusty patron. He begs not to be treated roughly (445) and it looks as though he flinches before the old lady's hand. She plainly feels that his portrayal of pathetic helplessness has gone on to bathos (456); she implies that he has sobbed (458), and this seems all too probable in the light of his final 'plan of action'. The scene ends, as such a scene formally should, with the hero's resolve, but in this case the resolve is to creep away empty handed if things should look at all rough (506–7). A vengeance hero aggressively engaged in his intrigue, when he has gained entrance to the enemy's palace, may hide there, but κρύψας as a participle of retreat is unthinkable in such a man. And Menelaus not only imagines this undignified skulking for himself, he acts it out, crouching in some shadow or bit of shrubbery in the very next moment, when he hears Helen and the chorus coming back.

Such is the champion promised to Helen by Theonoe and the gods. It is not surprising that for a moment he makes an open farce of her already ridiculous tragedy. He and Helen, as soon as she is back on stage, play a scene from conventional suppliant drama, but Menelaus falls into the wrong role, and it is the wrong scene that they enact. The champion has arrived, but what we get is the pursuit scene, with the innocent maiden in flight before a bestial villain figure. And given Menelaus' costume, the affair must have looked rather more like the satyr pursuit of Amymone than the fearful scene with the Egyptians in Aeschylus' *Suppliant Maidens*. If the champion won't dress the part, the poet seems to say, anything can happen.[3] And now we recognize a final reason for his earlier removal of the chorus, since for this anomalous situation, an unknown stranger was the first necessity.

The aberrant scene of pursuit is ridiculous but brief; it quickly melts into a recognition scene that becomes a bridge

---

[3] On clothing as one of the motifs of the appearance and reality theme in the *Helen*, see A. N. Pippin, 'Euripides' *Helen*: A Comedy of Ideas', *CP* lv (1960), 152.

between the *Helen*'s two positive actions, linking its now mori-
bund suppliant plot to its triumphant rescue. Like the four scenes
that preceded it (the claiming of sanctuary; the arrival of the
champion; the gatekeeper scene; the pursuit), this one belonged
to the tragedian's stock of standard stage situations. And here
again, as in the four other cases, this particular tragedian has
used the convention to rouse expectations he means to frustrate
and perplex, before they are fulfilled.

The process of recognition begins with an air of stage nor-
malcy.[4] Menelaus is the first to feel the truth, having glimpsed
his 'token', Helen's unmistakable flesh (and how like he is, at
this moment, to Xanthias, at *Frogs* 414). His own identity is
obscured by his ungodly outfit, but at 560 Helen recognizes
him; she could hardly have refused much longer, equipped as
she was with Theonoe's special information. The scene seems
to be over—it has been all to easy—when suddenly Menelaus
remembers the thing that must make this recognition different
from all others. He sticks at the word 'wife', recollecting that he
has one already; he orders Helen haughtily not to touch so
much as his *peplos* (a hard line for heroic delivery when one
has no such garment to boast of), and then, in the scene's
next phase, he becomes the reluctant partner while Helen plays
the aggressor. She knows where her own strength lies, and she
argues that in such a case as theirs the senses bring the only
valid proofs. Menelaus all but surrenders at 581, admitting,
'My mistake was in thinking I had another wife.' But then
unfortunately he insists upon continuing to try to reason where
Helen would teach him to feel. And the preposterousness of the
truth is too much for him. He can accept only for a moment the
proposition of the two Helens with its unfortunate corollary,
that it was the wrong one whom he fought for and took at Troy.
It occurs to him to ask what the wrong one was made of, and it
is upon the concept of a lady made of air that he chokes. He
loses his grasp of all that Helen has said, erases it from his mind,
and begins to feel personally outraged. 'I still don't see how you
were able to be in two places at once', he objects (587). Unwisely,

[4] For the set elements in a Euripidean recognition see H. Strohm, *Euripides*
(Zetemata 15, Munich, 1957), pp. 77 ff. The fact that there is a steady pattern is
there firmly established but the value of the discussion is somewhat diminished by
the author's refusal to separate recognition from intrigue and the resultant exclusion
of the highly developed recognition of the *Ion*.

Helen chooses to answer with a version of the play's favourite
onoma-soma sophistry, saying, 'Oh, one's name can be everywhere
while one's body never moves', and this elegant response proves
to be more than a simple sacker of cities can take. 'Stop!' he
wails, 'I have trouble enough already' (588–9). And with those
words Menelaus prepares to do the unthinkable. He, a partner
in a recognition scene, having recognized, turns his back and
begins to walk away. Just so he had earlier thought of walking,
or rather scurrying, away from danger though cast as an adventurer. And just so has Helen already walked away from her
suppliant seat at the tomb.

Here is a new sort of catastrophe, the exact opposite of the
established tragic catastrophe where kinsmen who fail to
recognize threaten to do terrible harm to each other. What
threatens at this point in the *Helen* is that the kinsmen, though
they have recognized, will do nothing at all to each other. The
dramatic illusion is almost broken while the poet teases his
audience with a sense of imminent artistic disaster. The whole
play seems to have disintegrated as each of its scenes showed
signs of doing, and it looks at line 593 as if the Egyptian Helen
will be left like a piece of unclaimed baggage while Menelaus
goes off with a morsel of cloud.

This threat has of course been smilingly prepared by the
dramatist, and he deals with it now by means of one more
delicately distorted conventional device. The catastrophe of
negation is interrupted most appropriately by the disappearance
of something that never quite existed. The interruption comes
just in time to forestall Menelaus' exit. The Old Sailor hurries on
and captures the attention of all with his report of a miracle.
The Helen whom he was guarding, the Helen brought back from
Troy, has risen up to heaven, and the old man, in good messenger
fashion, recreates the marvellous moment, repeating the very
words of the ascending *eidolon*. The phantom Helen thus speaks
out, and her last words on earth are a kind of death-bed confession. She reveals the deception that went into her creation,
and testifies to the identity and the innocence of the true
Egyptian Helen.

This kind of manipulated revelation, so different from an
internally necessary discovery of the truth, is a threat to
Aristotelian tragedy even when it occurs, like the revelations of

Artemis in the *Hippolytus*, at the very end of a play. Euripides, however, has boldly brought a voice from an invisible machine, the voice of the exodus, into the thick of his play. Menelaus hears it, and his wrong-headedness and hostility are transformed at once into comprehension and love. The artistic crisis is resolved, the recognition scene can go on, and the play is saved by the off-stage voice of a dissolving ghost.

The recognition duet, so long postponed, is now sung in full, and it is satisfyingly like other such duets, though embellished at least once with an erotic *sous-entendu*.[5] Before he goes on to the intrigue, however, the poet provides a brief pause which sets this recognition apart from all the other scenes of its type. The Old Sailor, in dim reflection of an Aeschylean chorus, calls a halt to the play's events so that he may attempt to understand them (700 ff.). He has two speeches allotted to his reflections, and in each he tries to read the general lesson of this particular adventure. His words are clearly serious on some level, and they remind us that Euripides, in the *Helen*, is not simply dancing on the grave of the genre he has outraged, but looking for a new mode of expression for another kind of thought.

The Sailor's first speech is excited by his reluctant perception of the deceit of the gods ('Do you mean to say we suffered as we did, senselessly, for a cloud?' 707) and by his enthusiastic recognition of the true Helen here in Menelaus' arms (709). The conjunction of this happy present with that ignoble past brings some of Solon's old saws to his mind (note his insistence on σπεύδειν at 718 and cf. Solon, 1. 43 and 73), and these he tests against this new experience. The Elegy to the Muses had taught that what a man struggled for and took by force would not last, while what came of itself, and so from the gods, would endure forever. 'Yes', the old man seems to say, 'that's true, but god is a very strange fellow and mixes us up more thoroughly than this simple rule suggests. Sometimes a man strives (and seems to succeed) while his counterpart, the one to whom things came

[5] Note 644–5, which I would give to Menelaus, followed by 646–7 from Helen (for a different assignment and interpretation, see A. M. Dale, *Euripides. Helen* [Oxford, 1967], ad loc.). This gives us: Menelaus: 'But this splendid disaster has brought me to you—a tardy husband indeed, but all the same, I mean to enjoy my luck.' Helen: '*Do*, by all means!' (cf. Mae West's celebrated 'Help yourself!') 'I pray for the same thing that you do; it would be wrong, in a married pair, for one to suffer when the other was content.'

easily, is suddenly destroyed. Look at the two of you', he says. 'You strove, each in his way, but while Helen got a bad reputation, Menelaus did win the war and gain a facsimile of his prize. And now suddenly everything you both desired has come of its own accord!' Through the turbulence of his thoughts he perceives that, though the world may show examples in which strife seems to have been crowned with success, such success will not be real. Strife may bring you a phantom Helen, but only the gods, in their sly deceitfulness, can confer the object of desire in unimpaired perfection. Even without the special trick of the phantom prize, it is obvious that there would have been no glory and no true success in bringing home a Helen who had actually been at Troy, since she could never again have been a young and faithful wife. Whereas now, by a miracle of divine trickery, Menelaus once again has a wife who brings no dishonour to her husband or her father or her brothers. And this final reflection leads the old man to a jubilant reminiscence about the wedding of his mistress, an event he can again feel proud of, after twenty years of shame (721–5).

Such are the old man's thoughts about the present happy moment. They are most satisfactory, but he cannot help going back to the past, and the years at Troy. Menelaus urges him away, but he lingers, still turning it over in his mind.

I'll be off, my lord. But look here, doesn't this show what a shabby business it is that the prophets run? It's nothing but lies! There's not an ounce of truth in all their fires or their messages from birds—who but a fool would think a bird could have anything useful to say! Just notice—when his own people were dying for a cloud, even Calchas failed to warn the army, and so did Helenus, who watched his city sacked when there was 'nothing' at stake! You'll tell me, I suppose, that this was all because the gods meant neither side to know the truth, but if it's their intention just to lead us on, what point is there in prophecy? Gods who deceive should be approached with gifts. Let's pray that they'll be kind but waste no time with soothsayers. They are only seeking their own livelihood; nobody gets rich without lifting a finger, just by the aid of prophets' fires. If you want to consult anyone about what to do, I say: Take the advice of settled opinion, and listen well to good counsel (744–57).[6]

---

[6] Many editors and Miss Dale most recently have deleted large sections of the Old Sailor's two speeches. Their reasoning is in essence that Euripides should be

It is clear that the poet has given the sailor's reflections the marks of the old man's character, and yet they are not mere characterization—nothing in Attic tragedy is. These lines stand out with conscious emphasis, divided from the rest of the scene by brief choral remarks at 698–9 (the gnomic summary of the recognition scene) and 758–60 (the chorus's approval of the old man's conclusion). The audience is alerted, before they begin, by the sailor's 'What's that you say?' at 706, delivered so urgently that the speaker disregards the tragic rule of speaking in full trimeters.

The sailor does not make it clear whether he thinks Calchas and Helenus knew and refused to speak, or did not really know the truth, though he seems to mean the first of these. It makes very little difference because his essential concern is with man's behaviour in a universe where the gods deceive; *how* their deceptions are wrought is beside the point. His second speech thus finally reinforces his first. If striving after gain is useless, how is man to shape his life? How does he acquire those goods Solon was praying for, the ones that come of themselves and remain in a man's possession? You might have thought the answer was to consult a prophet, and so learn what wars to wage, what seas to sail, what trenches to dig for treasure—but no, the present instance proves that this is not the way. You must take the gods' deceit as the first fact of your universe; you will strive to please them in the appointed ways, and lead your life according to the best rules men have made. This of course does not mean success, but it is at least a reasonable and dignified plan. Success, as the chorus points out in its

making an attack here, that the Old Sailor doesn't attack, and therefore that his words cannot belong to the play. It is indubitably true that the speech is not an address on 'the futility of war' nor is it an exposé of the 'frivolous cruelty and irresponsibility of the gods' (Dale, p. 117), but who has determined that these are the only subjects which could be treated at this point? Miss Dale felt that the speeches are too characteristic of the man, that they contain too much *ethos* and not enough *dianoia*, which also seems a curious reason for rejecting them. Since there are no internal difficulties serious enough to warrant deletion, the two speeches must be respected. Lines 755–6 in particular have been called 'irrelevant' (Dale, ad loc.) but what they do is bring the grand examples of Calchas and Helenus down to the everyday level. The trick of the lines lies in the fact that the οὐδείς of 756 is a man who consults the prophet looking for an easy prosperity. Thus the statement moves from the professional to his client: '(For the prophet) soothsaying is clearly just a way of earning a living, (and for his client it is a waste of time) for no one gets rich just by following the prescriptions of prophesy.'

approving codicil, finally depends upon the friendship of the
gods (758–60).

When he has reached his conclusion, the old man leaves the
stage, and his departure marks the belated end of the recognition
scene. Such a scene, in high tragedy, brings a new perception
not only of a human face or an altered situation but of the truth
behind the situation; it is often a recognition of the face of god.
Euripides has not allowed his two sub-tragic principals any share
in such an exalted experience (indeed, neither has been troubled
by any serious misconceptions of god), but he has, by means of
the old sailor, granted it to his audience. They have thus early
received a revelation about the nature of the gods that rule the
Helen, and they are clearly expected to hold it in mind as they
watch the rest of the play.

At 777–8 Helen exclaims, 'Miserable man, have you been
kept safe through all these years, only to be slaughtered now?'
and thus she officially marks the transition from recognition to
intrigue. Theoclymenus' standing threat to her chastity has now
become a fresh threat to Menelaus' life, but when Helen reminds
us of this, her words are paradoxically reassuring. A recognition
scene in the middle of a suppliant piece was a disturbing development, but a recognition scene as the preliminary to an action of
intrigue and escape is a comfortable experience. Helen's words,
so like those of Iphigeneia to Orestes (*IT* 873 ff.), encourage
the spectator to believe that this peculiar play, after all its
vagaries, is now about to settle down to become a correct
escape intrigue. The initial suppliant action would have
demanded in its development an open confrontation of champion
with villain, and perhaps the use of public force to drive the
pursuer from the stage; now, however, as if to signalize his shift
from suppliancy to a sophisticated rescue plot, the poet creates
a moment in which the principals discuss the use of force, but
reject it in favour of a crafty plan (813). Helen had never dedicated herself at the tomb of Proteus (she is precisely *not* his
property) and she does not therefore have to be solemnly raised
and defended and transferred to the public keep. She is instead
to be abducted once again, and that with a minimal risk. At
line 811 Helen speaks to Menelaus in the conventional phrase
of one who urges a non-heroic stand upon a hero; she might be
Ismene or Chrysothemis, but instead of being brushed aside,

her advice is taken. Once more, however, the presence of a prophetess nearby, and the possibility of obtaining certain knowledge, disrupt a conventional development, this time that of an intrigue. Helen means to deceive Theoclymenus, but she remembers that there is someone inside the palace who cannot be deceived. Theonoe cannot ensure success, but she can condemn the plan of escape to certain failure by making the villain as impervious to lies as she is herself. And so, before the intrigue proper can get under way, this superfluous priestess must in some way be silenced by the principals.

Theonoe is a stumbling block in Helen's path, and she is in addition a dangerous extravagance in the economy of the escape plot. Her power and her position make her something like the ruler in a suppliant piece, something like Athena in the *Eumenides* (note 1005, where we are explicitly reminded of this). All of which means that she is the last figure we should expect to meet in a play that has just destroyed its own suppliant elements and announced its intention of converting itself into a rescue drama. But since the priestess cannot be deceived she must be persuaded, and so Theonoe forces a kind of tragic rhetoric upon the two characters who seemed just now to have escaped at last from the weight of serious roles. They are bent upon escape from Egypt as well, but they are made to play one last distorted suppliant scene before their poet will let them taste the pleasures of deceit and open flight.

In the persuasion scene Theonoe takes the judicial role that ordinarily belongs to the ruler of the place where suppliants are claiming sanctuary. She hears two pleas, but these, instead of being one for the defence and one for the prosecution, both come from the 'suppliant' group. The priestess has momentarily taken the stance of champion, thus forcing Menelaus for a second time to assume the posture of the villain in the formal choreography of a suppliant scene. The actual villain is still lurking in the wings, and the present scene is constructed around his absence in such a way as to make the real threat seem to be not physical brutality but the possibility of self-righteous inhumanity in the figure of the judge.

Helen is chief suppliant, and she begins with a speech that strikes the note of heavy secularity which is to pervade the scene. She defines herself as a piece of property left on deposit with

Proteus. Such property must clearly be returned to its rightful
owner when he makes his claim; any other action would be
unjust. Helen glances for a moment at Theonoe's peculiar
situation, pointing out that injustice from her would be especially
repulsive because she has the management of sacred things in
her hands. She then turns to her own sufferings, surely extensive
enough to warrant a bit of good luck now. She would like to
repair her reputation, play the mother at last to the abandoned
Hermione, and profit a little from her husband's salvation.
Helen's points all have their clear, traditional labels: *dike* and
eusebeia both indicate that this is the moment for an act of *charis*
from the priestess, and such an act will bring Theonoe a reward,
for good fame (*kleos*, 941) will be hers. The whole speech is
predictable, economical, and tasteful; anyone could have written
it and anyone could have spoken it. From it we learn nothing
new about either Helen or her play. It was necessary to the
symmetry of the scene, but it has been made so as to offer no
challenge to the speeches that follow; what it does do is remind
us of the conventions of the scene of persuasion—conventions
from which the poet now means to stray.

When Helen has finished, the chorus pronounces her words
properly touching, but adds that it is longing to hear what
Menelaus will say 'to save his skin' (945).[7] The women are only
uttering a conventional referee's phrase, but in this case their
curiosity is especially suitable since no one yet knows what kind
of a creature Menelaus is. He steps forward at this moment very
eagerly and begins by describing the unmanly postures he will
refuse to take. These prove to be the very ones he did assume
earlier when he was faced with the old lady, and the effect is
distinctly comical. The audience, however, cannot yet be sure
whether this echo, so plainly contrived, is meant to deliver the
coup de grace to Menelaus' heroic pretensions, or whether it is

[7] 'Only Theonoe can speak these words' Miss Dale reports (op. cit., ad loc.),
then scrupulously brings forth the passages that show that it is the chorus who should
speak them. The two-line interruption that in a sense passes the speaker's wand
from one character to another is a commonplace with the chorus, and so is this kind
of frank curiosity (cf. e.g., *PV* 631), whereas there is no precedent for such a speech
from the magisterial figure in this type of scene. Miss Dale does not discuss the special
example of a trial scene provided in the *Eumenides*, but two things can profitably be
noted there: 1. that the chorus, even though it is in this case a party to the trial, yet
exercises the prerogative of designating speakers (*Eum.* 574–5); 2. that Athena
never once interrupts while the two parties are in debate.

offered now as the measure of a change that has come about in him.[8]

Menelaus' early words are full of pompous bluster; he sounds, indeed, much like that other pseudo-Heracles, the Dionysus of the *Frogs*, and he proves to have, also like that Dionysus, a taste for literary criticism. He and Helen are both playing from the tomb of Proteus in a tableau strongly reminiscent of Orestes and Electra in the *kommos* of the *Choephoroi*, and this gives Menelaus his chance. First he makes sure that everyone will notice what he is doing: 'I shall now make my speech at your father's tomb, using the *pothos* convention!' (961).[9] Then he strikes an attitude and begins an 'Aeschylean' prayer:

> Ancient sire, inhabitant of this polished tomb,
> render unto me the wife I claim,
> her whom Zeus sent here to be preserved for me . . .

But the absurdity is too much for him. He breaks his stance and looks about with mock apology:

> Well, naturally, I know that *you* can't give her back—you're dead!
> But surely this woman will not wish to hear her father slandered
> when once he had the best of reputations;
> the decision rests with her.
>
> (962–8; cf. *Choeph.* 489–90; 479–80)

---

[8] At 947–8 he says, 'I would not cling to your knees and supplicate, I would not wet my cheek with a tear,' and he comes back to the question of womanish tears at 991, his whole disclaimer perhaps a dim parody of that of Prometheus at *PV* 1003–6. A. Y. Campbell, however, asserts that Menelaus does weep between 990 and 991, and that his earlier repudiation of tears is meant to enhance his 'breakdown', making it 'dramatic and moving' so that it will prove Menelaus' courage to be that of 'a "Man of Feeling" and not the stolidity of a tough'; see his *Euripides. Helena* (Liverpool, 1950), pp. 114 and 116.

[9] The word πόθῳ at line 961 has always been a problem, for it is in Miss Dale's phrase 'as difficult to account for as to emend'. The translation offered here supposes that the word is a technical term belonging to the art of acting. It seems likely that, just as there was a vocabulary of conventional gestures among the actors of the Attic stage there was also a system of conventional vocal tones, so that a high pitch might convey one emotion, a low quaver another, etc. This is strongly suggested by the Schol. B. at *Or.* 176, with his report that the chorus' song there was of a sort ordinarily sung at a certain pitch and loudness. If the most common combinations of gesture pattern with vocal pattern were thought of as the histrionic modes, and came to have names, then one of these might well have been the '*pothos* strain', the manner used for speeches that expressed a longing for an absent friend or protector. The chorus at *Trach.* 103 may be identifying their mode in this way; at any rate it seems that the φρὴν ποθουμένη of this line belongs to them and not, as Jebb claims, to Deianeira; cf. Dionysus at *Frogs* 66 with his πόθος Εὐρίπιδου. Callinus 1.18 suggests the possibility of folk-songs of praise in something like this strain.

And then, in case anyone has missed the point, he repeats his trick, this time leaving his parody without commentary and achieving his effect through an exaggeration of the old repayment *topos*:

> Hades' depths, I summon you—be my ally now!
>
>   (cf. *Choeph.* 1-2; 18-19)
> You have got a splendid pile of corpses,
> thanks to Helen here. They fell by my sword and were paid you as
>   your wage.
> Now, either give them back—send them up alive!—
> or else make sure this woman shows her father's piety
> and gives me back my wife!
>
>   (969-74).

These two open attacks upon the diction of tragedy suggest that Menelaus' use of bombast in the rest of the scene is likewise a form of parody. They join with his later scorn when, at Helen's suggestion that he report his own death, he sniffs, '*That* has a familiar sound!' (1056).[10] He will liberate a lady and go home to reclaim a throne, but he wants to make it plain that he is no preposterous hero of high tragedy. Once he has shown what he thinks of the tragic genre, he is rid of his old embarrassment at finding himself here on stage. He had earlier been unable to get properly through a gatekeeper scene; he had made a farce of Helen's suppliancy and had threatened to ruin the recognition by simply walking off. Now all this is changed; although he has been formally replaced as champion by the judicious Theonoe, he successfully plays the suppliant and treats the Priestess with just the right combination of deference and moral authority.[11] When he announces now that he will fight his rival and die if necessary, before he will give up his wife, he is quite credible

---

[10] This explicit consciousness, on the part of a stage figure, of the genre in which he works, may have been typical of some of the personnel of satyr drama. At any rate Silenus, in the *Cyclops*, opens with a quick series of references to other satyr plays; see P. Waltz, 'Le drame satyrique et le prologue du "Cyclope" d'Euripide', *L'Acropole*, vi (1931), 278–95. Here in the *Helen* Menelaus' literary consciousness is part of the general technique of holding the audience at a distance by insisting that it regard the drama always as a work of art, never as an experience for themselves. It is thus related to the motif of musical modes that runs through the choruses; to the use of a figure like Helen, more portent (26) than woman, as the principal; to the Mountain Mother ode that gives an aetiology of comedy (see Pippin, op. cit., 155–6), and to isolated asides like the ποιητῷ τρόπῳ of line 1547.

[11] Note his absolutely correct use of the threat of miasma at 982; cf. Aesch. *Supp.* 456 and, in distorted form, *Ion* 1311.

and in the scenes that follow he proves to be, by report at least, a worthy champion at last.

Apparently, then, the echoes from the gatekeeper scene have been made to sound here so that the audience may measure the change that Menelaus has undergone since his first entrance in this play. They prove that he is like an Orestes, though he doesn't wish to be, in that he has been led from a reluctance for his task to a firm resolve, by way of a recognition. In Menelaus the usual effects of recognition have been exaggerated because the poet is for the moment using his bizarre fiction to show what a recognition scene can do for a play. The usual restorative powers of the rites of recognition have been in a sense doubled here because Menelaus' reunion with the true Helen is at the same time a separation from the phantom of Troy. It thus marks not only the beginning of a period in which the gods will favour him, but the end of a period in which he was most particularly their dupe. As far as we can tell, the quality of initiation that a recognition has does not lead Menelaus to any new understanding of the gods or of his mythic fate, but it does mark his re-integration into the life of the play at a new and higher level. Helen has claimed him as her husband, and in so doing she has transformed him, taking a spineless Silenus figure and making a rescue hero of him. His ridiculous nudity will now be covered with regal dress, and the cringing coward who gave chase to the princess will become a man of action. In the moment of escape he will sweep (1609) Egyptians from his decks much as Heracles, in the *Busiris*, swept others from their bloodstained altar.

Theonoe's part in the persuasion scene is overtly far more conventional than that of Menelaus. Her entrance is marked by extravagant visual effects, but she proves to have the undeviating austerity of principle that makes for decisive tragic action. Her torch-bearing priestesses bear witness to her alliance with the supernatural, and yet at the same time they minimize any mystical significance she might seem to have by making her office so markedly Egyptian and exotic. It is not her relation with the gods that is in question here, for all the sailor's talk of prophecy, but her relations with the members of her family.[12]

---

[12] The question of the value and the proper use of prophecy is raised by the fiction of the *Helen*, but it is not central to its meaning. The Old Sailor had seen that prophets belong to gods who are capable of deceit, so that whether they hide the

Her own sense is that she has in this moment a terrible freedom. She knows that there is a scene like the present one being played in heaven, where Hera and Aphrodite are putting their respective cases before Zeus[13] but she does not know how he will decide (878–91). And so for her the case is an open one which she must judge alone.

Theonoe has evidently been ordered by her brother to inform him if Helen's husband should threaten to appear, and her first impulse is to honour this royal and fraternal command (892–3, with Reiske's τί φῇς). Helen and Menelaus, however, urge a second and higher command, that of justice and piety, which orders her to carry out the will of her dead father. She must not speak, she must keep silent and in this way see to it that the commitments Proteus entered into are honourably fulfilled. Theonoe thus must choose between two forms of compliance: a safe obedience to a present, physical force, or a treasonable cherishing of an unseen, spiritual law. It is Antogone's choice, and Theonoe hesitates no more in making it than the daughter of Oedipus did. She will honour her father and save her brother, against his will, from his own impiety (1020–1).

Theonoe's is the only serious choice in the play, and in this company of less than tragic figures the essential questions surrounding the noble choice arise in her case with peculiar sharpness. Why would a feeble human creature ever do as this girl is shown to do? Why would a man or woman ever choose the past over the present, the unseen over the seen, death over life,

truth or whether they reveal it they are, heard rightly, simply reminders of the total dependence of mortality upon an incomprehensible providence. He cited an example in which men were encouraged to continue in a foolish war by the silence of a prophet; Theonoe now embodies another example, in which one of those men is enabled at last to bring that war to a close by the silence of a prophet. (Or looked at from Theoclymenus' viewpoint, a man is kept from an unjust private war by the prophet's silence.) The examples cancel one another out, as far as the value of prophecy goes, and in Theonoe's case we are urged to consider the woman who has voluntarily put aside her mantic office, never the office itself. Her prophetic power happens to have placed her where she has a choice, but this fact is not exploited by the poet; it is as a human being that she decides, and it is as a human being that she is saved, in a carnal illustration of her own beliefs and of the chorus's more commonplace assertion that in justice there is a hope of salvation (1031).

[13] It would seem that we are meant to conclude from this earthly tableau that in the parallel scene in heaven there was likewise a surprise. Apparently there, as well as in Egypt, the two who approached an arbiter were in agreement rather than at odds, which is to say that Aphrodite had, as Helen prayed she would (1098), decided not to play pursuer any longer.

and tragedy over melodrama? The answer here is supplied in
two forms, one pragmatic, the other supernatural.

The Old Sailor, in the course of his musings on the deviousness
of heaven, had concluded that one should rely for guidance not
on mantic arts but, having prayed to the gods, upon *gnome* and
euboulia, one's own conventional sense of right and the advice of
respectable peers. He had arrived at this prescription by testing
the wisdom of the sages against his own experience, and it is
frankly a practical rule—it is the best one can do under the
circumstances.

This rule Theonoe follows to the letter as she makes her
choice. It called for prayer, and her life has been given over to
prayer; it called for a rejection of prophecy, and she at this
moment puts aside her own mantic prerogatives. Without
trying to know what the gods intend, she finds her way entirely
by the secular means that the old man had prescribed. When
she speaks of her *physis* and her will (998), of her innate sense of
justice (1002–3) and her knowledge of customary practice, she is
describing the elements that have formed her *gnome*, and when
she combines her knowledge of her father's will with the respectful audience she gives to Helen and Menelaus, she is listening
to the counsels of *euboulia*. The sailor, however, was thinking
primarily of situations in everyday life in which a choice was to
be made between two paths to what appeared to be a profit,
whereas Theonoe is making a very different sort of choice.
She must decide not where to look for treasure or whether to go
to war, but whether she will preserve her life or risk it for a
principle. And the old man's practical method has indicated a
course that almost certainly means death. How then can it still be
wisdom, and how can one find the strength to fulfil its command?

These are questions that the sailor's discourse did not answer;
in fact, its notion of a deceitful heaven made them peculiarly
difficult. Theonoe, however, gives them a brief and sufficient
response, and as she does so she sets the stamp of seriousness upon
this elegant and iconoclastic play:

> Injustice will be punished, either here, or there
> among the dead, for though the mind of man shall die
> it has its deathless part, the remembering will
> that sinks immortal in the immortal air.
>
> (1013–16)

As she describes the ultimate sanction that makes noble con-
duct necessary, Theonoe takes the kernel from centuries of
religious speculation. The idea of punishment after death was
an old one, familiar everywhere, but the remarkable thing about
Theonoe's profession of faith is its absolute austerity. She leaves
out every inessential detail, and for her the ideas of reward or of
the presence of the immortal gods are quite unnecessary. She
sees only the flawed mortal, one who is now a mere abstraction
from his most abstract part, in bare confrontation with an
accusing elemental purity. (Notice her opening ritual; what
she works there is the reception of 'the pure breath of heaven',
867.) [14] This vision is not antithetical to conventional Olympian
religion, but it is a description of another part of the cosmos;
Theonoe can, while entertaining it, also imagine a punishment,
in this life, that might come from Aphrodite (1006–7) and she
can urge her friends to pray (1024 ff.). In the same way,
Theonoe's vision is not antithetical to the play in which it stands,
though it comes as a revelation wholly unexpected.

Theonoe and Menelaus, then, by the time the central scene
is done, have established absolutely divergent tones. Menelaus
has found his way from rebellion, through parody, to a new,
comic definition of his role. He has entered the camp of Odysseus
and the satyr-drama heroes. Theonoe, on the other hand, has
reiterated, with great dignity and one blinding flash of total
comprehension, all that Menelaus and the play have so far
attacked. She is a pure tragic figure, and only because she is so
are the adventurers allowed to play out their comedy. In the
blocking of the scene, Theonoe took up the position of the wise
local ruler, and Menelaus that of the violent pursuer, so that he
and she together have almost deprived the still unseen Theoclymenus of every conceivable function that might have been
his. When he does at last appear he is as naked, in his way, as
Menelaus was on his arrival, and this effective deposition of
Theoclymenus was of course the overt aim of the persuasion
scene. Theonoe's choice of father over brother disarms Theoclymenus so that he cannot properly play even the duped villain
of the escape scenes that follow. She deprives him not only of the
extraordinary supernatural aid of her warning, but also of his

[14] On the philosophical background of her statement, see Pippin, op. cit.,
159–61.

natural defence, his intelligence. He would ordinarily be suspicious, and he begins to be so now,[15] but his misplaced confidence in his sister's knowledge and obedience makes a simpleton of the king.

This diminishment of the villain has several important results. First of all, it works to diminish also our sense of Menelaus' boldness and even of Helen's courage and cleverness in deceiving the young king. Secondly, it entirely destroys the suspense ordinarily generated by scenes of intrigue, leaving a kind of emotional vacuum which the poet has filled in this case only with verbal wit.[16] Thus a serious formal imbalance develops in the play's penultimate scenes. The spectator does not by this time expect that the tragic possibilities of the rescue plot will be realized, but he finds that without any real opposition, even the comic melodrama he was prepared for cannot quite continue. Only when this weak Theoclymenus is wholly left behind and Menelaus is fighting against his subjects is there anything like a confrontation of equals, and even then, though the Greek ship is filled with blood (1602) it is only the blood of a good messenger speech. Within that speech, every effort is expended to make the escape as absorbing as possible, but it is still true that the spectator inevitably feels that the success achieved at line 1618 has been far too cheaply won.

It was Theonoe who deprived the play of its villain, and so of its suspense and its heroism, not to speak of its pity and its terror. Thus it is with perfect poetic justice that she, the one tragic figure here, the one human being who made a choice and so has an ethical flavour, is the one who is made to pay. It is paradoxically her job to prove that physical evil does still exist on these boards, so that we may once again believe that human virtue matters. Were she brought on stage in person as she struggles with this force, she might efface the heroine who, in spite of her wit and her restored reputation, has still so very little more than face to offer. And so the minuscule central scene from Theonoe's tragedy is played by proxy, and the loyal servant who stands in for the priestess represents the final liberty that the

---

[15] I would agree with Miss Dale that two lines have been lost between 1226 and 1227, the second of which must have expressed some doubt on Theoclymenus' part, along the lines of 'how do I know he's telling the truth?'.

[16] On this scene, see Pippin, op. cit., 153–4.

Helen will take with the settled scene conventions of the Attic stage.[17]

The servant feels none of Menelaus' rebelliousness or embarrassment when he finds himself playing high tragedy. He savours his role, and plays it with noble simplicity. In the space of twelve lines, nine of them split, the tyrant and the slave reiterate the salient points of Theonoe's choice: the two justices (1628; 1633); the exertion that leads to evil (1629); the supremacy of the conscience (1630); the noble act of treason (1633). Then the servant, in three lines, expands upon his own decision, which is Theonoe's too, to embrace death (1639) if it be the concomitant of the noble act (1639–41). The tiny scene is hardly more than a repetition of the litany of tragic self-sacrifice, but it adds one last point of faith necessary to heroic action, for the villainous king and the noble slave between them mark out the distinction between chance and the will of heaven, between melodrama and true tragedy. The slave believes that whatever *tyche* may give or take away, *to chreon* can remove or restore at will, and the finale of the *Helen* will bear him out in this.

Theoclymenus' hand is raised against the slave, and so against his sister, and a full tragic catastrophe is about to be played out. The intended familial crime is a knowing one, and so it can be interrupted only by chance or by a divine agency—a recognition is here impossible. An interruption by chance would make melodrama, one by heaven makes a kind of tragedy, and Euripides, having caused this bit of tragedy to erupt at the end of his nontragic play, gives it its deserts. The Dioscuri appear in the machine and shout the formula of interruption;[18] Theoclymenus freezes, the servant rises, and the instruction from heaven begins:

---

[17] Miss Dale would follow LP and give this role to the leader of the chorus, calling the masculine forms at 1630 and 1640 'generalizing'. She argues that a new figure could not simply pop out of the palace at this moment; that he could not reasonably be supposed to be *au courant*, and that he would be unidentified. It would seem, however, that unless this scene is supposed to repeat the absurdity of the earlier gatekeeper scene, this interposing figure must be male. Also it seems that he must come out of the palace (not up from behind Theoclymenus, as would be the case with the chorus leader) because he evidently blocks the king's way; Theoclymenus says ἀφίστασ' ἐκποδών (1628). As to identity, the natural thing would be to use one of the mute figures who had come out with Theonoe before, in which case his priestly robes would immediately identify him, and his understanding of the situation would be explained.

[18] Their opening command (ἐπίσχες, 1642) is the conventional one for the interruption of a catastrophe; cf. *Ion*, 1320; *Androm.*, 550.

The purloined marriage that provokes your rage
was never meant to be, while this girl, Theonoe,
your sister and the daughter of a nymph divine,
has in no way done you wrong, but has honoured heaven
and her father's just command.

(1646-9)

As soon as they can the airborne brothers make this discrimination between the two actions of the play, explaining that Helen's
happy escape was destiny's creation, while Theonoe's near
disaster was the work of a principled human choice. As they
continue, however, they make it clear too that the fulfilment of
the one action and the interruption of the other equally express
the will of Zeus, for chance has played no more part in the negative than it did in the positive drama.

By a miracle Theoclymenus is taught to admire his sister, and
he in turn congratulates the twins upon the character of theirs
(1686-7). Theonoe will evidently continue to purify the atmos-
phere and to act as priestess and prophetess, for her betrayal
of her mantic duty is in the finale described by gods, just as it was
earlier by Helen, as a form of piety (1648-9). Menelaus is to live
forever among the heroes of the Blessed Isles (1676-7) and
Helen, at the end of a happy life, will become a goddess of divine
rescue (1667). With the promise of immortality thus explicitly
made, the ultimate transportation of Helen and Menelaus from
Egypt to Sparta becomes an almost allegorical affair. Their
salvation, like that of a satyr play, has been granted to creatures
at once excessively flawed and excessively fortunate, to mortals
who are plainly the darlings of the gods. Helen, after all, is
Zeus' daughter, as Silenus was Dionysus' foster-father, and it is
only Theonoe, with her fully mortal virtue, her vision, and her
miraculous salvation, who pulls Helen's story back from the
realms of irrelevant absurdity.

By casting Helen as a suppliant heroine who picnics at the
sacred spot, and Menelaus as a champion whose role is pre-
empted by the villain's sister, Euripides suggests that faith and
courage are not so frequent in this world as suppliant tragedy
might have you think. He also announces, with this distorted
action, that he is in no mood to praise the polity.[19] So much for

---

[19] Since the achievement of the normal suppliant plot is the substitution of civil
protection for the protection of the sanctuary, it ordinarily asserts a close connection

the suppliant action; his rescue plot he does at least bring to a normal fulfilment, but by drawing its monster's teeth he subverts it from its ordinary effects. The lonely mortal hero who faced demonic nature in defence of a princess has become simply one more in the roster of Helen's kidnappers.

The figure of Helen, with her phantom double, allowed the poet to play long and lovingly on the theme of appearance and reality.[20] She is, as the Old Sailor saw, the loveliest and the costliest example of that divine deceit which makes life agonizing but also, the poet adds, makes it exquisite. He shows us a magical, irrational world where men are foolish, vicious, absurd and beautiful. It is constantly being rearranged by divine manipulation, and it is redolent of the presence of gods who exploit men's weaknesses more often than they punish them. Somewhere in Egypt, however, there is a mortal of another sort, one who can still act the part of the protector of suppliants even though this means that she must also become the heroine of a secular sacrifice and face a death like Antigone's. This tragic *arete* is an exotic thing, a lonely, distant and barbarian phenomenon that draws its strength from a special vision of eternity. It neither enhances nor denies Helen's world, but it does somehow penetrate it, so that gods, men and events are all rescued from the sordidness of irresponsibility. Theonoe cannot make a tragedy of the *Helen*, but by intruding upon a charming *jeu d'esprit* she alters it, saving a serious poet from frivolity.

between the will of heaven and the justice of the *polis* or the ruling prince; thus, for example, Danaus can tell his daughters to celebrate the Argives as if they were gods (Aesch., *Supp.* 980 ff.).

[20] On appearance and reality, see F. Solmsen, '*Onoma* and *pragma* in Euripides' *Helen*', *CR* xlviii (1934), 119–21; also Pippin, op. cit., 152–4.

V

ION

THE *Ion* is different from all the plays so far discussed, and from those to follow, in that its multiple actions are played not in sequence but simultaneously. Creusa moves as principal through all the phases of a fully developed vengeance plot with catastrophe interrupted, but she is also the victim-heroine of a release, and meanwhile Ion plays the primary role in an oddly displaced but still definable drama of return to wealth and power. The interruption of the vengeance action and the fulfilment of the other two depend ultimately upon recognitions, and the play is so organized that when the heroine of the vengeance piece shall recognize the hero of the return, the rescue will come about and the plots will melt together just as the two principals do in their embrace of mutual discovery. The perfect co-ordination of this complex is the secret of the *Ion*'s apparent classical unity, while the actual diversity of the plot accounts for its extraordinary richness and vitality. The play as a whole has a single and powerful sense of positive overturn because the interruption of the negative plot and the fulfilment of the covert plot of release are both encompassed by the all-embracing action of return.

The mixture of return, rescue and vengeance was of course no new thing on the Attic stage. It is implicit in the *Choephoroi* and in the Sophoclean *Electra*[1] although in these cases the total effect is negative since the release is likewise muted, while the vengeance serves the return and is completed. The lost *Cresphontes* was much closer to the *Ion*, since there, as here, the woman who was to be released plotted vengeance against her unrecognized son, while he pressed his claim to his throne. In that play, however, as in the Orestes plays, the all-embracing praxis is a

---

[1] There have been some recent attempts to prove the Sophoclean *Electra* to be very late; they are not fully convincing, however, because they depend upon a presumed likeness between this play and the *OC* and the *Philoctetes*, a likeness which reduces itself merely to their all having 'happy endings'; see A. M. Dale, *Euripides. Helen* (Oxford, 1967), p. 134 and *Collected Papers* (Cambridge, 1969), p. 228.

mixed action of return and vengeance, and the boy's murder of his rival is completed. This means that the *Cresphontes* too was, in its ultimate description, a play of negative overturn, and so quite unlike the *Ion*.

Ion's return to the city from which he had been exiled has been given the non-violent form that actions of return probably had in archaic drama.[2] His establishment upon the throne is not to be touched by any drop of blood, and upon this purity the Pythia explicitly insists. Vengeance may be proper to some, she seems to say, but this boy is to go to Athens unspotted and accompanied only by good omens (1333). He does not have to kill to inherit, nor does he have to undergo any fairy-tale test of strength, unless his mother's attempt upon his life should be viewed as a kind of trial. All that is necessary to this return is a recognition.

Ion's return action is, in its freedom from any stain, unlike that of Cresphontes and much more like that of Theseus in the lost *Aegeus*. In Ion's case, however, the vengeance plot that mingles with the return is not only dissociated from the hero, it is given as its principal a woman who is unlike Medea in that she plots a blind and not a knowing crime. Medea had to be punished, and the exile of the sorceress will have added a kind of harshness to the joyful conclusion of the *Aegeus*, whereas the sweetness of the *Ion's* triumphant close has no such bitter admixture. Instead it gains an added flavour from Creusa's happy overturn as she moves from blindness into sight, from guilt into innocence, and from emotional bondage into the freedom of confidence.[3]

---

[2] An action of return apparently provided the praxis for the Sophoclean *Telephus* and for the Euripidean *Aegeus* and *Alexander*; the satyr play *Sphinx* was probably a parody of this same type of action. In the simplest form of this plot the exiled principal moves from bad fortune to good by means of a recognition which allows him to claim what is rightfully his own; more complex versions could include ordeals like that of Jason, or displays of strength like the athletic contests of *Alexander* and *Telephus*. In dramas of compound action the plot of return was frequently combined with vengeance, the murder being either the deed of the principal, as in the case of Orestes, or the deed of another directed against the principal, as in the *Aegeus*, or both, as in *Cresphontes*; at least once, in the *Larissaioi*, it was an accident. The return action was also combined sometimes with an action of rescue, as in *Antiope*. (In *Agamemnon* and *Women of Trachis* fictions of flawed returns are used in the service of plots of divine vengeance.)

[3] Compare also the *Alexander*, where the homecoming is pure, the vengeance blind, defensive and interrupted, but where there is still not the *Ion's* accumulation of

The best foil for the *Ion* would be Sophocles' lost *Creusa*, about which we can only speculate. The older poet's was probably the elder play[4] and it was presumably set in Athens, the proper scene for Ion's return. With the Erechtheid palace in the background, the theme of Ion's coming rule would be stronger, and the justification of the queen's attempted crime an easy thing. The boy would come somewhat ominously, like a Theseus or a Jason, and the ruler, this time no usurper but the legitimate queen, would react with natural suspicion. Creusa's intrigue in this setting would be plainly a defence of her own house and it would, in addition, be free of any impiety. Her blindness would be of the simple sort, created by events as Deianeira's was, and so she could have been reconciled in the end with joyful propriety to an Ion more knowing and more assertive than is Euripides' young heir.

The Sophoclean play, whatever its date and whatever its quality, at least serves as a reminder that there was another, more traditional, Athenian version of the events that make the fiction of the Euripidean *Ion*. In shifting the setting of his play away from Athens and off to Apollo's capital, Euripides has made a central, overwhelming innovation, and he is careful to announce this change of scene as soon as possible. 'Here I am at Delphi', says Hermes at line 5, and his next sentence begins, 'Athens is *another* famous city . . .' (7), so that even the dullest member of the audience will notice at once that an important alteration has been made.

Euripides meant to write a Delphic play, and in this matter at least there is no question of his success. Everyone who reads the *Ion* is struck, if by nothing else, by its evocation of the great shrine with its complex ritual and its awesome natural glory. This effect is the work of the poetry, but even the wood of the scene building, fitted out to represent not a palace but the temple of Apollo, will have worked a kind of magic on the myth.

positive effects, since the end of the play will inevitably have been shadowed by the sense that Alexander was to become Paris and that all Cassandra's prophecies were true. On the reconstruction of this play, see J. O. de G. Hanson, *Hermes*, xcii (1964), 171–81.

[4] The old man's criticism of Creusa's plan at *Ion* 1021 ff. and Ion's words at 1269 sound as if they were playful criticisms of a previous play, and since Sophocles is the only other tragedian known to have used this fiction, the most efficient conclusion is that it is to his *Creusa* that Euripides here refers.

The action was inevitably altered when it was played against a sacred screen, and this Euripides knew well. The temple setting first of all made possible a new Creusa, a woman whose crimes were no longer simply blind but were touched now with religious error. When she acts on this ground, the Queen of Athens is no longer a simple defender of her house. She has not stayed at home, as the woman of tradition (the woman of Apollo's plan) would do, but has come to Delphi like a weaker Neoptolemus, half intending to confront the god with his injustice. When she intrigues against Ion in this setting she necessarily plots to kill Apollo's acolyte on Apollo's sacred ground, and this fact alters the whole quality of her guilt, making it deeper and more difficult to dispel.

Unlike Creusa, Ion gains in initial innocence when he is placed upon this sacred spot, and his unworldly childlike purity is the subject of the song that marks his first entrance, at the dawn of this drama's day. The Delphic setting has altered the time of the play, shifting it backwards ever so slightly, so that where an Athenian piece would have imitated the opening of the hero's adult life, this temple play gives us instead the closing moments of his enchanted childhood. It is as if we saw Perseus just before he left the satyrs, or Jason on the last day he spent at Chiron's cave. The Delphic setting gives ocular proof that the child who was exiled long ago has had a happy fate and it announces that this play will concern itself with what the boy is leaving behind, as well as with what he is going to claim.

Delphi means not only a gain in innocence for Ion, but also a gain in good fortune. He belongs to that race of semi-divine children whose stories ordinarily contain torments and exile and danger.[5] The heroes of tales such as his move from rough childhoods into secure maturity, from bestiality (or at least from low-life scenes) into civilization, from the upland wilds down into a polished city life. Sometimes these pastoral places were, it is true, the site of virtues forgotten in town, virtues which the exiled princes took back with them, like the lessons of Chiron, when they went to claim their thrones. Even in these cases, however, the return to the throne was experienced as a kind of initiation, a passage from a lower to a higher form of life. Ion's

---

[5] See M. Nilsson, *Minoan-Mycenaean Religion and its Survival* (Lund, 1950), Chapter 16, 'The Divine Child'.

history is formally like the others' and yet he has never known torments, danger, or even insecurity. He has had no animal wet-nurse or shepherd guardian, nor has he slept in a cave or a hut. The prophetess has been his Amalthea, the priests his rustic company, and he has eaten from the altars and dressed from the god's rich treasuries in a place where all the world was ripe for his acquaintance. The poet has been able to replace the wilderness with an ornate and cosmopolitan shrine; he has turned the usual tale of bucolic obscurity into a triumphant account of urbane though pious pleasures. The one motif he has retained from the traditional locale of the lost boy is the sense of pastoral purity. This he is at pains to attach to Apollo's shrine, where, indeed, it is at home. His hero will carry an immaculate Delphic purity of heart down to Athens with him, but he will not experience, as he goes, an overturn from bad to good. He will move instead only from an unworldly form of happiness to another, worldly, one.

Euripides has arranged that a return, a vengeance, and a rescue shall take place simultaneously on the terrace before Apollo's temple at Delphi. He intimates in the prologue that his plot will be compound, and all but announces that whatever curiosities we may find in its multiplicity have been created with specific intent. This is done through Hermes, who outlines the drama Apollo means to have performed and then invites us to watch with him and see what will actually happen when a divinely authored piece is played upon a human stage. Apollo's action is thus labelled as the primary one, and since Athena testifies in the end that it has passed successfully through the depths of the mortal counter plots and issued forth as it was meant to do, the critic's first exercise is to identify its streams.

Hermes gives us Apollo's plan, which is to make of Ion as nearly as possible another Erichthonius. That child of divine parents was removed from the secular world, after the failure of the Aglaurids, and cared for by his spiritual mother, Athena, in her Acropolis temple. When he came of age he was given by her to the childless Cecrops, who adopted him and secured the throne of Athens for the new Erechtheid race. Ion likewise has been spirited away by his divine parent, and brought up unknown in a temple; now the time has come for his return to his city, where Xuthus is to be his Cecrops. Apollo faces one delicate problem, however, which Athena had not been troubled with. He cannot publicly acknowledge his boy on earth, though he has done so in heaven, for this would mean the loss of all his long-range aims. Xuthus must make Ion his heir, and Ion must be able to bequeath the Erechtheid name and property to his own sons, if Ionian power in the Aegean is to be established. If he is to conform to the customary patterns of inheritance Apollo's child must seem to be not merely an adopted son, but Xuthus' own by blood, and Apollo for this reason must practise a deception upon the Attic king.[6]

Hermes outlines a drama of return that will have two acts. First there is to be an oracle to Xuthus, producing a false recognition between him and the god's son; later there is to be a true recognition between the boy and his mother. We learn later (1349 ff.) that the god had meant the Pythia to give her ward the box of recognition tokens on the day of his departure, in preparation for his discovery by his mother, when he should have arrived in Athens. The god's drama will be complete when Ion is securely installed as heir to the Athenian throne. This, then, was to be a simple action, turning entirely upon recognition, with its only elaboration arising from the deception of the king, which was to cause a doubling of its one incident.

As this archaic piece is actually played it is better theatre than one might suppose, for it turns out that there is a second source of complication in the heir himself. Ion is reluctant to leave Delphi,

---

[6] Creusa is thought of as an *epikleros*, the sole female heir of her father. Normally she should have married the male who was her closest paternal kin so that the royal property would remain in the family, but Creusa had no male relative and so her foreign husband would, according to custom, take on the status of an adopted son in the Erechtheid family. However, neither an *epikleros* nor an adopted son had testamentary power under Attic law; both could pass property only to their own legitimate heirs by blood; neither could lawfully secure it to an adopted child or even to a bastard unless he were legitimized. In this particular case, then, Apollo's device must be one for securing the legitimization of a bastard, which would have to be done by consent of both parties in the marriage. The bastard is of course Creusa's, but since Xuthus would have no conceivable reason for allowing such a child to interfere with the rights of his own potential heirs, he must be made to think that the child is his. Creusa, having recognized it as in fact her own, will not then resist the idea of his legitimization as the son of Xuthus (659–60, where Xuthus looks forward to persuading her of this). Only by this roundabout means could Ion legally inherit his portion of the Erechtheid power. The imaginary situation is built up from concepts that Athenians had known at least since the time of Solon, and thought of as being very old: see W. K. Lacey, *The Family in Classical Greece* (Ithaca, 1968), pp. 139–46; M. Broadbent, *Studies in Greek Geneology* (Leiden, 1968), pp. 228 f.

for an interesting complex of reasons that offer a charming commentary upon the god's notion of how the return should be plotted. Because of the peculiar nature of his fate until now, because he has been so favoured, because of Apollo's graciousness, in other words, Ion is blissfully happy exactly where he is. His monody at the beginning of the play voices a sense of wellbeing mixed with ecstasy that is shared by no other creature of the Attic stage.[7] In addition to his contentment Ion has a sense of Delphi and its contrast with the outer world; he knows that it is partly the purity of Delphi that ministers to his joy. And most of all, he has a sense of Apollo himself; he has invented the pretty 'fiction' of being the god's son, and this means that he has fixed all of his curiosity as to his actual parentage upon his mother. He is not nearly so pleased at discovering a mortal father as he should have been, and he longs still for the sight of the woman who bore him.

All of these responses, which are the fruits of Apollo's education, create the friction and the suspense of the divine plot of return. It is to be noted, however, that this Apolline play of return is always of the sort we would call comic. Indeed its first great scene, the recognition between the boy and the king who is to be his mortal father, almost flounders into farce because of Ion's haughty identification of himself with Apollo and his shrine. The eager old soldier is repulsed by a fastidious boy—'Are you quite sane, sir, or has some god played havoc with your wits? . . . Please remove your hand from the garlands of the god . . . Your jokes, sir, fail to please!' (520; 522; 528). It is only when Ion realizes that attachment to this importunate creature implies a Delphic birth, a free-born mother, and consanguinity with Zeus, that he consents to listen to his claim.

The next scene begins as one of persuasion, in which Xuthus would explain to Ion all the glories that lie before him in his new life. Xuthus, however, is soon interrupted and the scene almost reverses itself as Ion, fired now by his Erechtheid ambition as well as by his Apolline dedication, makes a double rhetorical resistance to the idea of leaving Delphi. First he argues that Athens will be no proper place for him, as the bastard son of a foreign king; he touches on the difficulty afforded by Xuthus'

[7] The only comparisons are with the brief song of the huntsmen at the beginning of *Hipp.*, and with the parodos of the *Bacchae*.

royal wife, and then turns into the positive side of his argument,
a plea to be allowed to stay behind at Delphi:

> Think of all my pleasures here!
> I have leisure, first and best; society but not a crowd.
> Here there is no base-born man to strike me from my path
> (and that's a thing I could not bear—to yield before the mob).
> I pass my days with gods and men in prayer and conversation
> aiding those who come rejoicing, never hearing lamentation.
> Each day I lose a friend, but new ones never fail;
> for them I am a novelty and they are fresh to me!
> And that one thing most prayed for among men—
> inhering justice (though it go against one's will)—
> this is conferred on me by my own nature
> and the harmonizing custom of this place
> where I serve god. Father, when I reflect upon my life
> I know that I am better here than there.
> Do let me stay!
>
> > (657 ff.)

Xuthus' response to the boy's reluctance is a worldly 'Come
now, you must learn to appreciate good fortune.' He proposes
that they be as careful of Creusa's feelings as they can, and
reminds Ion that it is she who has the giving of the throne.
With his mention of the queen we dimly perceive that, though
the god has apparently not foreseen Ion's resistance, he has yet
provided in his plot for its removal. Creusa is the key to the real
success of the return; when Ion has found her out, he will know
himself to be a true Erechtheid and a full citizen of Athens. He
will discover in her a focus of love that will make Athens in some
degree a fair substitute for Delphi, and he will learn that he
carries Apollo with him in his own flesh, wherever he may move
in the secular world. All this lies in the immediate future;
meanwhile it is the boy's natural gentleness that allows the
action to go on, for it makes him obedient to his new-found
father in spite of his doubts about Athens.

The second phase of the plot of return, the true recognition
between mother and son, is forced by the counter-plots to be
played at Delphi instead of at Athens, but there is nothing in its
content that seems to have suffered by this change of scene. At
line 1369 Ion stands toying with his box of tokens, the gift of the
Pythia. He is thinking of opening the basket that was his infant

bed and looking at the objects within, to see if they carry any
mark that will lead him to his lost mother. He is watched here,
as he might have been at Athens, by Creusa, who overhears his
soliloquy:

> When my soul turns to her, tears come;
> I think of how she bore me in painful secrecy,
> how she betrayed me, and would not take me to her breast,
> how I, without a name, took service with the god . . .
> His gifts have wrapped me round in full sufficiency
> but oh, the chance was cruel! There was a season when
> I should have lain luxurious in my mother's arms,
> tasting of her sweetness, but in that very time
> I never knew her care. And her distress was equal;
> her life was emptied of her rightful joy . . . etc.
>
> (1369 ff.)

Creusa's first real view of the basket brings a full recognition
to her, and it then becomes her task to prove to the doubting
boy that she is his mother. This she does by identifying each
object before it is held up to her view. She describes the bit of
weaving, and the gold Erechtheid snake necklace, and when she
succeeds even in foreseeing the unwithered chaplet, the miracle
that the box contains, the uphill work is over and the rejoicings
can begin. Creusa sings, exactly as she would have, had the
scene been played according to the letter of the Apolline plan:

> My house has its hearth, my land its king!
> Erechtheus is restored,
> and the line that sprang from earth
> no longer shrouds itself in night
> but looks upon the sun!
>
> (1464-8)

The discovery of the Erechtheid mother leaves only the
rediscovery of Apollo as father, and the divine return drama will
be done. Creusa begins the revelation, and at the first mention
of the god's name the boy, who has resisted this new account of
his parentage, bursts out, 'Go on! this is a noble and a happy
tale you tell!' (1485). The mother and son marvel at the un-
accountable twists fortune has taken with them, but then Ion
remembers Xuthus and the contradictory oracle he has received.

Suddenly he doubts what Creusa has just told him, and feels his
divine paternity degenerating into a lie. She swears; he cites
the god's word that he is Xuthus' son, and a final stalemate
blocks the resolution of Apollo's piece.[8]

The divinity who appears to dispose of this last difficulty is
the same one who might have been expected to play *deus ex
machina* had the second phase of the return drama been played,
as planned, at Athens. The goddess Athena acts in a double
capacity since she is the representative both of the god who is
sending the boy home and of the city that will receive him, and
she can thus reassure him on the two points of his doubt, his
paternity and his future role at Athens. To Ion she says:

> This woman bore you and Apollo was your father.
> He has given you to Xuthus, though you are not his son,
> that you may have a place among earth's best-born men.
> This was his conspiracy . . .
>
> (1560–3)

And to Creusa:

> Take your son and go to Cecrops' realm;
> see him safe upon the throne!
> He is an Erechtheid prince, the heir legitimate
> and so will justly rule my land.
> His fame will spread through Greece, and his continuing sons,
> four, from a single root, will give their names
> to four regions and to the people four
> that crowd about the foot of my acropolis. . . .
>
> (1571–9)

The return action has come to its triumphant fulfilment, and
the exodus of the *Ion* shows the departure of that royal procession
which will, in a few days' time, enter the city gates of Athens
accompanying the new heir. He will seem to be Xuthus' son,
but he and Creusa know his true heredity. He has found his
throne, and the last words spoken before the final *envoi* of the
chorus constitute a kind of coronation for him. The goddess of
the city commands: 'Assume the ancient throne!' and the prince

---

[8] Note how like this situation is to that between Menelaus and Helen, where the
memory of the Phantom Helen acts upon Menelaus just as the memory of the false
parent, Xuthus, does here upon Ion.

responds: 'I will, for it is rightly mine' (1618).[9] Apollo's will is done.

Crossing this positive action, influencing it, yet curiously powerless to alter it, is Creusa's vengeance drama. In the beginning her piece seems conventional enough, its only anomaly an apparently over-long preparation of the situation that demands her action. Like other vengeance principals, she arrives from a distance at the place where her rival is in power, but in this case she only discovers her enmity after she has come. (Her coming, however, was dictated by a second enmity, which will prove to have its importance.) The standard vengeance victim is a usurper, and this is what she is presented with, in the person of her husband's bastard son. She has, like so many vengeance principals, a comrade (lightening the criminal load of the hero is always one of the dramatist's chief problems in these plots), and he provides the first formal aberration of her case from its type. Medea, we assume, poured her own poison into Theseus' cup, and Cresphontes' mother herself raised the axe to split her son's head open, but the assassination of Ion is left to the ancient tutor of Erechtheus. The old man thus technically separates Creusa from her crime, and at the same time he endows her with positive qualities that act as antidotes to her guilty intention, for with him a strain of near comedy, not unlike that brought by the old nurse into the *Choephoroi*, enters Creusa's vengeance plot. At the beginning of the great episode of revelation and intrigue, when the murder will be planned, the queen and the tutor play a miniature scene (725–46) that matches them, for sympathy and humane fallibility, with the Ion and the Xuthus of the preceding episode. The old man hobbles and quavers, and Creusa, as she encourages both his steps and his feeble jokes, is plainly a woman who knows how to love as well as to hate.

Creusa's vengeance is to be interrupted and it is therefore, by the best tragic rule, blind. Her vengeance must in fact be absorbed by the return plot and be lost in her own happy future, which she is to share not only with Ion but with his genial presumptive father. The poet thus faces a special problem for he must

---

[9] His response is also a kind of promise. Because of the ambiguity of the word *axion*, it might almost be rendered 'I shall be worthy of it, since it is worthy of me'. (I have followed Hermann's disposition of the speeches here.)

maintain the seriousness of the threat of death, and yet so lighten
the responsibility of the woman who plans it that she can go
home in this joyous company. His solution is to increase Creusa's
blindness, until it goes far beyond a simple mistake of identity.
He sees to it that she is fed with misconceptions and lies, and in
order to keep this process, in turn, from becoming too sinister
to survive within a promising drama of return, he uses the
irresponsible chorus and the foolish old man as his agents,
making it plain that both are motivated by misguided but
genuine love for their queen.

Both the chorus and the old man are self-deceived; they think
that they speak nothing but the truth, and yet the revelation
that comes to Creusa, the 'threat' that makes her crime necessary, is false in every way. And the poet has so arranged his play
that senseless and destructive lies shall come hard upon a truth
that the audience has both heard and seen. The very first
thing that the women say—and their speech is illegal, since they
were sworn to silence by their king—is that Creusa is never to
have a child (761–2). This statement is purest emotional invention; nothing that they have overheard has given them the
slightest grounds for such a prophecy, yet they convince Creusa
that it was spoken by the Pythia herself. Trophonius, in fact,
has already promised the contrary, saying that neither the king
nor the queen will leave the shrine childless, but everyone joins
in forgetting his words. Athena, in the end, settles the question
in detail, promising Creusa three future sons as well as her
present one, but at this earlier point in the play, thanks to the
chorus, her future barrenness is assumed, and it becomes one
of the chief factors in the anguish that leads to Creusa's crime
(789).

When the women imply that Ion is Xuthus' natural son (775),
their suggestion is equally untrue, though here their mistake is
more nearly justified. This second falsehood is seized upon by the
old man and on it he builds a fantastical story of intentional
disloyalty, slowly ripening conspiracy, and present danger for
the queen. The audience has just seen a ridiculously happy
man plotting with his 'son' to give Creusa as large a share as
possible in their new felicity (654 ff.), but it must listen now while
the foolish old tutor describes that same man as the blackest of
villians, busy plotting his wife's death and the deposition of her

line. His own fiction quite carries the old man away, and he
ends with a ringing call for a revenge which will be Creusa's
only escape from the terrible father and son (844–9).

The tutor is full of fancy and he is urging a vengeance that is
to precede, not follow, the suffering of an injury, but still he
speaks much in the vein of the other bad counsellors of tragedy.
Creusa's response, however, is quite unprecedented. Instead of
taking up the old man's suggestion and carrying the scene on
into the phase of intrigue, Creusa produces a total reorientation
in the spirit of the action. What she does is redefine the enemy.
The perfidy of Xuthus has just been urged upon her, and she
answers, illogically but with absolute emotional relevance: 'I can
show you a better case of faithlessness than that!' She removes
Xuthus, and replaces him with Apollo as the author of her
suffering, justifying the change by a new revelation. If she is to
be barren in the future, and if she has lost her husband's confidence, there is no reason to continue to protect her own
reputation, and she can attack that of the god. Unfortunately,
Creusa's sense of the niceties of truth is no stronger than those
of the chorus and the old man, while her emotions are far
stormier, and so she adds, with her monody, a third major
falsehood to the premises that point to Ion's murder. She reports
the death of her own son as it if were a verifiable fact, and finds
in that long-ago death a new and absolute reason for a present
killing. It is a simple matter of repayment: with ironic accuracy
she equates the new son, given to her husband, with the old son
who was taken from her, and finds that the present gift makes
the past robbery doubly reprehensible. She accuses Apollo,
saying:

> You took your joy of me,
> then gave a living son
> to one who'd never pleasured you
> and left the child of yours and mine
> to die, a witless babe,
> the helpless prey of birds!

> (913–18)

As dramatic utterance, her song is matchless. All of Creusa's
true nature is revealed in its mixture of truth and falsehood,
love and hate, and in its unwilling testimony to the beauty of the

god she calls her coward lover.[10] No one who heard it could fail
to sympathize with the singer, and yet the audience is uncomfortably aware that the lies are proliferating and that they are
leading to a deed more terrible than they had supposed, a
direct attack not only upon a son but upon a god.

When the monody is finished, the old man comically insists
upon a repetition of Creusa's tale, and once again the death of
Ion is reported as an established fact. 'Where is your son then?
Speak and be childless no more!' 'He is dead, old man. Exposed,
and devoured by the birds.' 'Dead! Apollo played the coward
and abandoned him?' 'He did. He sent him off to Hades for his
schooling!' (950–3). The tutor is of the simple sort that sees
gods as slightly fleshier men, the sort whose theories Ion has
already described in his reflections upon Creusa's story of her
'friend' (444). Naturally then, his first reaction to Creusa's
accusation of the god is to propose that they should burn his
temple down. She answers that she is afraid. He next proposes the
death of Xuthus, but Creusa knows in her heart that her husband
is not her enemy. It is the boy she would attack, overtly as one
who usurps her father's throne, covertly because he has belonged
to Apollo and is now Apollo's gift.

With Ion chosen as victim, the intrigue proper can begin at
last. The dramatist had reached a point, at line 846, when killing
was called for; now, some 120 lines later, the same call comes.
Creusa's monody and the subsequent scene that investigated it
have resulted in no material change, but the audience now
knows why Creusa is ready for the crime. Xuthus has been
removed to the background where he belongs; it is not as his
boy, but as Apollo's boy, that Ion now must die. Nowhere else
is a vengeance crime thus redefined in the scene of its conception,
and nowhere else is the physical intrigue made as it is made here.

Creusa and the old man begin at a pitch of determination,
introduced by her eager 'How? If I could—! There is a deed I
would do!' (979), but the following sixty-five lines work some
curious alterations in her position as vengeance herione. The
mock quarrel between the two conspirators reminds us that
though they are mistress and slave, Creusa is not assuming the
absolute responsibility that ordinarily goes with the vengeance

[10] For a more detailed analysis of Creusa's monody, see A. P. Burnett, 'Human
Resistance and Divine Persuasion in Euripides' *Ion*', *CP* lvii (1962), 95–6.

role. She is not going to commit the crime, and the poet spends his intrigue scene distracting us even from any consideration of the old man who is to be her agent. Eight lines suffice for the actual scheme (1029–36) and almost all the rest of this extraordinary scene of stichomythia is given over to a description of the implement (987–1017). When the poet has finished with it, the poison has effaced the poisoner, and the audience has been given the sense that this liquid may have a power other than its proprietor understands.

Creusa's poison is a thing she has always worn on her wrist; it is almost a part of herself, and it well represents her essential mixture of nobility and rebellion. It comes from a monster especially created by the poet as an enemy of the gods, and this is a reminder that Creusa, when she uses her poison to defend her house, will be attacking a god. On the other hand, the poison was given by Athena to Erichthonius, and this means that, though she is a rebel against Apollo, Creusa yet has divine favour and protection. There is one point, however, in the poet's description of the poison, which is not so easily accounted for. He was innovating in his aetiology here (and boasting of the fact, as at 996–7) in order to bypass the unwanted figure of Perseus and to give himself the rebellion of the giants as the poetic context for his assassination weapon. He chose, however, to keep one motif from the old Medusa tale, and it is one that seems, in its new surroundings, quite gratuitous. The duplicate presence of a matching, healing elixir, drawn from the right side of the monster's body, cannot have been dictated by tradition since there is no tradition at work here, and it is certainly not dictated by any mechanical necessity in the present tale. In the old story it had its part to play, and was said ultimately to have entered Asclepius' medicine chest. Here it has no practical function, but it is yet forced upon our attention by repeated reference (1003; 1005; 1011; 1013).

The unused curative drop inspires Creusa to observe that 'good and evil do not mix' (1017), a remark that betrays how little she knows of herself and humanity, and that also gives us the clue to the symbolic function of this unspent boon. It is here in order that it may represent how little humanity knows of its own god-given qualities. By dwelling on this drop, Euripides has reminded his audience of the possibility of healing, and of the

healing god, and by so doing he has enhanced our sense of
Creusa's temporary human perversity. She has been given the
paired powers of life and death—she wears them on her wrist—
but it is only of the second that she thinks. The audience is
teased by the sense that the good drop is here for some purpose,
but it is introduced, then lost to the plot, like the elixir of life
that the satyrs lost in the Sophoclean *Kophoi*.[11] It is a part of
herself that Creusa will not use, and her human deficiency in
mercy has to be made up for by a merciful god. The antidote
rests untouched in Creusa's golden armlet and in its place
Apollo will have to send a dove, to drink the poison up.

When Creusa's bracelet, the extraordinary weapon of this
crime, has been given to its extraordinary agent, the queen goes
into hiding and the chorus calls upon the witch-goddess,
Einodia, to speed the gorgon poison to its mark. Their lyric is
unusually dramatic, as suits these meddlesome ladies who have,
by breaking their king's command, set the vengeance plot in
motion. The song is reminiscent of the Bacchantes' call for
vengeance (*Bacch.* 977 ff.), but these women are demanding a
death that is not to be accomplished, and their ode is composed
so as to keep the listener in awareness of the singers' error.
Creusa's Apolline son is described as a low foreigner, the
opposite of Erechtheid nobility (note the echo of the responding
lines, 1060 and 1073), and one whose presence would outrage
the divinities of the great Eleusinian procession. The spectator
of course does not need to be undeceived, for he has known all
along that this murder will not be done. He expects an interruption and so he can enjoy the poet's ironic play with the blindness
of the women, but with Creusa absent from the scene of the
crime, he begins to wonder how a recognition can be brought
about.

The premonition of difficulty is justified when the messenger
rushes in, his first news that the queen and all her people are
now hunted criminals. The catastrophe has been interrupted
but the recognition has not taken place, and this unprecedented
state of affairs causes the audience to join with the chorus in its
cry of 'How was the plot discovered?' (1116). 'The god discovered it', is the answer, but the chorus again asks 'How?'

[11] The story was also treated by Epicharmus, Aristias and others; see Aelian
NA 6. 51.

and the full response comes in a slow and ornate tale isolated from the rest of the play by an introduction heavy with seemingly irrelevant physical description. This long *prooimion* tells of a piece of space set aside and withdrawn even from the sacred air of the rest of the shrine. It is the scene of the banquet and so the scene of the crime. It is decorated to become a tiny cosmos and dedicated to human festivity, and yet it is a consecrated space where both contents and container belong to the god. As the messenger slowly sets this imaginery stage, a powerful sense of anticipation is created and with it a conviction that the piece to be mounted in such sacredness will be a kind of miracle play.

The unseen drama begins at last, just as Ion's feast is drawing to its close, with the entrance of Creusa's old man, who is playing Hephaestus at some banquet of the gods, hurrying among the good-humoured guests with pompous zeal. He manages to get all the cups within his keep, and when the slaves are passing everywhere with wine, he takes Ion's goblet, poisons it, and presents it to the boy. All are about to pour the common offering when a blasphemous word is spoken and Ion, with his instinctive piety, calls for fresh wine to be prepared while the ill-omened drinks are emptied on the ground. At this point, as soon as the poisoned wine is cast away, the defeat of the assassination is assured and Ion has been saved—by chance? by the blasphemer? by his own piety? by the god? These questions hardly have time to arise, for the actual interruption is almost unnoticed in the continuing scene. Ion is not yet to recognize Creusa as his mother, but he must recognize the assassination attempt and thus Creusa as his assassin, and these recognitions have been arranged so that the audience, meanwhile, will recognize the identity of the boy's saviour.

In a moment of mysterious silence[12] a band of sacred temple doves, possessions, like everything else here, of the god, come fluttering in. They are wine-loving doves, and when they settle to sip from the pools of discarded drink, one of them dies Ion's death. The boy at once understands; he recognizes the presence of poison, identifies the old man as its source, and soon has the confession that implicates the Athenian queen. The audience,

[12] Compare *OC* 1623 and *Bacchae* 1084 for other such silences marking the intervention of the supernatural.

however, has known all of this all along; its attention is fixed by
the bird:

> None felt any harm except for that one dove
> who settled where the boy had poured his goblet out;
> she took a taste and then the pretty feathered thing
> fell into convulsions and gave a frenzied cry
> we could not understand. All that host of revellers watched,
> marvelling at her agony; they saw her die,
> breath rattling in her throat as she stretched out
> her scaly, coral-coloured feet.
>
> (1201-7)

In this redeeming bird the spectator recognizes the agent of
Apollo. The messenger has understood it likewise, and both are
confirmed by Athena, who announces in the end that Ion's life,
like his mother's later, was saved by the god's contrivances
($\mu\eta\chi\alpha\nu\alpha\hat{\iota}\varsigma$ $\dot{\epsilon}\rho\rho\acute{\upsilon}\sigma\alpha\tau o$, 1565). The dove's death purchases a new
life for Ion, for the bird not only absorbs the poison but proves
that it was present and so allows the boy to take his first steps
towards a true understanding of his situation.[13]

A blind vengeance whose interruption does not cure the
blindness of the parties involved is obviously likely to repeat
itself, and that is what happens in this case. Creusa does not
repeat her attempt, though she might have done, given the
opportunity; instead Ion duplicates it by trying to take her life
in return. This is the result of the carefully arranged interruption
that was not a recognition; it is the mechanism which allows the
poet to write his climax scene; it is indeed the special achievement of this ingeniously complex plot. When Ion reciprocates his
mother's violence, the return hero steps actively into the
vengeance plot, and in so doing he transforms both himself and
that secondary action.

---

[13] The dove story belongs to a common folk-tale type; Stesichorus (*PMG* no.
280 = Aelian, *NA* 17. 37) repeats a version in which a bird saves his benefactor from
drinking poison by knocking the cup from his hand, and from this parallel we can
learn three important things about the Euripidean variant. First, as the cause of the
salvation, Euripides has substituted a pious deed, pleasing to god, for a merely
good deed, pleasing to the bird. Second, Euripides has insisted that there be a death,
and has made the bird ransom the boy from death with its own life. Third, Euripides
has given the poison an active, almost magical function, as it makes itself manifest
first through the bird and then upon the person of the old man, and so leads directly
to the accusation of the queen.

The young man who leaps from the banqueting table, seizes Erechtheus' old tutor, extracts a confession and then angrily accuses his enemy before the assembled Delphians is no longer quite the same person as the almost tranced boy of the early morning scenes. His brush with death has so altered him that when he next appears before the audience, he is momentarily able to play the villain's role in a wholly unexpected suppliant tableau. The city has condemned his assassin to death by stoning, and Ion comes to arrest his new-found enemy. When he discovers that she has put herself out of the city's reach by clinging to the altar on the temple terrace, he is outraged. He orders her off, and when she refuses, he threatens her with death. He seems to hold a drawn sword; at any rate, his arm is clearly raised against the suppliant when the Pythia bursts upon the scene crying 'Hold!' (1320), and even then he is disposed to argue with the priestess' injunction (1328, 1334).

Ion's interrupted gesture makes him the equal of his mother; each of them has now willed the murder of the other, yet each can call his attempted crime 'unwilling' (1500) since he did not know his victim. The two loving destroyers can thus feel a like remorse and a like sense of awe at the chance that has saved them from becoming each both slaughterer and slaughtered. Their crimes take on a new aspect, for together they have willed an act of self-destruction, and together they have been rescued from that act. All this means that their embrace, when it comes at last, is far more comfortable, as well as far more touching, than it would have been, had recognition come when only one was guilty.

Ion's violence, in fact, effects another sort of equality between himself and Creusa, for both are now guilty of an intended religious crime. Creusa's suppliant gesture formally makes of her pursuer an exact replica of herself, a mortal who would blaspheme in action by attacking one of Apollo's creatures upon consecrated ground. Here is the fullest measure of the change that seems to have been wrought in Ion by the day's events, for the boy who swept the porch at dawn and filled the stoups with pure Castalian water, the boy who boasted at noon of the purity of his Delphic life, is ready at evening to desecrate the altar of Apollo. The transformation is so radical that many critics have rejected it as wholly against nature and therefore bad characterization, while others have tried to deny Ion's plain intention to

seize a suppliant woman.[14] Denial is impossible, however, for
Euripides has created a moment, at line 1320, when his innocent
hero will stand frozen, his posture one of extremest impiety; only
after the Pythia's first words will he begin to relax. The effect is
sensational but not melodramatic, for it has been rationally
prepared and it is absolutely necessary to the ultimate resolution
of the drama still going forward.

Ion has not revolted from his god, he has not even, by his own
account, suffered a loss of faith, but he has grown sophisticated,
and this is Creusa's work. He explains his raised arm himself,
with an attack upon the law of sanctuary that echoes the Furies
of the *Eumenides*:

> This is a fearsome law, established for us
> by the gods, yet neither proud nor wise.
> Is it sense to house corruption at our shrines?
> It should be exorcised! When vicious hands reach out
> and touch the god, is that a pretty sight?
> Only the just should claim the altar's safe refuge
> when they have suffered wrong. Surely god
> cannot intend the noble and the base
> to be received alike, protected and inviolate!
>
>   (1312–19)

Ion has decided to look for wisdom and for social utility in
heaven's laws, and to set them aside if he does not find these
qualities. His new attitude is the same one he had described in
his earlier speech about gods as mortal women's lovers, but there
he had been careful to label it as not his own (444).[15] Now he has
succumbed to the world, and he thinks of an Apollo so shrunken
in stature, so parochial in power, that he needs human censors
to watch him and human guardians for his divine purity. He
sees Apollo now much as Creusa sees him, and this is of course

---

[14] Norwood, *AJP* lxiii (1942), p. 111: 'crude psychology'; Wilamowitz decided
that Ion, brought up as he has been, could criticize the right of asylum but could
not raise his hand against it, and that therefore the action comes to a complete stop
here, marked by a pause (*Euripides. Ion* [Berlin, 1926], p. 150, ad 1312). On the
contrary, the Pythia obviously bursts out of the temple, breaking the conventions
of the tragic entrance by failing to identify herself in her haste to stop the threatened
act. Her cry of 'Hold!' halts a movement that has already begun; cf. *PV* 697;
Choeph. 896; *OC* 856; *Androm.* 550; *Or.* 1069; *Phoen.* 896, and the parody of passages
of this sort at *Frogs* 522.

[15] Note the same argument in the mouth of the villainous Copreus at *Held.* 259.

her doing, for she has told him the fiction of a child left to die by a careless and cruel divinity.

This bit of poetic justice lies at the heart of Euripides' magical scene. The suppliant is herself the source of the blasphemous error that almost costs her her life, while the pursuer is the victim of a deception that his own existence ought to contradict. Lies have encouraged him to apply logic where it has no place, and his logic teaches him to defy an ancient *nomos* which is all that stands between him and the most repulsive of human crimes. Ion has presumed to understand god, and his presumption must be set aside by pure illogic, by the direct intervention of the god whose intentions he has so completely misconstrued. Apollo *does* mean that the guilty as well as the innocent should find refuge at his altar. His purity is of a sort that cannot be tainted, and his protection, like that of the Suppliant Zeus in the Aeschylean play, is effective even to one who has set himself against him. Creusa's rebellion, her lack of faith, have expressed themselves in her fiction of the baby devoured by birds. Her slanders have imposed themselves even upon her; they have also made her living son her pursuer, and they have forced the god she hates to save her once again.

Creusa, in compensation, has been forced by her own elaborate vengeance plot to make a gesture of faith. She throws herself upon the mercy of Apollo, the god she has been calling merciless, and in so doing she symbolically reenacts her first union with him. She has complained that the god took her when she was unwilling (893)[16] but now she says, 'To him I dedicate myself as sacred property' (1285; cf. 1289 where the same idea is repeated). She is the same woman, her defiance is not yet gone; she still carries on her covert dialogue with the god she has taught herself to hate, and when Ion asks her what pleasure she expects to find in dying amongst the garlands of the god, she answers with the old double bitterness: 'The pleasure of providing pain to one who tortured me!' (1311). Her suppliant posture alone has not healed her unfaith, but it has satisfied the poet and the god. Creusa has been made to cling to the altar of

---

[16] Or rather, she has said that she cried out to her mother when he took her (893), a mark, presumably, of her unwillingness and perhaps also a conventional detail in a story-type that derives from Persephone. Hermes said in the beginning that Apollo took Creusa 'by force' (11).

the god she had defamed, and that is enough. She is raised, as
few suppliants are, not by a secular prince but by a divine device.[17] When she sees the tokens that the Pythia brings she
willingly offers herself to her son, as she had offered herself to
the god a few moments before, and the pent-up recognition is
released at last.

Creusa is different from other vengeance principals because,
before this final interruption, she suffers an apparent negative
overturn. An ordinary vengeance piece, interrupted or not,
showed a hero who moved directly from planning to doing
without himself experiencing any real overturn; that was saved
for his victim. Here, however, there is a visible transformation,
as the woman who entered with such marked pride of power
becomes a wretched criminal who must huddle at an altar under
threat of death. Creusa's drama has taken a special form because
her crime was in many ways more like that of a rebellious
theomachos than like that of the wronged hero of a vengeance
piece. Apollo was the true object of her obsessive enmity; Ion,
even by her own representation, had not yet done her any harm
and was hated by her chiefly for his connection with the god.
Creusa has been guilty of a spiritual crime and so she is brought
low, but in the end her impiety is treated with persuasion instead
of nemesis, since she is needed still as mother of the four Greek
tribes.

The god makes a point of saving Creusa from an open blasphemy, just as he saved her from killing and being killed. He will
not allow a confrontation, for fear she might with further blasphemy put herself beyond even his mercy (1557–8), though in
fact her rebellion is by this time at an end. Her knowing war with
god thus goes unpunished, as does her blind attack upon her
son; it has after all left the god untouched while it devastated
her own life. And the dramatist has made sure that no one's
sense of justice will be offended by her happy fate, for he has
made of her impiety a kind of external torture from which she
is released.

It may seem perverse to regard Creusa as the heroine of a
drama of release, but she necessarily trails behind her the shreds
of such a fiction when she enters on this stage. She is a princess

[17] But cf. Alcmene, who seems to have been similarly rescued, from a fiery altar,
by the intervention of her divine lover, Zeus.

of the type of Auge or Pasiphae, and the chorus explicitly reminds us that she belongs to this familiar category (506–8). She is one of the fabled mortal women who bore children to the gods, though her past shows marked differences from these women's standard tragedy. The human mothers of divine children are usually persecuted even before the miraculous birth; they and their children are threatened by a cruel tyrant figure, then rescued, either together or separately, by the interested god. In the cases where the mother and child have been separated, a subsequent drama is possible, for if the mother is imprisoned, married off to an insufferable prince, or sold into slavery, she may then after a prolonged period of torment be accidentally discovered by the very child whose birth provoked her woes, recognized, and rescued by her hero son (cf. Tyro and Antiope). Like Semele released from Hades, she is taken back to a place of power and security, where she will share her son's prosperity.

Creusa clearly is such a figure, and yet she has been made to vary from the type at almost every point. Nothing has ever marred the outward good fortune of her life. She carried her divine child and bore him without pang or publicity; no villainous father threatened either his life of hers. This point is made strongly at the outset (ἀγνὼς δὲ πατρί, 14) and it is repeated each time the birth story is told. Creusa alone brought about the separation between herself and her son, and then she continued in her life of pomp and luxury; no shadow of the chains and dungeons, the slavery and exile that ordinarily shaped the mother's life, ever fell on hers. Creusa has lived in the palace of her fathers, she has ruled as Queen of Athens, and has shared her throne with a brave and kindly man. And yet, for all this, she *has* been tortured. Her sufferings have been translated from the physical to the spiritual plane, but they are none the less real for that. She is like her fictional sisters, for through all the long years she has been imprisoned in her own despair, the slave of her anger against the god.

The day of the *Ion* is the day of Creusa's discovery by the son who should release her from her torment. She very nearly makes him a fellow-prisoner instead, by telling him her lies about the god and tempting him to join her in her doubt, but that is only normal complication; the rescuing hero should be himself endangered before he finally sets his mother free. The special trick about this rescue is that, where others require as a rule three phases—recognition, intrigue, and escape—this one is entirely accomplished within the recognition.

As soon as she recognizes the wicker cradle she had left her baby in, Creusa experiences a revelation something like that of Heracles in the *Women of Trachis* when he learns the nature of the poison on his robe. In one moment of comprehension she sees that this is the point to which her whole life was leading, that all was necessary as preparation for this. She sees that there has been no cause for fear, that neither she nor her child has ever been abandoned, but that both have been constantly under Apollo's watchful eye. She learns, in other words, exactly what Hermes had taught the audience at the outset when he said of Xuthus and Creusa: 'Loxias has shaped their case and brought their fortunes to this point; their fate was not forgotten, though it seemed to be' (67–8). Creusa's illumination is expressed at once in her final telling of the sacred tale of Ion's begetting and his loss. She has told it three times already, demonstrating how her gathering doubt and anger could influence her memory, but now she tells it afresh, and with a strange new emphasis.

Before Xuthus had been given a son, Creusa spoke of a baby exposed, one whose ultimate fate was unknown; it might have been eaten by beasts, though admittedly there was no trace of blood (352); it might have been saved by a miracle (357–8). When she had been stung by what seemed a fresh insult from the god, she offered a new story in which the frankly suppositious beasts of her first report appeared as a nightmare flock of feasting birds, to whom the god had abandoned his child (916). In the conversation with the old man that followed her song she continued to speak of a dead baby, now as a child that Apollo had sent away to Hades to school (953). And in this conversation she had added another detail about her own part in the fate of her son. Before, she had treated the moment of leaving the child only as one of suffering for herself, but in the scene of intrigue she capped her case against the god by announcing that she had exposed the infant in full expectation that it would be saved. Thus she finished by creating a version of the abondonment of the infant in which she was wholly innocent, wholly the sufferer, while the god was cruelly guilty both of betrayal and of a grotesque example of kin-murder.

Face to face with her living son, Creusa goes over the story yet once again. She has need of forgiveness now, and for that, nothing but the truth will serve. The place of the boy's begetting now gets a new epithet; it is no longer simply the Long Rocks or the Cave of Pan, but with an entirely altered association, 'the cliff where the nightingale sings' (1481). The only attribute given to the rape itself is 'secret' (1484), for the Apolline paternity of her son is now a subject for boasting (1487), and the Apolline villain has entirely disappeared. Curiously enough, the death and even the birds remain, but they are associated now with her own part in the tale, instead of with the god's. For the cruelly careless father we now have the mother made cruel by fear, and Creusa's story at last agrees with the one that Hermes told, for what Creusa confesses to Ion is that when she left him in the cave, she left him there to die.

> I hid you from my mother's eye and having nothing else
> I wrapped you in my loom's first web, my maiden handiwork;
> you had no bath, took no milk from my breast,
> instead I set you out at once, a feast
> of sacrifice for birds, my gift to Hades' king.
>
> (1489-96)

Creusa has in the moment taken upon herself the crime she had imputed to the god; she has escaped from her own torturing fictions and has recovered the past as it was. She can once again see the god that her own monody had shown to the audience, a golden god, blinding in his beauty, and she immediately comprehends his present plan for his son (1539-45). She can even see that her own actions may have made the divine benevolence more difficult (1543-4). Apollo has used the wicker cradle, so long preserved, to force one recognition between mother and son, another between Creusa and himself. And when the queen of Athens has discovered the identity of Ion and the nature of her own divine partner, her shackles fall away as if she were some Bacchante liberated by one of the wine god's miracles.

Creusa had loved the child she bore but never nursed; fear had led her to betray that love, and she turned it into hatred for Apollo, forgetting the beautiful god who had appeared to her and remembering only the creatures of her own imagination.

On the day of this play her hatred of the god spawns lesser hatreds for her husband and for the boy the god has given him, but the strength of her emotion still has its source in her maternal love. And this is why we can so easily accept her perfect re-orientation as the drama ends. As soon as the miraculously preserved tokens tell her that Ion is her child, her hatred reverts to its original form and she loves again as she had for a few moments, some sixteen years before when the child was born. It is easy for her now to love her husband too, and above all to love the god once more. It is she who voices in the end the ecstatic devotion that Ion sang of when this play began, saying in her last full speech:

> Listen now to me.
> Where once I blamed I wish to praise,
> lauding Apollo who restores the child he had abandoned.
> These gates are lovely in my eyes, this temple and its voices
> that once seemed enemies! My hand is happy to caress
> the god's great brazen ring as I salute these doors
> and say farewell!

> (1609–13)

Apollo has been directing the return action, but he has been one of the players too, albeit an invisible one, in the actions of vengeance and of release. Indeed, he seems always to be at the very heart of the play, just as his temple is at the centre of the playing area, and there is a sense in which we watch a tripartite consultation of the oracle, as Xuthus, Creusa and Ion receive his words and react in their different ways. Apollo, however, does not merely speak in this play, he acts. Once in the past he had appeared on earth in something like a man's form and made the child about whom everything now turns, and on this stage he moves to defend his creation. He acts here by means of a dove and a priestess, as he had many years ago by means of his brother, Hermes. And finally he sends Athena, who represents him in his prophetic capacity, but who also announces once and for all the fact that he has taken an active part in the adventures of the principals.

Apollo is one of those principals, and it makes not the least difference that he is invisible. Nor does it matter, dramaturgically, that he is a god. His permanent though unseen presence in the action redeems the two interruptions of Creusa's vengeance plot from the charge of melodrama or bad play-making, and it also works a technical miracle that Aristotle never realized was possible. When Apollo, through his priestess, forces that heightened recognition to which he is himself a party, he reconciles the formal disparities of the compound plot. It is he who causes the positive and the negative actions to explode simultaneously in a joyful scene of extremest pity and terror, and it is he who adds the final surplus of success to the mortal's deeds. By becoming himself a party in the final reconciliation, he enhances the return and the new rank Ion is to have among men, while by the same stroke he so thoroughly annihilates Creusa's rebellion that it is as if her whole vengeance tragedy had never taken place.

Many moderns have been bothered by the mechanical importance of Apollo in this play. He is defined sometimes as an irresponsible divinity, sometimes as a mere mask for disorderly chance, but he is considered all to frequently to be external to the human action and therefore unjustifiable as a cause. This attitude springs from the modern inability to think mythically, and from the modern assumption that Euripides must have shared with us the limitation of imagination which we call 'healthy scepticism'. The fact is, however, that the poet has made for this play a god of undoubted power in human affairs, one who is at the centre of a great cult, and one who is worshipped in a particular way by the mortals here portrayed.

Apollo's divinity is the essential point of the play. We must therefore consider how it has been described, especially since so many critics believe that the portrait has been purposely and grossly flawed, that it may disparage all divinity, or at any rate the god of the Delphic cult. Indeed it has been argued that with this play Euripides meant to reduce the spectator to a bitter atheism, or to a bitterer belief in a malignant and mocking heaven, but this essentially Victorian attitude, based upon disapproval of the seducer god, is now giving way. If nothing else contradicted it, the overt intention to praise Athens and her allies should have shown its impossibility, as does also the ingenious manipulation of the multiple plot for the creation of an unprecedented pile of positive effects in the end. This does not mean, however, that the portrait of the god is not a curious one. The poet seems, for all the Delphic detail, to be describing the nature and the working of divinity in general, and his revelation is, at first sight, a difficult one to take in.

The specific 'attacks' upon Apollo that are mounted in the play—on the scores of ungratefulness, abandoning children, refusing oracular aid, or supporting the law of sanctuary, etc.— are all part of the dramatic clash. They are in every case scrupulously neutralized by the continuing action, denied by other speakers and made the subject of recantation in the end. It is not in these old rhetorical bones that the unique difficulties of this god are to be found. There is no awkwardness in a god's having engendered a child and made him the centre of a providential plan; this is standard sacred history. And when the god proves to have been careful of his mortal accomplices, to have been moved by serious purposes and not by lust, and to have willed the best for all, he is surely exonerated even from the irrelevant charge of ungentlemanliness.

Apollo's intentions have been in every way divine, but the play does seem, by its very structure, to question his absolute foresight and control. He can foresee and prepare the massive shapes that loom in the future; the coming history of the Aegean is under his eye. And he can on the other hand shape the least detail of a personal destiny; he has arranged Creusa's marriage and her barrenness, so as to bring her husband to Delphi as if by appointment, exactly on the day he is needed. And yet what we see on this stage is a mixing of events Apollo has intended with others that apparently he has never for a moment foreseen. His plan is temporarily balked and ever so slightly altered by obstructions he has in a sense created but seems not to have foreknown.

There is then some quality of consciousness that is lacking in this god. When Creusa learns too soon of the divine gift to Xuthus and tries to kill her son, Apollo can stop her easily. He can likewise stop Ion, when he means to violate an altar, but as far as we can tell, he has not expected either of these mortal actions. What he does not know, then, is the strength of passion in the human heart. He does not understand pain and pride and resentment and doubt; he cannot feel the physical wound of a mother deprived of her child, or the confusion of a boy who must take his first steps in an adult world. Most particularly, he cannot suspect the meanness and folly of lesser mortals, and so he has not calculated on the lies and treason of the low-born chorus, or the eager amorality of the doddering tutor.

This kind of lofty unconsciousness would be repulsive in a mortal character and so those who insist on overlooking Apollo's divinity (even as they criticize it) call him a heartless god. They are of course entirely accurate, since gods do not have hearts, any more than they have tears, ambitions or a sense of time. Apollo's lack of comprehension is not an invidious detail in a characterization patterned on the human personality. It is rather a necessary aspect of his divinity. Ion's speech, in which he chides the god, is proved to be mistaken in its assumptions; with its conclusions reversed it becomes a true description of the nature of a god. He is not like men; he cannot be accused of their crimes or measured by their justice or called to account by them in any way, because their flawed nature is not his. It is the one thing he cannot even know, though he can always transcend it, and so he does, in the action of the Euripidean *Ion*.

VI

ANDROMACHE

THE *Ion* is easily the most classical of the tragedies of mixed plot. Its two opposite actions of vengeance and return are of the same extent and are played with perfect simultaneity, while its third, muted action of release illuminates them both. The effect is that of a single praxis deepened and enriched through a multiple embodiment, for the two protagonists meet always as echoing equals, and both have been given a rare definition in which consistency, solemnity, vitality and beauty are mixed. It is quite otherwise with the *Andromache*, the play that forms a link between the pieces already discussed and a second group of tragedies in which a negative action dominates. In the *Andromache* the poet openly eschews any attempt at regularity and proportion and strains for effects of a very different sort, effects produced by extreme and wilful distortion of both situation and character.

The *Andromache* is shaped—for it does have a shape, albeit an odd one—by one central experiment, that of role-changing. This peculiarly Euripidean practice will appear again in the *Orestes* and has already been noted in an undeveloped form in the *Helen*, where Menelaus was made to fall short of his role, even to try to abandon it, before he finally came to terms with its heroic postures.[1] Here in the *Andromache* the poet goes much further, using the blatant multiplicity of his plot to create a kind of repertory situation in which a character may, while keeping the same stage name, appear now in one and now in another of the conventional parts during the course of the play.

---

[1] This does not mean that *Andromache* necessarily follows *Helen* chronologically. Because of the scholiast's note that the play was not produced at Athens, dates ranging from 430 to 417 and places as far apart as Argos and Dodona have been suggested for the production. All the arguments that begin with the assumption that the play is political propaganda are, however, equally unconvincing, and the dating to the mid-twenties, derived from metrical statistics, may as well be kept; Webster would assign *Andromache* to the years between 428 and 424 (*The Tragedies of Euripides*, p. 118).

Human morals and human actions seem under these circumstances to have a sickening fluidity, and this effect, gradually
invading the mind of the spectator, is plainly central to the
dramatist's concerns.

The baldest scheme of the *Andromache*'s mutations will serve
as an advertisement of the poet's subtler practices and intents.
He begins with a suppliant tragedy played by a helpless heroine,
two villains, and a royal champion. This action is brought to a
successful conclusion and is followed at once by a rescue piece
in which one of the tormentors from the first drama now plays
the helpless heroine in the company of an invisible villain and a
champion who comes from the outside. This action also succeeds,
though we do not get its final scenes for it is broken in on by a
third drama, a tragedy of divine punishment. The unseen
villain of the previous piece comes on as the hero of this one;
the champion from the previous piece plays the agent of destruction, while the royal champion from the initial suppliant drama
takes a secondary role as a helpless old relative. In the course of
these modulations of function and of ethos only one character
remains true to the original role and character assigned to her,
and this is Andromache herself. She is likewise the only one of
the troupe who will remain in this strange scene, a country
neither Greek nor non-Greek, when these three contorted actions
are complete.

The refusal to search for any artistic intention behind such
odd methods of casting has led to the widespread conclusion
that this play is an awkward failure.[2] In general it is said to lack
elevation, nobility, and any sense of patterning in its events; in
particular it is accused of a total collapse in construction in its
second half. To some admirers of Euripides it has seemed an act
of piety to pass over the *Andromache* as quietly as possible, as if
its author had asked that it be burned. Indeed, the most ponder-
ous of the handbooks of Greek literature supposes that Euripides
withdrew the play from Athenian competition and sent it to the
provinces because he knew it to be hopelessly bad. With reason,

---

[2] 'Downright insanity', said Verrall; 'worthless' is Wilamowitz's report, and others
have added further adjectives: chaotic, cheap, sensational, *assez vulgaire*. The highest
contemporary praise comes from Kitto, who hails the play as good melodrama
('a deadly play', *Greek Tragedy* [New York, 1961], p. 233), and from Garzya, who
thinks it a fine study in the 'Pathologie des Eros' (*Euripide. Andromaca* [Naples, 1963],
p. xxxv note 26).

runs the scholarly conclusion there, for the Athenian public would never have put up with such flimsy construction and such irresponsible innovation.[3] All these judgements spring from the assumption that the irregularities of the *Andromache* were accidentally produced by a poet whose attention was somewhere else; no real attempt has been made to discover the exact means by which this 'chaos' is created, or the ends it effectively serves.

The first action, which extends to almost two-thirds of the play's length, is the one section of the tragedy favourably noticed by critics.[4] It gives the play its name, and it should establish whatever rationale the whole will have; it is also easy to approach for it closely follows a traditional form. Andromache's scenes make up a full suppliant tragedy and in fact provide our best example of what was surely a familiar variant upon the Aeschylean plot pattern.[5] When the pursuers appear, as they do here, before the champion has been secured, the drama becomes of necessity a bitter one with its rhetoric tuned to conflict instead of to persuasion. The champion, when he does appear, will make a highly dramatic entrance, he will save the pursued from a palpable danger, but his importance in determining the ethical flavour of the action will be severely limited. This type of plot, then—the form chosen by Euripides as best suited to the *Andromache* he meant to write—minimizes the usual tendency of suppliant drama to praise the polity. It tests and tries its central figure to the utmost, bringing him within a hair's breadth of destruction, and it leaves its spectator with the sense of how ready evil is to triumph everywhere. The champion does appear, but the fact that he would have been wholly useless even a moment later must act to reduce his stature and the audience's sense of peace. With its secondary emphasis thus transferred from champion to villain, this kind of suppliant action draws close to the tone and the ethical potential of the rescue plot.

Euripides evidently found that even this evil-oriented variant of the suppliant action was not adequate to portray the cruelty and error that were to be a part of his *Andromache*. He contrived

[3] Schmid-Stahlin, i:3, p. 400.

[4] Even Friedrich says categorically, 'die Andr. bereits in der ersten Handlung ihren Gipfel erreicht und in der zweiten merklich abfällt', *Euripides und Diphilos* (Zetemata 5, Munich, 1953), p. 53.

[5] Compare the suppliant situation in *HF*.

to redouble their effect by splitting his villain in two and writing not one but two separate scenes in which Andromache must struggle with her pursuers. This doubling of the villain's role also shows that the poet was not interested merely in the melodramatic possibilities of the more sensational suppliant plot, but that he had other intentions in mind. Menelaus, after all, was all he needed to create the suspense of the last minute rescue, and Menelaus is so used. Before he even appears, however, a long and passionate scene of conflict is played between Andromache and a very different figure, the princess Hermione. This initial confrontation is mechanically gratuitous, but the whole suppliant action takes its ethical colour from its magnificent and shocking exchange.

Andromache has delivered a terse but graceful prologue speech in which, after sounding all the names from the glorious past, she turns to her present situation with a single name from the new generation—the name 'Hermione'. She explains the cause and the extent of her present danger with perfect clarity, ending with the fact that lies behind it all, the temporary absence of Achilles' son. A serving woman then brings the news that Molossus is not safe; she is sent at once to summon Peleus, and then the prologue is capped with Andromache's one act of self indulgence, the elegy of lament that is her only remaining pleasure and which is for many readers still the jewel of the play. A parodos of Sophoclean immediacy and brevity follows, to be interrupted by the entrance of an unexpected and extraordinary figure.

The Spartan princess seems scarcely older than a Juliet, but she has decked her childishness with all the gold her limbs could bear in order to confront her husband's slave. With her first words (147), uttered in defiance of some imagined criticism, she ironically repeats Andromache's own description of herself as a bride, long ago, and the echo seems to make of the two women a paradigm of *tyche*'s habit of overturn. Hermione's good fortune, however, like Andromache's hopelessness, is only apparent, and beneath the contrast of their states a permanent likeness appears in the fact that both are the spoils of war. The worn-out woman of Troy and the gilded Spartan girl have been brought into a shocking intimacy as prizes of the same heroic bed. Finally, though she is herself one of the pursuers in this suppliant plot, it is Hermione who expresses a sense that danger threatens. She too is a kind of exile, and she believes that she must get the better of Andromache, or be herself driven out from her present home. And she, like Andromache, cannot expect friendship from the Greeks, since, for anyone who has suffered from the Trojan war, the daughter of Helen is no more to be loved than is Hector's wife.

The girl and the woman are beautifully distinguished, the one in her finery and her fearful pride, her ignorance of life and her dependence upon worldly power, the other as bare and harsh as a rocky cliff and as impervious,[6] a creature made wise by too much life and almost scornful of the world. The scene between them, however, is no mere exercise in double portraiture. Something actual is at issue here. Hermione has come, though she knows that Menelaus will soon have Molossus in his power. She knows, in other words, that her enemy is vanquished—why then is she here? She answers this question in her first few lines by admitting that she has not quite decided yet what she will do with her rival. She can take Andromache and have her put to death, but she herself suggests a second possibility—that Andromache shall become her slave. And by coming out at all she opens a third alternative which Andromache is quick to recognize. She might be persuaded by Andromache to abandon the quarrel and leave unused the absolute power she now has. Hermione's mind is divided because she has not yet determined to her own satisfaction the exact nature and extent of Andromache's offence. Her official charge is treasonable witchcraft, and if she kills, this will be her rationale, but even as she names this crime she betrays her real concern:

> You mean to seize this house and to usurp my place;
> your sorcery makes me distasteful to my lord
> and barrenness has settled in my womb.
> Women of Asia are deep and skilful in such arts.
>
> (156–60)

---

[6] As if in playful reference to Heraclitus (fr. 118), Euripides has made Andromache's essence dryness, and this makes her presence at Thetis' shrine all the more a curiosity. In general in this play reason is dry and passion is wet: Menelaus will later use water to describe his own pig-headedness (537), and Peleus will remark that dry ground (Andromache) may bring forth better seedlings than deep earth (Hermione, 637).

Evidently Hermione is not so much barren as neglected, and her true belief is that Andromache receives the marital attentions that are denied to her. For this crime she has a second punishment in mind; it is not death but perpetual torture, for she would have the Trojan woman as her slave, to do with as she will.

Andromache meets the official charge first with a brilliantly bitter speech of self-disparagement. 'Is it my charm, my wealth, or my friends, do you suppose, that fire me with ambition to move into your place?' (196–8). She proves, after the fashion of Creon in the *Tyrannus*, that she could not reasonably be thought to be guilty of conspiracy since she would have nothing to gain. Then she turns to the true charge. Hermione is tormented by jealousy, as Andromache cooly perceives; she is like any jealous woman—sure of her rival's guilt, but thirsting to be told that her own suffering is groundless. Andromache surely knows this, and she has told the audience earlier that she has long since left Neoptolemus' bed (37). She could appease the girl's curiosity, as she has that of the spectator, but she chooses instead to keep absolutely silent now upon this interesting point. She has said that she will not prove a traitor to herself (191), and evidently to swear to Hermione that she is not her sexual rival would debase an erstwhile queen of Troy. And so, instead of assuaging the girl's passion, Andromache chooses to attack. She takes it upon herself to teach Hermione that jealousy is lechery and, as such, a thing of shame, and of course her argument only seems a confirmation, to the girl, of her suspicion that her husband still frequents the captive queen.

Hermoine is neglected, says Andromache, not because of the power of any rival but because of two linked vices in herself, pride and selfish sexuality. Virtue, not beauty, commands conjugal love, and feminine virtue in marriage means compliance and submission in every realm of life. 'For example', she says, 'I was loved by Hector. Why? Because, forgetting pride and lust, I entered with him into the erotic adventures that came his way, and took other women's children to my heart' (222 ff.). Throughout this scene Andromache is fighting, with both wisdom and cunning, for the life of her son. She means to suggest, with her talk of taking bastards to one's breast, that for Hermione both virtue and self-interest demand that Molossus shall be spared.

Unfortunately, though she knows the state of Hermione's passions, she speaks to her only in the language of reason, and ends by goading the Spartan girl into a decision to kill both her rival and the boy.

The quarrel between the two women, though technically unnecessary to the staging of the suppliant action, is thus handled in such a way that it becomes a part of the causal chain leading to disaster. It is quite unlike anything in any other surviving suppliant drama,[7] though it closely resembles the first confrontation between Jason and Medea. Here, as in that scene, the spectator is invited to feel pity for both parties, and here as there he feels the sands of his moral certainties shifting beneath his feet. The two women have been set side by side, like two figures from the niches of a church—Queen and Slave, Greek and Barbarian, Rich and Poor, Wife and Concubine. The irony is obvious, since Hermione is the slave of her ignorance and her pride, a barbarian in respect to Molossus, poor in family (being not only without a son but also without a true father), and finally a wife by title alone. And yet a simple reversal of labels will not do. It is easy enough to show that Hermione's lines on the typical 'barbarian' customs of incest and family crime should not have been spoken by a member of the House of Atreus, but this does not make Andromache's doctrines any more Hellenic. Her version of wifely submission has not only made her rather more concubine than wife, rather more slave than queen, even in Hector's day, but it has also finally brought her to submit with equal complaisance to Hector's murderer's son.

As a representative of reason, Andromache has none of Jason's damaging self-interest, but she is flawed enough to make us see that there is no simplistic way of reading this magnificent scene. The Trojan queen believes that her mind can perceive an absolute Virtue and an absolute Vice, and can know that certain acts are shameful, others fine, wherever they are done (244). This is a noble view,[8] but the truth is that the poet has forced

---

[7] Its nearest parallel is the scene between Oedipus and Polyneices in *OC* but there it is the suppliant, not the pursuer, who is brought to a new decision (to curse his sons), and that decision lies outside the formal economy of the suppliant plot.

[8] However the poet has caused her to undermine it with an argument based upon its opposite, the relativity of morals, when she asks Hermione what she would have done had she been married into a polygamous society (215 ff.).

her to argue on very difficult ground, since in this case it is a wife's resentment of her husband's mistress that is to be recognized as immutably shameful, while the concomitant immutable virtue is illustrated by complicity in a husband's adulteries.

The poet has made his women introduce the unsettling idea that morals may be relative,[9] and he himself has added an indication that the human mind is imperfect in its perception of the truth and therefore imperfect as the mirror of absolute virtue. Andromache's exercise of her mind in this scene has defeated her own ends and brought about the condemnation of her son. Her reason has proved that Hermione is her own enemy and that there is therefore no 'real' quarrel between the two women, but Andromache is nonetheless being destroyed by that quarrel. Both the Greek and the barbarian, both the lustful and the temperate, both the villainess and the heroine are being victimized by Hermione's jealousy, for though Andromache's reason has demonstrated that jealousy in general is a shameful thing, it has forgotten to testify to this particular jealousy's lack of substantial cause. Hermione's jealousy has made a suppliant of Andromache and an untutored pursuer of the girl herself, but it is a phantom emotion, created from false suspicions and encouraged by silence. At the climax of the play the spectator will learn one further truth about this curious motive force: that the man who is its subject no longer even exists.

Such is the 'superfluous' scene in this suppliant tragedy. It pictures an unusually proud and active suppliant, but Andromache, after all, can be portrayed again in the course of the following scenes, and the true function of this scene is clearly the description of Hermione. The very fact of such a description is surprising since in no other suppliant drama have we been invited to look so closely at a villain. Of the sons of Aegyptus we need know only that they are singleminded, of Creon at Colonus that he is a hypocrite, of Lycus at Thebes that he means what he says. Here, on the other hand, is a pursuer of subtle complexity,

---

[9] See 173–6; 215 ff. and cf. 437 and 693. Compare also Peleus on the effects of a Spartan education (595 ff.) and Hermione on the influence of her women (930). The idea that the *nous* can fail of proper ethical perception is recognized by Andromache, in Hermione's case, at 252, and is given an objective reflection in the fact that the two women each claim to be *sophron* (235).

one who is weak and divided in her mind, one who can rouse our sympathy even as she resolves upon the killing of the heroine and her helpless child.

By creating a knowing evil-doer who is yet pathetic, the poet prepares his audience for the mutation of label and function that Hermione is to undergo in the play's next action. He also, however, threatens the tragic quality of his suppliant action, for escape from such a pursuer will necessarily lack magnificence, and any blatant triumph over her would be inhumane. As the first episode closes the spectator becomes aware of an unaccustomed series of negatives in this suppliant situation. Andromache is seated, not at an altar nor at a temple, but at the shrine of a nymph; she is a foreigner in the *tempietto* of a very local, very minor divinity, and for this reason she seems to be appealing rather to Neoptolemus' grandmother than to a god. The supernatural power is thus not very strongly present here in Phthia, and neither is the secular, for the ruler is absent and the state seems almost to have disappeared with him. Repeated calls have already gone out to Peleus before the play begins, and they have brought no response. The threat to the principal is indeed not truly a public affair but one that belongs to the woman's quarters, and it is based upon the negative fact that Neoptolemus does not frequent his wife's bed. Andromache soon says to Menelaus, οὐ χρὴ 'πὶ μικροῖς μεγάλα πορσύνειν κακά (352; cf. 387), and the same rule might have been applied to her own tragedy. She cannot in this situation give her suppliancy any positive meaning, for it is not because she stands for anything that she is thus made to suffer. The Danaids at least thought they were defending the principle of chastity, the women of Argos were demanding the right to bury their dead, and old Oedipus clings to his sanctuary because he knows his body and his death are powerful and must not be wasted, but Andromache has come to Thetis simply to escape a jealous woman and her father, and the poet has told us that in a sense this threat is unreal, since Hermione's whole view of her situation is false. The details of the scene thus make a kind of guerilla attack upon the normal suppliant plot, and in this sense this first episode makes a programmatic statement of the subversive intentions of the entire piece. It is nevertheless a fully tragic scene, never falling for an instant beneath the anticipated level of nobility and seriousness, and in this quality it will not find its equal again until the last episodes of the play. Hermione is both pathetic and dangerous because she is genuinely self-deceived, but her father and her erstwhile suitor are creatures of a different sort—men who are not what they claim to be, who do not even try to speak the truth, who intentionally deceive others and who cannot successfully sustain the tragic tone.

The next figure to appear after Hermione has withdrawn[10] is so devoid of the tragic quality that he functions almost like and old-fashioned sign-board, carried on stage to tell the audience that it has entered another forest altogether. Hermione was an innovation—a rich and serious one—among the personages of the suppliant plot, but Menelaus, who belongs there formally, is an intruder who perverts the exalted tendency of the action beyond recovery. He comes on, having seized the Phthian Molossus as Neoptolemus once seized the Trojan Astyanax, but he is no enraged victor seeking vengeance for a father's death. He does not, like the sons of Aegyptus, embody simple violence (and incidentally the will of Zeus as well); he does not, like Creon in the *Colonus*, represent expedient patriotic intelligence; he is never hard or sinister after Lycus' fashion, nor is he even frankly bestial, like Helen's Theoclymenus. Even in his villainy he is weak and debased. Menelaus begins by kidnapping Andromache's child and ends by abandoning his own; in the interim he deceives a suppliant and lifts his hand to kill a woman and a child as they beg for mercy, and yet with each outrage he seems less dangerous. Peleus is evidently disgusted by his womanishness (note the repeated use of *aner* words at 590, 591 and 592), and Andromache, his victim, cruelly remarks that only in the *gynaeceum* could he offer any threat. Menelaus is a sordid bourgeois creature, weak, vain and sly—a uxorious man who is yet unable to be loyal even to his own daughter. He is, as Andromache says, a terrible example of the sort of man who can gain a reputation in this world (319).

Here, as in the previous scene, a statement of truth has no effect at all, but this time it is not passion so much as vain stupidity that is impervious to reason. As soon as he appears,

---

[10] Garzya (op. cit., p. xxii, note 15) suggests that Hermione should remain on stage through this scene, but her silence would be extremely awkward, and the effect of splitting the villain would be lost.

Andromache's tireless logic proves, according to his own definition, that her pursuer is a stupid man. His stated purpose is the
defence of his daughter, but his actions, as the woman at the
nymphaeum demonstrates, are leading to that daughter's
inevitable injury. When Andromache has finished, Menelaus,
just as if she had not spoken, begins an endless ditty of praise for
his own hard sense, just precaution, wisdom and prevision. He
bolsters his high opinion of himself by using as many old saws
as possible. 'If I don't do the best for all that's mine', he says with
unconscious accuracy, 'then I'm no wise man but a common
cad!' (379). Like his daughter, he is a relativist, and he squares his
present action with his Trojan reputation by announcing that
whatever one wants is that moment's Troy (369). 'All is common
among friends', he murmurs suavely as he prepares to murder
his son-in-law's favourite (376–7); 'any slave of mine would be
equally his' (374–5).

With Menelaus the real world has invaded the tragic stage,
and he and Andromache finally face one another almost as life
and art. She keeps her stature, finding her way to self-sacrifice
by the light of her unquenchable rationalism, but she inevitably
loses something of her first vitality and ethical immediacy, and
she becomes, thanks to her unworthy enemy, only a kind of
breathing image of Sapientia, appearing to the audience now
much as she did to her exasperated young rival in the previous
episode (266–7). Menelaus, on the other hand, is grotesque but
sickeningly full of life. He is a common figure outside the theatre
and he is, in that world as he appears to be in this, a born
survivor. When Andromache points out that if he violates a
shrine he risks divine punishment (439), he shows his perfect
understanding of this disturbing fact. 'I'll take that when it
comes', he says, not believing for a minute that he stands in any
real danger, and in truth he does not, since the gods of tragedy
cannot notice the everyday vermin of the earth.

Under these conditions Andromache's so-called 'anti-
Spartan speech' (445–52) becomes a kind of parabasis, delivered
over the head of the dwarfed Menelaus to an audience all too
much like him. She finds herself the single 'barbarian' in a
world of 'Spartans' because all the Greek world talks, like
Menelaus, of wisdom and enlightenment, but rejects them when
they appear. She alone, guided by her unspoiled *nous*, knows

virtue from shame and chooses to have nothing to do with the latter. Naturally, then, she seems to be a creature from an alien world, and is to be put to death by a 'civilization' based on passion and stupidity. Her alien world is not so much Asia, however, as it is the tragic stage. In full tragic regalia she moves solemnly from her sanctuary in order to save her son, only to find that Menelaus has done what no one in the genre should do—he has simply told a sordid lie. Molossus' life is not saved; it depends upon Hermione, who apparently signals from the palace door that her husband's heir shall be put to death at once.[11]

At this signal the first of the play's three echoing arias of lament begins. This one is a duet between the mother and son, interrupted and brought to a close by heavy choriambs from Menelaus' throat. The two bound figures fall supplicating at the Spartan's feet, and Menelaus, with sword upraised, is coolly wishing Molossus joy of his mother's company on the trip to hell, when ancient Peleus appears. Achilles' father, like old Iolaus in the *Heracleidae*, has evidently experienced a kind of rejuvenation in this crucial hour.[12] His mere command ($\epsilon\pi\iota\sigma\chi\epsilon\varsigma$, 550) interrupts Menelaus' crime, and when he raises his sceptre (588) Menelaus unmistakably jumps back; a hard stare would have accomplished as much, as the old man later boasts (762). The salvation is thus effected at once, and the rest of the scene is very nearly farce. Peleus finds it difficult to maintain a truly elevated tone when he is forced to dispute with such a one as Menelaus is, and he is drawn into some rather low remarks about Helen ('you should have paid that woman just to stay away', 609). He does, however, show himself to be of the same cast of mind as the woman he is rescuing; he too will test popular notions of right and wrong against an absolute standard of good and evil (compare his 586 with her 242), and he too likes to

[11] Note that somehow, at 494 ff., the chorus knows of Hermione's decision; there is some visible sign of a sentence of death. Apparently the servants took Andromache and Molossus inside, leaving Menelaus without; the two victims then reappear while the chorus is still singing, heavily bound (perhaps literally yoked). Hermione might stand behind them in the doorway and make a signal—the conventional gesture for a sentence of death—to indicate her decision. If she did this, the spectacle of her guilt would be heightened, with a corresponding heightening to be felt likewise in her later remorse and her easy forgetfulness of it.

[12] Note how the chorus that follows (766 ff.; see especially 789 ff.) reminds the audience of the deeds of his youth.

play with the 'essential' meanings of words (witness his lines on true versus chronological age, 761 ff.). With her objectivity he can say, 'What senseless customs exist in Greece', when reflecting on the fact that the man before him was once in command at Troy (693).

Menelaus, meanwhile, wholly betrays the suppliant convention. It is one of the typical difficulties of this plot that the figure representing unbridled violence must be quickly put to flight, and one solution was to make this figure only a proxy, a mere herald who could not resist the champion. Another solution, suitable to the appearance of a ruler in the threatening role, was to arrange for an off-stage war in which he would be defeated. Here, however, there is neither the dignified and ominous retreat of the herald, nor any din of war; instead we see a regal villain who yet struts and chatters like a lackey and tries to make amends. Menelaus offers his alliance to his conqueror, proposing that together they shall defeat the 'threat' of the chained figures at their feet. He sets out to prove that he has been acting in Peleus' own interest, his assumption being that the blood of Achilles is of no account and that a line of rulers sprung from Andromache and Neoptolemus would of course be a scandal to Hellas. Forgetful of his own recent fright before an ancient and unarmed foe, he tells us that the Trojan War was a boon for Greece since it taught every combatant to be brave.

Euripides gives his Spartan prince the speech of a Punchinello who has just ducked one blow and is about to catch twenty more, but since the *Andromache* is not a farce, the audience must forgo the pleasure of seeing Menelaus thrashed. What it does see is the villain sidling away with all the foolishness of a satyr coward. 'It wasn't my idea to come here in the first place', he whines, 'and I don't mean to get into any foolish trouble. I really must run; I haven't all the time in the world you know, and there is trouble in the Peloponnese!' (730–4). He cannot at this point discriminate even between 'enemy' and 'friend', but equally abandons both his daughter and her rival in the depravity of his haste to get away. He is a loathesome and ridiculous man, one who will not be seen again in this play, but one who has irreparably lowered its tone.

When Menelaus has gone Peleus raises the suppliants and promises asylum until Neoptolemus shall return. All three actors retire and the first action is complete. A pair of victims, likened to ewe and lamb, chained and about to have their throats cut, have been liberated and commanded to rise by a miraculously old man now miraculously vigorous. Peleus has associated himself with a wind from heaven (554–5) and has struck a curiously Dionysiac note when he turned on Menelaus with scorn to say, 'Did you think you had a bull or a lion here, that you chained them so securely?' (719–20). And yet, for all of this, Andromache's release does not seem to hold the solemn promise of a true *lusis* action, any more than it sounds forth in praise of order and the city's institutions. And this is because Euripides has chosen to show a very peculiar sort of threat. There was evil here, and it brought Andromache and Molossus to the brink of death, but the evil was commonplace. It is not mysterious or fated or absolute, but instead, as embodied in the Spartan daughter and her father, it is a mixed and wilful thing, sometimes pathetic, sometimes even ridiculous. It is ugly, but not terrible, based upon misapprehension and self-delusion and working through cowardice and deceit. It did almost cause a catastrophe, and yet it dissolved before an old man's frown. When the threat is as ephemeral as this, the champion suffers a loss of scale and the rescue is deprived of the demonic power that it should have, as the reinforcement of an altar's taboo. In spite of his rejuvenation the saviour here is merely a genial private figure; he is not an adequate representative of the saving city since its real power is not his. In addition neither he nor that city has taken any physical risk, and so the salvation is not quite a serious thing. Andromache's suppliant drama, though technically it is a success, has been so managed that its normal increment of tragic emotion has signally failed to accrue.

Andromache is saved but the quarrel between the two women has not been resolved, and though Menelaus has gone, Hermione, the second pursuer, remains somewhere inside the palace. The fates of both women finally depend still upon the return of Neoptolemus and so, when the chorus has offered a valedictorian tribute to the youth of Peleus, a wholly separate but not irrelevant action can begin. We might expect now a full rescue for Andromache, after her temporary salvation by the ancient king, and a rescue it is that follows; it centres, however, not upon the misused queen but upon her rival, making its heroine the same girl who had determined just now to kill the Trojan woman and her son.

This second drama has been compressed into a single episode in which some but not all of the usual rescue motifs and scenes occur. What is staged is entirely familiar but it is, in effect, strangely altered by the absence of the scenes that are left unplayed. The heroine's danger and helplessness, for example, are described in what appears to be the conventional manner and at great length, first by the nurse and then by the girl in a lyric monody, but for all this apparent thoroughness, a serious omission is felt. The violence that threatens the heroine is never satisfactorily defined. The nurse is afraid that the princess may kill herself, while Hermione is afraid of she knows not what—whatever her husband may decide to do to her when he hears of the attempted crime. A palpable rescue hero soon appears for her, but her 'monster' never has any substance at all. Indeed, the unseen villain of this piece has an aspect that is perversely both noble and just, and this means that Hermione's rescue from him is condemned beforehand to an ethical as well as a dramaturgical vacuity.

As soon as he comes on, Orestes marks another serious omission in the shaping of this thumbnail rescue piece. He has come not unwittingly, but with a plan that concerns Hermione, and now he pronounces his own name at once, thus declaring that there is to be no recognition scene to work its gracious magic on these escaping principals. The girl, on her side, not only knows him but at once sees in him the opportunity of immediate flight. Death is no longer an interesting alternative, since Orestes can remove her from her husband's roof and put her out of his reach, and there is no need whatsoever for the usual elevating mutual resolution to die, if escape should fail, since there is no obstacle here to a smooth departure. It may even be possible to substitute a new and indulgent husband for the angry one and so close the entire affair with all her losses cut. Hermione wastes no time, and the two go off, unopposed and unregenerate, escaping from a situation where neither an evil villain nor a friendly god had had a chance to make his presence felt.

This excessively efficient rescue has been deprived of all claim to the sublime. The poet has dissociated it from heaven, from fate, from any sense of immutable law, even from established mythic patterns, and has made of it a sordid and apparently ephemeral vignette. He has refused to give it even the gauzy fairy-tale scrim that might have made Hermione seem, for a moment, to be an abandoned Ariadne or an Andromeda lifted out of the serpent's reach by the miracle of Perseus' tiny wings. He will not romanticize, nor will he on the other hand allow his flat and distorted action to turn into parody so that the spectator may distance himself from its miserable hollowness. Hermione's rescue, for all its anti-tragic quality, is treated with a full seriousness and this is why it seems to follow like a correction upon Andromache's earlier escape. With this new action the poet forces a temporary cynicism upon his audience, urging them to think that virtue is only a tragedian's dream, while this present meanness is the daylight view of things.

Neither Hermione nor Orestes is overtly out of place on the tragic stage; both have moments in which its diction is natural to their tongues, and yet they do at last break the Aristotelian rule. They are not 'good of their kind', they are simply 'of their kind', and that is no special one, but merely the human kind. At the centre of the stage, caught in an extraordinary situation, are a man and a woman who are at present illuminated neither by any light within nor by the Pindaric glory that ought to stream down upon the head of one caught up in heaven's schemes. Hermione is painful to us, not because she is badly drawn, as some critics say, nor because she is a hypocrite, as most of the others agree. She has the power to disturb even our memories of Andromache and her escape because she is both candid and accurately delineated, and because she is so much 'like us'. She can, in common with most men, put aside a genuine recognition of error when tempted by a comfortable escape from the consequences. Her remorse is perfectly real, and it is very brief. It is this pair of facts that cause in the spectator a new sort of pity and terror entirely foreign to that of classical tragedy. Orestes does not have Hermione's shallowness, but he has instead such total ambiguity that he becomes a living illustration of the problems of moral relativity posed in the initial episode of the play. And he is also, in his evasion of any ethical label, so life-like that the very possibility of didactic theatre seems to be shattered by his presence on the stage.

In spite of its banality there is nothing careless about the shaping or the style of this rescue piece. It begins with a miniature two-part prologue, a scene that is plainly a fresh introduction but one that is also artfully linked to the action that has gone before. Hermione sings a monody that is her version of the duet in the first section and of Peleus' lament in the last, and as she does so she makes a poetic recompense to the victim of her earlier threats. Her song thus tenuously attaches the rescue to the supplication, bridging what will soon be felt as an abyss. With direct reference to her previous scene, Hermione now tears at the costume she had put on to shame her rival; she is no longer dressed to kill. With bloody nails she attacks her own beauty, as she would have that of the Trojan queen (856; cf. 259). She makes herself now overtly shameless, as the other woman had shown her to be in her private thoughts (832; cf. 220), and she wishes for death while reminding herself that she has no shrine where she may play the suppliant (858). Later she supposes that if she does not die, she will become the slave of Andromache, thus returning upon herself her second threat against the queen (927; cf. 165). She closes in a fashion worthy of the heroine of the opening piece, finishing her song with a fantasy of flight dressed out in the conventional figures of the longed for tragic death. She would rise like a dark-winged bird, or sail between sombre headlands into the Black Sea, where heroes disappear (862–5).

Even after Orestes has appeared, Hermione continues for a few minutes to be thus a figure of remorse in action. Assuming the posture she had forced upon Andromache, she throws herself as a suppliant at the feet of the newcomer and greets his arrival with words that echo Andromache's salute to Peleus (892–3; cf. 573). The same nautical imagery of salvation is employed, so that, where Andromache in chains had been a ship becalmed into whose sails Peleus breathed a saving wind (554–5) that saw her into harbour (749), here the frenzied Hermione is a storm-tossed crew that sights Orestes as its haven unhoped for (891). The figures themselves are sadly worn, but their repetition works here to suggest that Hermione is a weak sister to the Trojan queen. This parallelism at first seems to promise some sort of exaltation for Hermione, and the audience naturally suppose that, though she is tainted by crime she will yet be shown to be worthy of a release like Andromache's. Perhaps her crime will be made to seem a fated one? . . . but no, in that case, it would have been complete, like Hypsiplyle's. If only it had been blind, like Creusa's attempt on her son . . . ! Moved by Hermione's anguish, the spectator searches thus hopelessly for some way to soften his view of this new heroine, only to discover that in the present scene with Orestes she has forgotten her old pain and is in the act of betraying the audience's sympathy. Hermione did for a time recognize and claim her guilt, but now, as she explains herself to her champion, she refuses all responsibility for her action. She listened to evil counsel, she says, and evidently feels herself to be wholly exonerated by this excuse.[13] She now regards Peleus' opportune arrival, the arrival that saved her from even more serious guilt, as a piece of rotten luck, and she describes his salvation of Andromache as 'siding with the base' (914). She has learned nothing from her crime or from her remorse, and she appears now as a child in terror of its deserved punishment, one who waits for a just parent whom she yet means to cheat if she can.

The confused spectator turns to Orestes, trusting that the champion will bring some revelation that will allow him to see this heroine as worthy of release. His expectations, however, are more than disappointed, for Orestes simply leads him onto even less familiar ground, then lets him sink at last in what seems to be a bottomless moral bog. He is a champion of foxfire, constantly changing aspect and direction in a most disquieting way. Orestes has come from Delphi and is going, he says, to Dodona; evidently he carries still some of the emblems of his permanent suppliancy. Hermione enhances this suggestion of consecration when she begs for his protection with arms that wind around him like the wreaths of wool upon a suppliant's staff (894-5). As soon as he speaks, however, this creature of Apollo strikes a vulgar note of personal intrigue. He is curious about the most intimate details of Hermione's marriage, and justifies his prying by explaining that, having heard certain gossiping reports of her unhappiness, he has come to learn the truth. As he explains himself more fully, however, he begins to find a more successful tone, suggesting that the loss of Hermione was the bitterest part of what he suffered in consequence of Apollo's matricidal

---

[13] Compare Phaedra, who was not only counselled but tricked, and who derived from these facts no diminution of her intolerable sense of guilt and shame.

command, and reminding us of how first Menelaus and then
Neoptolemus had gratuitously wounded his honour. As long as he
thought Hermione happy, he says, he let his honour go unavenged, but now he has come to put an end to her misfortune
and to his own heroic shame. He speaks quite movingly of his
past suffering, and makes a great point of his delicacy in not
wishing to approach Hermione until he knew that she was indeed
as miserable as he. His words, always a shade too personal,
wholly fail to provide a more comfortable view of Hermione's
morning's work, but they do suggest a new approach to this
curious second action, for the princess ceases to be its principal.
We feel now that Hermione is only an accessory to some Orestean
drama to come.

Having taken the centre of the stage, Orestes repeats in a new
form the trick that Menelaus played in the previous action, for
he suddenly alters the whole aspect of things by announcing that
he has lied. He has purposely misled both Hermione and the
audience by representing his actions as well as his intentions as
other than what they really were. Orestes had made his principal
aim seem to be the recovery of Hermione, and had pretended
that a knowledge of her spiritual state was necessary to any
action of his own. Now he boasts that he has already taken care
of her husband, and we are forced to the realization that the
death of his rival was always central to his purpose, that taking
Hermione was only a part of his vengeance, and that he has
secured her by an unscrupulous manipulation of her will. He
could have told her at the outset that she had nothing to fear
from her husband since he was dying or dead, but by prolonging
her fear he has made sure of her alliance with himself.[14] He has
forced her to see him as her rescuer, when in fact she needed
none; he has made her go down on her knees to beg him to carry
her away in secrecy, when presumably she might either have
stayed in safety or have been sent home in state. There is a sense,
then, in which, instead of making a flawed Hermione whole

[14] Orestes' deception is here superficially like that of his counterpart in Sophocles'
Electra, since he might reasonably wish to discover Hermione's state of mind before
admitting to his conspiracy. Here, however, the crime, in so far as it is to be executed
by Orestes, has already been committed; here the criminal is not seeking a sister's
support in the coming act of avenging the murder of a king and father, he is seeking,
as his private reward, the wife of the victim he has already slain, avenging an insult
to himself.

enough to be worthy of a release, Orestes invents a release which is itself so flawed as to be worthy of Hermione.

Orestes' unexpected words about a death for Neoptolemus are uttered as he and Hermione leave the stage. They are undiscussed and unclarified, left floating in the uncertainty of the poet's mythic innovation and the vagueness of the speaker's future tenses.[15] Nevertheless they constitute the most audacious *coup de théâtre* to have survived from the Attic stage. There is little time for reflection upon them before the final action begins, but they come upon the listener like the flash of lightning that renders a familiar landscape wholly unrecognizable. This death must be worked back into the two dramas that have already been played, for Neoptolemus was a secondary though invisible figure in both of them, just as he is the principal of the tragedy to come. The threat from which Hermione was rescued was the righteous anger of a hero husband, and this fact has rendered her whole rescue piece morally senseless, just as the failure of that husband to appear has undermined its mechanical structure. This was disturbing enough, but now the entire action is made to topple into a causational void. In the moment of its consummation we learn that the reason for the escape—that paradoxically just threat that so troubled the princess—does not exist. Neoptolemus was strong, and Neoptolemus surely had the right to a terrible anger against his wife, but Neoptolemus is or will soon be dead. And if this is the case, the heroics of the morning are as much affected as these noonday melodramatics are. The old suggestion that there really was no quarrel, no cause for jealousy between Hermione and Andromache, is borne out now by an even larger negative, when there is no Neoptolemus. The two women have been spending the worst or the best of themselves in a situation that made virtue and vice cruelly equal in their irrelevance. Their sufferings were sharp, the decisions they took

---

[15] A. Lesky was the first to point out the obvious fact that there is a perfectly reasonable chronological sequence here (see now his *Gesammelte Schriften* [Bern, 1966], pp. 144 ff.). The murder belongs to the stage past, although Orestes himself does not know whether it has been done or is about to be done. Some ten or eleven days ago Neoptolemus left Phthia for Delphi; after he got there he spent three days in sightseeing, and during those days Orestes bound together certain Delphians in a conspiracy to kill him, whenever he should enter the temple. Orestes then quitted Delphi, and the murder took place soon after he left, perhaps on the following day, since a messenger in a hurry reaches Phthia only a few hours after Orestes, who had travelled at his leisure.

were concrete expressions of ethos; they have, on this stage, lived through moments as real as life can provide, and yet now an increase in our understanding of actuality has transformed both the wise queen and the erring girl into blind creatures who flutter uselessly in a vacuum of causation.[16]

The disappearance of the principals in an escape plot is customarily followed by a messenger speech. Only in this way could the best part of the action be imitated, for the messenger told of brilliant ruses, last minute reverses, bloodshed, bravery, and the exhilarating moment of freedom secured. In the *Andromache*, Euripides takes this formal convention and makes it the vehicle for yet another dramaturgical deception. The exit of Orestes and Hermione is duly followed by a messenger scene; it is introduced by old Peleus, who comes on saying that he has heard of the escape, and everything seems regular enough. But the breathless man who then arrives has nothing to say about the departure of the Spartan pair. His speech, in fact, comes from another play, not theirs; it is not from a rescue piece at all, but from a tragedy of divine punishment (an effect that certain words of Orestes have prepared us for; 977; 994; cf. 1008). The man from Delphi who bursts into our play comes from a *Neoptolemus* that has had its ealier scenes played out on another stage.

This closing tragedy is formally very different from the two preceding pieces, for it is neither complete but flawed, like Andromache's suppliant tragedy, nor is it maimed and diseased in all its extant parts, like Hermione's escape. The Neoptolemus play has lost its initial scenes, but from its two fully developed final episodes a classic tragedy of amplitude and elevation can be restored. When the messenger has finished, the spectator is in possession of everything he might have gained from monologues of elucidation, scenes of altercation, even from choral meditation.

---

[16] Note how the poet forced his audience to share the women's blindness, leaving them temporarily uncertain whether Neoptolemus is alive or dead. In the related question of the death of Achilles a like confusion has been created, not as to time but as to agency: Apollo killed him, according to Neoptolemus (53); the Priamids killed him, says Hermione (247); Helen killed him, says Andromache (248); Menelaus killed him, says Peleus (614–15); Paris and Troy herself, says Melenaus (655). In addition the chorus, in the first ode, adds a host of further suggestions as to his assassin: Hermes; all the gods; the three goddesses; and finally Hecuba (by not putting Alexander to death).

He has had the rapid revelation of the full praxis of a tragedy that is something like the *Hippolytus*, even more like Pentheus' drama, and yet peculiar to itself for its retrospective action and its remorseful principal. In the course of this one speech the poet has described Neoptolemus' death, and has conveyed as well the moral complexity and the mysterious terror of this man's war with god—a war he could not abandon even when he travelled to Delphi meaning to offer peace.

Once before, Neoptolemus had gone to Delphi; he had approached Apollo as if that god were no more than one of his peers in the anarchy of a heroic battlefield, and he had demanded blood-money (53). He had denounced the Delphic god in the sanctity of his own shrine, calling him the murderer of Achilles, and he had been allowed to go away unharmed.[17] In the years that followed, however, he had come to think that his attack upon the god had been a dangerous error; he feared the god's anger and decided to return to the Pythian shrine, hoping to discover how he might avert the divine vengeance that surely threatened him. And this is where the present play began. Neoptolemus' second visit to Delphi (the journey that gave Menelaus the opportunity to persecute Andromache) coincided with a visit that Orestes was making there. Exactly according to schedule, Achilles' son stepped into a divine snare that was to bring about, with tragic irony, precisely what the hero sought—Apollo's satisfaction.[18]

The Neoptolemus of the messenger's narrative has the full stature of a hero of tragedy. He is a warrior, a veteran of Troy, all that Menelaus only seemed to be, a point Euripides insists upon with the echo between lines 458 and 1123. Like Hermione, he knows remorse, but his remorse is not put aside; it moves him to action, and that action brings about his downfall. He is both by character and fate one who makes war on god, and even in his

---

[17] Euripides has simplified the reasons for Apollo's anger, putting aside the death of Priam and isolating, as Neoptolemus' effective act of blasphemous *hamartia*, his accusation of murder against the god (50–3; 1002–3; 1106–8; 1194–6). To go to Delphi with words of blame of any sort was an outrage to the god, an act of desecration to the sanctuary, and Peleus recognizes this truth in his monody, using an odd turn of phrase to say that Neoptolemus had 'hung up' his accusation like a votive gift for the god (1196).

[18] Note 1106–8, where Neoptolemus uses a phrase which can mean either as he intends, 'to make amends', or, as Apollo takes it, 'to allow vengeance to another'.

attempted conciliation he re-enacts his first, ineradicable crime. His punishment thus comes upon him with didactic appropriateness and is plainly labelled as the justice not of man but of god. The agent of his destruction has been chosen, as was Agave, in such a way as to make the hero's death a cruelly ugly thing, and yet, by means of tragic irony, the poet leads his audience to accept and almost to comprehend the catastrophe.

Neoptolemus' past actions, the very ones he wished to atone for, had made him an enemy at Delphi. Orestes, therefore, found it easy to persuade the Delphians that Achilles' son had come again intending harm, and meant to destroy the properties of the god. Thus as soon as Neoptolemus should resolve to enter the temple, his very piety would seem proof of new impiety, and Orestes' trap would spring. And this is the scene we finally get, lavishly described by the messenger. Since this is narrative and not dramatic poetry, the irony is necessarily largely situational, and it is very plain. Neoptolemus is at his most magnificent in the instant when the Delphians come upon him; he stands alone against a company of men, once more dancing the Pyrrhic (1135), once more 'taking the Trojan leap' (1139) in a counter-attack that turns his enemies back. This very prowess serves to remind us of the Neoptolemus who outraged both Priam and Astyanax, and once again it involves him in acts of desecration. In his most superb moment the hero unwittingly gives truth to Orestes' slanders, actually 'sacking' Apollo's shrine (note καθαρπάσας, 1121–2; cf. 1095), seizing the arms that had been dedicated to the god and using them in a battle with Apollo's priests. He sweeps the sacred objects from the altar and takes his stand upon it, making his leap from there (1138), and in the ensuing rout, as of pigeons by a hawk, he fills the peaceful shrine with a rowdy ill-omened din (1144–5).

Neoptolemus' new crime, like the old one, is a crime against god, and he makes his payment directly to that god. His death occurs, like that of Pentheus, in the midst of sacred rites, and the command for it is given, as in the Theban case, by a supernatural voice (1147–8: 'someone' speaks from deep within the *adyton* spreading awe and terror; cf. *Bacchae* 1095 ff.).[19] And then the

---

[19] On the ritual quality of the voice from the *adyton*, as conveyed by the verb φθέγγομαι, see R. Fuhrer, *Formproblem-Untersuchungen zu den Reden in der Fruhgriechischen Lyrik* (Zetemata 44, Munich, 1967), pp. 30–2.

community of Delphians, like the Bacchic band, executes the sentence with a death that does not dismember but seriously deforms the hero's body (1155). When he has told Peleus that the remains are even now being brought to Phthia, the messenger speaks out in his own voice, which is much the voice of Cadmus, and confronts a divine mystery with the inevitable mortal doubt. 'How can it be wise, in god, to remember injury as a base man would?' (1164–5; cf. *Bacchae* 1357). Thus he demonstrates the universality of Neoptolemus' crime, which was to treat a god as if he were a man.

The messenger withdraws and the character so markedly absent until now enters, as a corpse. Neoptolemus' outraged body is brought before Peleus and he, reduced now to a condition like that of the woman he saved in the first drama (note how 1077 was made to echo 717), sings his lament. At the end of the suppliant section he had spoken jauntily of his renewed youth but now, in despair, he sees himself as soon labouring in Hades, childless and alone (1216). He and his grandson make a pair of prostrate figures like those of Andromache and her son in their duet, but Peleus has a voiceless partner in his grief. Like the messenger, the old man looks at his grandson's death from a secular point of view, but instead of blaming Apollo, he blames Hermione. 'Oh marriage, marriage!' he complains (1186), and finds that by a terrible perversity marriage has not given him issue but has taken all his kin away (1177).

Peleus does not fully understand the situation but his errors, soon to be corrected, introduce the ultimate scene of the *Andromache*, a *deus ex machina* scene that miraculously stitches the three plots together while it drives all comparison with the *Bacchae* from our minds. It is not the cruelly appeased god of Neoptolemus' tragedy who now makes an appearance; it is instead the gracious feminine divinity of the opening suppliant piece, and she raises Peleus as he had raised the Trojan queen. 'It is because of our long-ago marriage that I am here', calls Thetis as she slips down through the pale evening air; she has never been angry, and she comes now with love, to work a kind of triple resurrection for the men of her family. Neoptolemus is dead according to the will of Zeus (1269); he must be buried where he will have honour and where his death will tell its tale, but the house is not, as Peleus had moaned, without an heir. Thetis

reminds him of Molossus, whom he himself had saved, and
promises that through that child there will be a long continuation
of their race (1250, directly answering 1177), the future of which
will be protected by yet another marriage, one between Andromache and Helenus. Even Troy will thus partake of the restoration of Achilles' line.[20] Then turning to the old man himself
his goddess wife reveals that he will be a god (thus correcting
his words at 1216–17) and that far from living, as he had said,
in a childless house, he will visit his own hero son Achilles where
he dwells immortal on the isle of Leuke (1260–2; cf. 1216).

'Do not grieve', the goddess says (1270), and Peleus responds,
'I shall not' (1276). He promises to bury his grandson and then
to keep his rendezvous with Thetis on the shore where he first
found her (1278), and on this note of immortal marriage the
play comes to its close. The rescue of Andromache and Molossus
has been made permanent, and there is to be an eternal rescue
for old Peleus as well. As the body of Neoptolemus is carried off
to be prepared for its hero's tomb, we realize that this final
tragedy has even transformed that mundane pair, Orestes and
Hermione.

When he spoke of his plot against Neptolemus Orestes had
seemed almost mad again. He had claimed that his crime had
a double causation, that Neoptolemus was to be punished both
for marrying a wife who had belonged to Orestes (1001), and
for demanding recompense from Apollo for Achilles' death
(1002–3). With what appeared to be megalomania he had
claimed that the death would emanate from god as well as being
implemented by himself (1004–6), and he had made his threats
with apparent incoherence, saying, 'He (Neoptolemus) will
come to know what it is to be my enemy, for the god is not com-
placent of outrage, but reverses the fates of his enemies' (1006–8).
Now, however, Orestes' confusion of himself with god and his

---

[20] As Wilamowitz noticed long ago, the τόνδε of line 1246 seems to show that
Molossus is visible here; indeed, the coordination of this demonstrative with τὸν μὲν
θανόντα τόνδ' at 1239 gives us Thetis' double gesture as it stretches toward both the
living and the dead. Campbell (CR xlvi [1932], 196 ff.) and Kamerbeek (Mnem.
ser. iii, xi [1942], 63) point out that Andromache should therefore be present also;
she and her son would have entered with Peleus just before 1047, and the σοι of
1041 could have been addressed to her. See, however, the arguments against this
version of the staging of the finale in W. Steidle, Studien zum antiken Drama (Munich,
1968), pp. 119 ff.

presumptious definition of his own role in Neoptolemus' death are proved to have a kind of accuracy, for the messenger speech has shown that Orestes was in fact acting as the agent of destruction in a divine vengeance plan. Orestes the man is in no way rehabilitated (see Thetis at 1241–2), but his meanness, his base nursing of an ancient insult, and his unscrupulous desire for Hermione have all been subsumed into the pattern of Apollo's will. Orestes was not principally an ignoble rescue champion or a petty vengeance hero, he was instead the appropriate agent of death in a tragedy of divine retaliation. Through him evil and human fallibility have been explained in the only way they can be, as serving a providential purpose that mortals cannot know.[21]

The poet of the *Andromache* has placed a pair of 'positive' human actions, suppliant and rescue, beside a single divine action of destruction. The two mortal recoveries from man-made evils represent quite fairly the best that man alone can do, and these are set out in comparison with the worst a god can bring about—a god-made catastrophe in fullest consummation. In the early phases of the play Euripides forces his audience to doubt the validity of tragedy itself, for he seems to find that men as they truly are can be portrayed only by a wrenching of traditional forms and an irrational assignment of roles. He suggests that mortals of Andromache's stature are wholly foreign to Greek soil, and he cheapens her escape from death until it seems not much lovelier than Hermione's disreputable flight. In the end, however, he has chosen to show Neoptolemus' tragedy and he has made sure that Apollo's act, often cited as an example of divine cruelty and injustice, shall fulfil itself in traditional beauty after the two examples of human exertion have dissolved in dubious makeshift. With Thetis he has indicated that life and art still have their own congruency, since both must borrow grace from the influence of a god. The heroes

---

[21] The effect upon the spectator is parallel to the effect upon Heracles, in the *Trachiniae*, when he discovers that Deianeira's apparent crime was only an act of criminal simplicity, a necessary part of his own fore-ordained death. Heracles, at that point, simply loses interest in his wife's motives—indeed in his wife—and we experience a similar drop of interest here, in Orestes. The chorus has prepared for the disappearance of the two escapees from our concerns by swallowing them both up in the general moral malady which they say has afflicted Greece since the end of the Trojan War (1037 ff.).

are dead and virtue is in exile, but heaven still confers its beauty on whatever it may touch, whether that touch shall come in anger or in love. And so it works within this play, for Thetis' words finally transform Andromache's almost accidental salvation, just as the messenger speech did Orestes' crime. Both are given at last a decent mantle of inevitability, and when the goddess includes the Trojan woman in her prophecies and gives her a role in the god-willed survival of Achilles' race, Andromache's escape from a petty and disgusting man does at last swell to the noble proportion that tragedy demands.

VII

THE *MADNESS OF HERACLES*

THE *Madness of Heracles* is another play of triple action. The mixture is the same as in the *Andromache* (indeed, it is the same as in the *Helen*) but the proportions and the order have been changed. Here the third and final overturn is from bad fortune into good, for the negative action has been made to fall between a suppliant drama and a final rescue piece, but here, paradoxically, the total effect is far more 'tragic' in the modern sense than was that of Andromache's play. Here there is little of that ultimate luminosity that sparkled from Thetis' apparition, for the goddesses who are seen on this stage are in another mood. Here the hero has had the role of destroyer forced upon him, and so his final survival is a far bitterer thing to an audience than was the divine destruction of Achilles' son.

The first remark always made about this play is that its parts have not been truly integrated. (The number of those parts is generally said to be two.) The old view was, with Swinburne, that the piece was simply an odious abortion; then there was a reaction, and unifying 'themes' were sought; now an élite group of admirers once more insists upon discoordination, but finds the play's special virtue in an internal war it is said to declare upon itself.[1] According to this reading, the opening of the play has been written with the intention of turning the audience into donkeys, that the poet may beat them severely

---

[1] See for example William Arrowsmith, in the introduction to his translation: '...The result is a structure in which two apparently autonomous actions are jammed savagely against each other in almost total contradiction, with no attempt to minimize or even to modulate the profound formal rift. That rift is, of course, deliberate . . .' (*The Complete Greek Tragedies*, ed. Grene and Lattimore, Vol. iii. *Euripides* [Chicago, 1959], p. 268). Compare Kamerbeek: 'What for a moment seemed to be a universe ruled by divine justice turns out to be the playground of arbitrary evil without any redeeming feature except for the endurance of man and human friendship.'(*Mnemosyne*, Ser. iv, xix [1966], 9–10). Kamerbeek does at any rate recognize that the number of the actions is three.

with his final scenes. He lulls them first into a stupefied complacency on the subjects of heroism, justice and the gods, then strikes with the whiplash of truth.

This thesis is attractive because it looks for a creative intention behind the notorious 'flaws' in the play's construction. Unfortunately, however, the *Heracles* refuses to conform to this particular pattern of dramaturgical revolt, and even more unfortunate is the fact that the attempt to impose this pattern has obscured the true radicalism of the piece. If this were a play that destroyed itself according to the above prescription, its opening suppliant action would serve as bait for the dramatist's hook and would have been written to be swallowed whole. It would represent the poet's attempt to create an action so *séduisant* that it would enslave his audience, and so good of its kind that when it was destroyed all the the traditional tragic values would seem to have been destroyed with it. It would be, in other words, a piece of perfect conservatism, and that consequently is what it has been called by critics eager to get on to the more exciting, 'truly Euripidean' parts of the piece that lie on the other side of the 'rift'.[2] The truth is, however, that the suppliant action is anything but conventional, its effect anything but soothing to an Attic spectator. Its outrages upon the settled cannons of tragic suppliancy are indeed so flagrant that we are forced to recognize a major intention of the poet in this marked deviation from the norm.[3]

When the opening scenes of the *Heracles* are compared to their natural foils in other suppliant drama, aberrations and distortions appear that are easily a match for those of the second half of the play. The experimenter of the *Andromache* is recognized

---

[2] Some, it is true, have paused long enough to complain of banality, dreariness, and excess, without seeing that if the initial scenes did indeed deserve these words the play that 'converts' itself, in Arrowsmith's term, would necessarily fail. V. Ehrenberg speaks of 'stale and boring rhetoric' (*Aspects of the Ancient World* [Oxford, 1946], p. 158); Arrowsmith calls the action 'slow, conventional, overwhelmed by the weakness of its characters' (op. cit., p. 266); later he speaks of 'a parody of a standard tragic movement', though parody would defeat the poet's presumed purpose of encouraging complacency. L. H. G. Greenwood (*Aspects of Euripidean Tragedy* [Cambridge, 1953], p. 122) likewise finds 'religious parody' here. There is a good survey of the literature on this play in H. Rohdich's *Die Euripideische Tragödie* (Heidelberg, 1968), pp. 71–80.

[3] One way to appreciate this fact is to compare the opening Euripidean action with the parallel section of Seneca's *Furens*.

in some characteristic exercises in this suppliant piece, and the chasm that has been said to yawn in the middle of this play seems suddenly much less broad. In fact, the two halves of the play, equally defiant of the conventional forms, prove to have positive ethical links that establish something very like a causal sequence between them. Megara's suppliant drama is an action purposely malformed so that it can lead directly into the grotesque scenes that destroy her.

When the play begins the situation of the Heraclid suppliants looks conventional enough. It is, like the plight of Andromache, of that most desperate variety in which the pursuer appears before the entrance of the champion, and here the danger is pushed to the extreme. This pursuer has already established himself by his violence as the local ruler, supplanting the prince who should properly offer protection, and the natural champion has meanwhile disappeared on a trip to hell. We expect the action to be ugly, and we expect it to try the mettle of the suppliants severely; we expect to see them overcome, perhaps, by force or deceit and almost put to death, but most of all we expect to watch them as, from their superior position of faith, they defy and even threaten their pursuers. The one thing we do not expect is to see them easily agree to leave their sanctuary.

The question of leaving sanctuary was in fact one of the standard motifs of suppliant drama. There was almost always some inopportune and unsuccessful attempt made to persuade the suppliants to move, for this provided the dramatic opportunity for a speech from the suppliant depicting his unshakable determination and unalterable faith.[4] Often threats were added, and thus there was an almost tangible measure of the principal's character and piety. If the dramatist needed to remove his suppliants before they had been ritually raised by their protector, if he meant to hand them over to their pursuers, he had to see to it that they were forced or tricked (unless he was able to arrange a recognition that would suddenly transform the enemy

---

[4] *Andromache* 129; 135; *OC* 162; 235; *Hcld.* 59–61; 344; and note especially Aesch. *Supp.* 492 and *OC* 176, where the persuasion is by friends and is met with a curious technical acquiescence in which the suppliants do move, but only from one sanctuary position to another. The one case where such persuasion is successful is *Helen*, and there the sanctuary is reoccupied as soon as possible.

into a friend).[5] It was plainly unwise to move too soon, even in the presence of friends, and it was almost impious to move in the presence of enemies, for, having made himself over to the god, the suppliant did not have the right to give himself up to the would-be violator of that god's properties.[6]

Now consider the unnatural suppliants of the *Heracles*. Their situation is, in tragedy's context, normal, but their decisions and their movements are in glaring violation of the rules of the suppliant plot. The opening monologue, as it should, identifies the suppliants and their altar, but sounds no word of prayer, praise or supplication, and when the action begins we are immediately aware of an anomaly. The role of leader of the suppliants has been split between Heracles' wife and his mortal father, and these two are quarrelling. The poet has taken up the old motif of attempted persuasion to leave sanctuary but he has altered its personnel and has magnified it until it becomes the material of his first two episodes. He has given the argument that belongs to an outsider to one of the suppliants and, in total violation of the usual, he has made that argument prevail. It is as if Ismene had persuaded Antigone to give up the burial of her brother or, closer home, as if Polyneices had successfully persuaded Oedipus to leave his sacred grove.

The *agon* of this suppliant piece has been located in a new place. Megara and Amphitryon dispute, she is victorious, and as a result the suppliants abandon sanctuary and deliver themselves to their pursuer. This astonishing pattern has replaced the

---

[5] Trickery can be seen in the case of Andromache; recognition in the case of Creusa, in the *Ion*. On moving in general, note Teucer to Tecmessa and Eurysaces (who treat Ajax's corpse as a shrine): φύλασσε, μηδέ σε κινησάτω τις (*Ajax* 1180 f.).

[6] Even in the presence of a protector the tragic suppliant is loathe to leave his place: Iolaus refuses Demophon's invitation to move to the palace, *Hcld.* 344; Danaus will leave only to move to other altars in the city (*Supp.* 492), and his daughters leave their suppliant boughs on the altar when they get up (506); Oedipus almost apologizes, but will not go to the palace (*OC*, 642 ff); Orestes, in *Eumenides*, goes reluctantly (85 ff.) at the command of the god of the place (74); the women of the Euripidean *Suppliants* are kept at their shrine even when all danger is past (947). On the suppliant as the property of god, see *Ion* 1285, and Nilsson, *Die Religion der Griechen* (Tübingen, 1927), p. 81, and notice how Megara is made to recognize this relationship, ironically, at 451. In this question the case of Pausanias is interesting; he was penned in and watched, at his altar, by the Spartans until the moment before he died of starvation, and was then carried out with no violence whatsoever, but the shrine and those who moved him were none the less polluted, for he had belonged to the god (Thuc. 1. 126).

archaic dispute between suppliants and champion (as in E. *Supp.* or A. *Supp.*) or the alternative dispute between suppliants and pursuer, both of which ended finally in their delivering themselves to their champion. The essential suppliant choice—to die, if die one must, as a consecrated being, and as a sure agent of damnation for the enemy—is here reversed. These people willingly divest themselves of all their supernatural force and choose to die as the ordinary secular victims of an impious enemy whose triumph they assure.

Critics have repeatedly described Megara as the familiar tragic wife, another but less interesting Deianeira or Tecmessa. They have been briefly touched by the life Heracles is presumed to have led her, forgetting that her unhappy biography is in no way relevant to her present situation. However sympathetic she may be as a woman, as a suppliant she is not only wholly unfamiliar, she is untenable. She is wanting in the primary quality of the suppliant, awareness of the divine, as a comparison with the Aeschylean suppliants makes disturbingly plain. Their constant reference to Zeus, the insuppressible prayer that breaks from them, finds not a syllable of echo from the wife of Heracles. Her idea of salvation is entirely secular and practical;[7] she seems in fact to be unaware of where she sits, of the boughs she must be holding and the crown upon her head. Her only prayer is addressed to her husband's ghost, and in it she calls like a necromancer for a revenant from hell (καὶ σκιὰ φάνηθί μοι, 494; cf. 516–17).

Megara's alienation from anything divine is the reason why she fails to sense her proper strength and so contests with her friend instead of with her enemy. The faithful suppliant has two powerful weapons; the first is the anger of Zeus against anyone who violates his law, and the second is the special pollution that the mortal can create by his suicide in the sacred place. These weapons properly allow even the weakest refugee to defy all

---

[7] Sitting at the altar of Zeus Soter, she can yet say to the children, σῴζω (72); at this place she still asks νῦν οὖν τίν' ἐλπίδ' ἢ πέδον σωτηρίας ἐξευμαρίζῃ, πρέσβυ; (80–1); she sees non-existent friends as the only source of salvation (84), and when she does at last find a mortal champion she only takes one more opportunity to insult the god (521–2). At 506–7 she again bypasses god to say that Time would be a saviour of hopes, 'if such there were', but concludes that Time does not know how to do his job. For her the only god is Heracles, and she and the children do hang upon him, when he comes, as they should have clung to the altar (627 ff.).

threats, to remain true to his staff and his garlands, and in the
end to win a salvation appropriate to his constant piety. Megara,
however, never attempts to use either of these legitimate
counter-threats; when Lycus proposes to move her by fire she
grows more eager to leave the steps of Zeus' altar, whereas the
same threat caused Andromache to hold fast to her sanctuary
and cry, 'Light up! The gods will know!' (*Andr.* 258).

A true suppliant is passive; he moves only when he is forced
from his refuge by his pursuer or when he is raised by his champion. Megara, on the other hand, abandons her altar of her own
free will and causes others to do likewise in an unparalleled
gesture of active unfaith. She is a non-suppliant, unable to
maintain the suppliant posture because she has no belief in the
efficacy of supernatural causes. She believes instead in a fixed
Necessity that is beyond all influence (309; 311) and suppliancy therefore quite naturally seems senseless to her. She is
proud enough to think that she can recognize this necessity, that
she can know her own saviour and that she can know him to be
dead. Megara is a materialist and so she chooses to move, in the
first piece of choreography that the *Heracles* offers, away from
the altar and into the palace. Within this movement she executes
a minor figure, the removal of the robes of faith and the assumption of those of the grave. For her, substance is *ousia* and spirit is
onoma (337–8), and her thoughts are constantly with appearances.
Thus she buys what she considers to be a seemly death at the
cost, in her own terms, of some hours of her own and her children's lives. She defies an ancient *nomos* and breaks faith with
Zeus, in order to procure for them all a few articles of clothing,
as Lycus reminds us with his scornful concession ('I don't grudge
you a *peplos* or two', 333). It is no wonder that the two enemies
understand each other, for her way of thinking is identical with
his when he openly rejects an ordinary form of propriety (*aidos*)
in the name of opportunism (*eulabeia*, 165).[8]

Megara charges old Amphitryon with too great a love of life,
and in the same way she argues that a voluntary death now will

---

[8] Note how her refusal to play the proper suppliant destroys Lycus' conventional
role. He does his best to be villainous, but the one thing we see him do is yield, like
Medea's Creon, to an entreaty that is not in his own interest. Since this is the case,
it is curious to find Ehrenberg, concerned to label this drama as 'melodramatic
theatre', describing Lycus as 'blacker than black', beside a Megara whom he calls
'noble and courageous', op. cit., 158.

bring good fame, whereas continued resistance will be a form of cowardice (287 ff.). He, on the other hand, identifies life and hope with courage, their abandonment with cowardice, and in his initial stance he embodies the true aristocratic confidence that Pindar expresses (cf. his 105–6 with *I.* 8.16: χρὴ δ' ἀγαθὰν ἐλπίδ' ἀνδρὶ μέλειν). Megara argues that Heracles in her place would do exactly as she does (290 ff.), that he would trade his children's lives and a chance to resist for a seemly burial; with this claim she prevails over the old man but she cannot do so over an alert audience. She pretends to act as the true wife of Heracles, but her husband repudiates her whole position as soon as he appears on stage. He is astonished that she has fallen into despair (552) and he specifically commands them all to cast away the ill-omened funeral garments that Megara was so eager to procure (562 f.). Before the play is over, he will have a chance to give her decision an active denial, for he will choose an apparently worthless life over an easy death precisely because to die by choice would be a form of cowardice (1347 ff.).[9]

Amphitryon is all that Megara is not, and he is in the play's terms right, since Heracles does come. He is an irrationalist, 'in love with impossibility' (318; cf. Ismene's description of her sister at *Antigone*, 90) and he is essentially a pious man. He is proud of his foster-son, but he has not, like Megara, allowed the gigantic figure of the hero to eclipse the face of heaven. He has in fact a close and powerful sense of Zeus, which makes him capable of blasphemy but saves him from her arrogant agnosticism. Amphitryon is however weak, and in this, his carpet scene, he is led against his convictions into an error that puts all their lives in jeopardy. (It is worth noting that for this he seems to feel shame at 322 f.) He listens to her sublimely irrelevant demonstration

---

[9] The final movements of the play have been planned as a visual corrective to Megara's error in the opening. Thus Heracles on the *eccyclema*, prone among the children and regarded by Amphitryon, is the doublet of Megara at the altar surrounded by the same companions and watched by the same old man (note 1214 where Theseus makes this likeness explicit). In this scene too the question is of moving the motionless, but Heracles annuls Megara's decision by giving himself to a friend instead of to an enemy and by abandoning the palace she was eager to enter, choosing a life that seems a servitude over a death that offers a kind of freedom, and moving off by one of the *parodoi* instead of going in through the central door. There is even a similar play with costume here, for where Megara changed her white robes for black ones, Heracles marks his acceptance of life by removing the tissue with which he had covered up his head (1226).

that what he irrationally hopes for cannot reasonably be expected (295 ff.), and lets her victory deprive him of his proper role. He cannot defy Lycus with threats of divine vengeance if he means to leave sanctuary; the only threat he has left is the commonplace one of fortune's reversal (216), and all he can do to save his own dignity is to deliver his discourse on the bow of Heracles (170 ff.).

Amphitryon allows Megara to move the suppliant group physically from the altar and he goes with them, forsaking the god he accuses of forsaking them. He allows Megara to strip herself and the children of their suppliant tokens and robes, and it must be that he also strips himself.[10] He allows Megara to rededicate them all, this time to death (480-84), and he finally allows her to turn his natural impulse toward prayer into a need for blasphemy. He, who has just agreed to hand the children over to Lycus, yet boasts to the god: 'I am your superior in *arete*, for I do not betray the sons of Heracles' (342-3). To the Saviour Zeus of the abandoned shrine he says: 'You do not know how to save your own' (346). He shakes his fist at heaven and reverses the usual prayer; he calls out not, 'as you helped us in the past, so help us now, today', but rather 'as you failed me in the past, so do you fail me today' (498 ff.).[11]

The old man's confusion is manifest, for his final statement comes to this: 'We do not rely upon Zeus; we leave his altar and arrange our own death according to Necessity; if Zeus allows what we now insist upon doing, he will prove himself to be a frivolous or an unjust god.' The Best Argument has been defeated by the Worst, and incoherence is the result. The suppliants have refused to supplicate; they have substituted black clothes for white and blasphemy for prayer; they are about to sacrifice themselves to man, not god, because they are by their own definition devotees of Necessity.

After such aberrations it is not surprising to find that the final

---

[10] Like Cassandra, he has had a very close relationship with the god, and his action will have the same heavy symbolism of futile mortal revolt that hers had, at *Agam.* 1266 ff.

[11] Note the irony of his repeated μάτην at 339 and 340. He means what Creusa meant—'where is the repayment you owe me for my complaisance?'—but the poet reminds the audience that he has taken his connection with Zeus 'in vain' in the same sense that one can take the name of the Lord 'in vain', i.e., without giving it its proper sacred meaning. The same effect can be felt at 501.

sequence of this drama of non-suppliants is marked by further deviations from the norm. The suppliant plot, as a piece of truly positive action, ends in the villain's defeat but not, as a rule, in his death. He may be converted like the Furies, ordered away like the various heralds, or defeated in offstage battle like the Creon of the *Colonus* or the Theban chiefs in the Euripidean *Suppliants*, but the action of the play does not usually include his slaying.[12] The suppliant champion will properly defend the suppliants, but leave the punishment of their pursuers to the wrath of Zeus Soter. Here, however, the champion is also a returning legitimate ruler, while the villain is the imposter who has stolen his throne, and the last scene is played as if it belonged to a vengeance tragedy. In a true suppliant action it is the moral authority of the state that paralyses the impious pursuer and finally puts him to flight, but here it is brute violence that wins the day. The assassination of Lycus thus delivers the *coup de grâce* to Megara's unhealthy suppliant piece, for just as the public battle that defeats certain suppliant villains emphasizes the social character of the traditional action, so this private bloodshed endows its preceding action with an opposite, anarchic effect. (Note what a point is made of the fact that Heracles is not to get in touch with any elements in the city until after the killing is done, 604–5. What a contrast with, say, Pelasgus!) Even as vengeance, this swift ambush of Lycus is anomalous, for it is unusually indiscriminate in its ferocity. In the brief phase of intrigue Amphitryon counsels his son on how to surprise the usurper when he is alone (599), but Heracles does not mean to stop there. He has already given a terrible description of his plan, which is to cut off Lycus' head and throw it to the dogs, then kill every man who failed to take up arms in defence of the Heraclids;[13] Dirce and Ismene are to be filled with blood (565–73).

[12] The one near exception is provided by Eurystheus, in the Euripidean *Heracleidae*, whose death is to be the first post-play event; this multiple plot has, however, already admitted elements from outside suppliant drama (most notably Macaria's sacrifice) and is itself a case of conscious deviation from the suppliant norm. It seems just possible that there was an ancient tragedy about the rescue of Danae, in which she and Dictys took the parts of suppliants (if Apollod. *Bibl.* 2. 4. 3 reflects a theatrical source), but even in this case their rescue would not include bloodshed, though it would presumably have encompassed the turning of Polydectes and his guests to stone.

[13] He points his threat at every man who was in his debt and who failed to dis-

This extraordinary scene that began with the assumption of the funeral garments, was interrupted by the return of the hero, included a kind of recognition and then veered away to intrigue, goes on to a brief recapitulation of the journey to Hades. It closes, however, with a movement built after the pattern of the *Choephoroi* killings, as the vengeance hero and those who are to serve as bait for his trap retire into the palace to wait for the unsuspecting villain. Amphitryon will be sent out to lure Lycus inside; he functions as Orestes' nurse did, but the particular trick he uses is worth noting, for it is a cynical pretence to piety (715) on the part of those who showed little enough piety when they were in truth seated at an altar.[14] The villain is successfully drawn within, and his cries ring out, as those of Aegisthus had, to the delight of the listening chorus.

The first section of the play thus ends with the unexpected violence of Lycus' death. The escape of the suppliant family of Heracles evokes an outburst of conventional piety from the chorus, but it cannot have left the Athenian audience, drilled as it was in the nuances of tragic hubris and religious crime, feeling very comfortable. By Amphitryon's own blasphemous demonstration, this outcome proves that Zeus is *not* a careless god, nor one uninterested in justice (212; 339 ff.; cf. 811–14), and this last notion is now a source of disturbing concern. How can such a god allow mortals who have flouted his suppliant *nomos* to profit by their impiety and faithlessness? Megara's doctrine of Necessity and her conversion of Amphitryon are reminiscent of Jocasta's temptation of Oedipus in the *Tyrannus*, and here as there an unwitting chorus gives subsequent instruction in the need for dread. A moral drawn ostensibly from the fallen, from Lycus as from Laius, proves to be fearfully applicable to his

charge that debt by protecting his family; since he was, as the conqueror of the Minyans, the benefactor of all Thebes (560), his qualification of indebtedness would technically exclude no citizen of the city.

[14] Nowhere else in suppliant drama is trickery used by anyone except the villain. Note that even Strohm, who views this scene simply as an intrigue and not as part of a suppliant piece, remarks, 'Die Intrigenhandlung des Her., mit ihrem dramaturgisch eng begrenzten Ziel, deutet über ihre wenigen Verse hinaus auf das Bild des Menschen schlechthin, wie es der Dichter am Beginn seiner Spätzeit gesehen haben mag, des Menschen, der trügen zu können glaubt und dabei von einer höheren Macht selbst betrogen wird', *Euripides* (Munich, 1957), p. 75. Amphitryon's deception may be compared with that used by Orestes and Pylades against Helen, *Or.*, 1437 ff.

surviving conqueror—there to Oedipus, here to the party of Heracles (*HF* 735–814; cf. *OR* 873–910).

This third stasimon begins with heavy Aeschylean echoes, describing Heracles as a kind of third-comer, a Zeus to Creon's Ouranos and to Lycus' Cronus (769–70). Lycus' death cries interrupt the song and then the ode almost parodies *Agam.* 369 ff., as the chorus asks, 'Who, himself a mortal, smirched the divine with disregard of *nomos* and launched his senseless argument against the blessed ones of heaven, saying that the gods are powerless?' (757–9). It is their intention to describe Lycus, the official violator of altars, but the audience has not heard Lycus propose any such argument, whereas it has heard just such things from the mouths of Megara and her father-in-law (note how θνητὸς ὤν at 757 reads back to Amphitryon's boast at 342). The chorus stops to call for a new song of rejoicing, then continues in the vocabulary of the *Agamemnon*, describing how gold and good fortune lead a man on into unjust acts; he mounts his new chariot of blessedness, then shatters it in a terrible overturn, because of *nomos* slighted (778–80). Again they mean to describe Lycus and his greed, but the specification of *eutychia* (774) as a snare carries a dread suggestion that Heracles too is in danger, for this is his attribute.[15]

This ominous sense increases as we listen to the final section of the ode, where the chorus responds to its own call for a new song and produces a hymn for Zeus and Heracles (780–813). First Dirce and Ismene, then the daughters of Asopus are summoned to the dance; next the cliffs of Parnassus are commanded to join in the song as Heracles' victory is celebrated at Thebes. For an instant the names of the two sacred springs sound forth with simple piety, but almost at once the harmony of the invocation is spoiled by a discordant memory, for these streams are no longer pure. Heracles had boasted (572) that he would fill them with blood, and he has just now made good that boast. It is their own pollution that Dirce and Ismene are called upon to commemorate, and this shocking truth makes the

---

[15] At 885 the chorus calls him ὁ εὐτυχής; the idea of *eutychia* is associated both with his past deeds (426; 613; 1221; 1300) and with his killing of Lycus (762; 885). In connection with this definition, note 475, where Megara gives his conquests the vocabulary of dangerous excess, and see Wilamowitz, ad loc., on the sense of πυργόω.

listener the more uneasy when he hears Heracles identified with
the Spartoi who massacred one another for the salvation of
Thebes. As the song continues he has time to wonder whether,
even at best, it is advisable to ask nature to uproot herself in a
gigantic pageant of the pathetic fallacy, when the occasion is
not a divine birth or an apotheosis, but merely the successful
termination of a peculiarly bloody vengeance killing. The spectator docs not know that the poet means to have this choral call
to celebration answered in grim exactitude when all nature
seems to join Lyssa in sending the madness upon Heracles
(861-2). He does not know that the punishment about to be
inflicted will be imaged sometimes as singing and dancing in
heaven,[16] but even in his ignorance he finds the final words of
the song obscurely terrifying. The death of Lycus proves to
these old men that the gods are pleased to concern themselves
with justice, and by their own demonstration this would mean
that the gods must concern themselves eventually with Lycus'
killer and with the cynical suppliants who were saved by him.

The second action of the *Heracles* is an expansion of the last
aberrant touch of violence that marked the opening piece. Its
peculiarity is most briefly described if we say that it is a deformed
vengeance action that has been labelled by one of its own divinities as a tragedy of divine punishment.[17] Its hero is, in a pragmatic sense, a doer, not a sufferer, yet his completed deed, when
it is recognized, is far more agonizing to him than the death of a
Pentheus or a Hippolytus would have been. His story is icono-
graphically like those of Lycurgus and of Ajax, with a pathos of
self-discovery added to a deed of violence in such a way as to
make another Oedipus of its principal.

[16] The theme of dancing occurs again at 681; 690; 763; 870; 871; 879; 892; 897;
899; 1027; 1303; that of singing at 680; 1027; 1085.

[17] When this central action is viewed as divine punishment, Megara is seen to
have played a curiously abortive version of the Deianeira–Phaedra role. Like them
she is necessary to the working out of the disaster, like them she has dominated the
play's opening scenes with a display of her own nature, like them she is destroyed
in the continuing action. However, the other two are, like Clytemnestra, true agents,
performing actions that are essential to the developing catastrophe, whereas
Megara's action has been superfluous. She is not so much the agent of this punishment as its very substance, and all that was necessary, from the gods' point of view,
was that she should have been ready to hand, with her children, when the madness
came. Her behaviour as suppliant has made not the least contribution to the
mechanics of the Heraclean catastrophe, but it has enhanced the claim of that
catastrophe to a kind of justice, and so it has increased its didactic power.

The first action was one in which the gods seemed to be absent, even non-existent, but this new action brings them down among the players. It is introduced by a second prologue that is remarkable not only for its position but for its form and content, for it is shared by a pair of goddesses who disagree. Iris and Lyssa have been sent on a mission of punishment, with Hera their commander and Heracles their object. Iris is eager for the job but Lyssa, who must actually induce the punitive madness, is reluctant and even critical of her superiors, for she sympathizes with Heracles and admires him for the benefactions he has brought to man. In the end of course she bows to authority, and sends down upon the hero a frenzy that is like all the storms of nature intermingled.

The scene between Iris and Lyssa is written with plain reference to the prologue of the *Prometheus Bound*[18] and thus, before all else, it leads the audience to look for likenesses between Heracles and the Titan rebel (cf. e.g. 1115; 1243; 1252-3). It also suggests a likeness between Hera, the deity it portrays, and the Aeschylean Zeus, and thus it finally intimates that there is more than punishment in store for the hero—that if we are to see him bound he will finally also be unbound.

The prologue scene between the two immortals dissolves into a brief passage of lyric exchange between the chorus and an invisible Amphitryon. It is formally like the passage that accompanied the murder of Lycus and his friends, and thus it draws attention to a likeness in the two deeds of slaughter. Next a messenger enters and begins a speech that takes the audience back a bit in time by supplying an imaginary preliminary scene of Heracles at the family altar. The speech describes all the events that led up to the killings the audience has just overheard, then leaves the hero asleep. The chorus sings

[18] Iris' vocative call to Lyssa (*HF* 833-4) is like Kratos' to Hephaestus (*PV* 3-4); her string of imperatives like his at *PV* 58; Heracles is to learn the rage of Hera and Iris (*HF* 840-1), Prometheus that his wisdom is stupidity to Zeus (*PV* 61-2) and that he must love the tyranny of Zeus (*PV* 10-11). Both must δοῦναι δίκην (*HF* 842; *PV* 8-9); both have defended the *timai* of men (*HF* 853; *PV* 30). Lyssa and Hephaestus are alike in their disclaimers (*HF* 858; *PV* 19); Lyssa is reluctant to proceed against friends (*HF* 846), Hephaestus against relatives (*PV* 14); both finally bow to necessity (*HF* 859; *PV* 72). There may well be other Aeschylean echoes that we cannot recognize; the Schol. at *Eum.* 26, records that Lyssa was a character in the *Xantriae*, where she was likewise associated with Hera, and it is possible that her personification is an Aeschylean invention.

of other child murderers, all of whom Heracles signally surpasses,
and then the doors open for the action's final episode, wherein
Amphitryon will play a scene with his son very like the one that
old Cadmus plays with his daughter at the end of the *Bacchae*.[19]
The fact that this compressed drama is finally a tragedy of
divine punishment and not the vengeance piece it seems to be is
formally reflected in the near suppression of the phase of intrigue,
and in the extended scene of final, post-catastrophic recognition.

The visual action of this second drama begins in the mind's
eye at a moment when the victorious Heracles is in the midst of
his ritual of purification. He had given the suppliant drama a
bloody ending and now he means to cleanse himself, but suddenly
he hesitates, and the others present can see that he is not himself
(931). As the madness comes upon him, he returns to his previous
mood of vengeance and realizes that his task is only half done.
He decides to interrupt his rites and to finish his retaliation by
killing his remaining enemy; then he can purge all the blood
away in one efficient lustration later on. As soon as he has taken
this resolve he loses all sense of reality and in his delusion he
sets out for Mycenae; he arrives there, finds Eurystheus and his
sons, and kills them one and all. In actuality, of course, he is
killing the wife and the children he had just saved.

Heracles' real crime is a thing wholly imposed and external
to him, but the illusory deed, like Ajax's attack upon the com-
manders, is in a sense still the hero's own. Lyssa has used the
Mycenaean murders as a distraction; they dazzle Heracles and
keep his troubled mind from recognizing the real work of his
hand, and they can do this because they are attractive to him.
Indeed, these imaginary killings are not unlike the killing of
Lycus and his men. They are executed in high good humour
(935; 952) and with a generous plurality. The hero makes no
nice discrimination among the enemies to be attacked and he
shows a violence that shades almost into impiety as he thrusts
away the hand of one who, he supposes, would make a supplicating gesture (967 f.).[20] This imaginary crime has a confusing

[19] Note also the likeness between the child's plea, at 988, to the frenzied Heracles,
and Pentheus' plea, at *Bacchae*, 1118 ff., to the frenzied Agave.

[20] The likeness between the two crimes has inspired the curious theory that
Heracles has been mad from the beginning; so Wilamowitz, Verrall, Grube, and
Dodds ("manic depressive type," *CR* xliii [1929], 99). However, the madness
quite plainly begins at line 931 (to be synchronized with 867). What has confused

air of reality about it because there were tales in which Heracles did slay Eurystheus and his sons, not in dream but in daylight violence. The poet has been careful to give the hallucination a ghastly kinship with the reality, and so the will of the sane Heracles seems always present, even as he commits his insane crime. He thinks that he is punishing the offences of others against himself, while he does punish those of his family against the gods and does also prepare his own grotesque and mysterious punishment.

The 'trip to Mycenae' and the slaughter of his own family have been separated by the poet that we may understand Heracles better, but practically speaking they are one and the same thing, and both were inaugurated by Lyssa. Likewise, both are halted by Athena. In the midst of the reported mayhem a miraculous figure appears; she is unseen, and yet the audience feels as if it had witnessed her epiphany because what the messenger tells them at 1002 ff. explains the cry that was heard at 906 and the shattering of the stage architecture that was witnessed then.[21] Inside the palace Athena had appeared and lifting a stone she had cast it at Heracles, felling him just in time to save him from killing Amphitryon. Her gesture repeats her more famous one during the battle with the giants and so reaffirms the statement of the second prologue, that Heracles is somehow an enemy of the gods. It is also the signal for the end

the critics is the gods' usual tact, for they have chosen to destroy Heracles in a fashion that is suitable to him. Violence has always been a part of Heracles' mixed nature, as it is of the nature of all men, and Euripides has shown Heracles' own 'sane' violence in the killing of Lycus and in its double, the fantasy killing of Eurystheus. The point, however, is not that *because* Heracles killed Lycus he was made to kill the children, nor yet that the two had the same cause, i.e. Heracles' madness. The point is that the god-imposed crime of madness has been made like Heracles' own willed acts of violence, because that is the way a poet's gods work. One might compare Phaedra's lust, as external to herself, as Heracles' madness, yet suitable to her heritage and to one aspect of her nature.

[21] I follow Wilamowitz in giving 906 to Amphitryon; there are those who believe that Athena was, at this moment, visible to all, hovering over the palace, but the staging problems (would she then visibly cast a stone? etc.) seem to militate against this. On the other hand, I see no reason to go to the opposite extreme and insist that there were no spectacular effects at all, when the partial destruction of the palace, so frank in its symbolism, could easily have been given a physical indication. For the conservative view, see A. M. Dale, *WS* lxix (1956), 101, where it is argued that 906 belongs to the chorus and does not refer to Athena at all, but to Heracles, the argument being based upon the purely subjective grounds that the line is 'out of key' for Amphitryon.

of the catastrophe. Heracles sinks at once into unconsciousness and the madness inaugurated by the two lesser divine figures passes away; it has been shaped and limited by the interruption of the daughter of Zeus. Athena's interference thus formally defines and ends the vengeance action which is also heaven's punishment of Heracles, though his true punishment, his remorse, is yet to be felt. Her appearance snatches Amphitryon from death and proves that Hera's rage is not the only force at work in heaven. Evidently more than one deity has the ear of Zeus, for Athena expresses in action the same quality of mercy that Lyssa's words had betrayed.

When the *eccyclema* appears the audience is presented with a ghastly heap of bodies and the figure of their destroyer. The deaths of Megara and the children have already been made horrible by the messenger's narrative, but they have at the same time very carefully been made tragic rather than melodramatic, for the poet has unobtrusively insisted that this fate was not only necessary to heaven but freely chosen by those who have suffered it. He has imaged Heracles like an Erinys with a torch (928) and has made him call up the very *keres* that Megara had chosen as brides for her sons (870; cf. 481); he has also shown the principals of the first action now vainly hiding at an altar (974; 984), or vainly supplicating the mortal champion they had preferred to Zeus Soter (986 ff.).[22] The spectator has thus been instructed in how he is to support the hideous spectacle of these deaths, but he is prey to an unresolved sense of pity and terror, for he does not yet know how he is to regard their living agent. The stage situation is deadfully misshapen, and it seems plain that the true *pathos* of this second tragedy is still to be enacted.

Heracles has appeared, as the vengeance hero should, among the corpses of his victims, unaware as yet that they are not those of Eurytheus and his sons. There he stands, as Orestes did at the end of the *Choephoroi*, but with two telling differences in the fixed tableau. Heracles is bound, not free; he is propped up against a

---

[22] The same kind of effect accrues from the ugly irony of 462 ff., where Megara spoke of the patrimony the boys should have had: a place in Eurystheus' palace for the first (463), who later dies as a proxy for the first of Eurystheus' sons (982); the club, called a δόσις ψευδής at 471, for the second who is to die by that club at 993–4; the kingdom conquered by the bow (472–3) for the third, who dies, shot through by that bow, at 1000.

pillar, deep in the tranced sleep that has followed his fit of madness. Instead of showing the fallen to the crowd, describing their crimes and ordering their disposal while he, like some Cresphontes, prepares to mount a throne, Heracles must have the bodies shown to him, and when he has discovered their identity, he sinks down among them and covers up his head. In his speech at 1146–62 he fully recognizes his victims, his deed and his guilt, and his wish for death marks the full arc of his overturn in an action that began just after his victory as a giver of life. The speech also serves, by a kind of enjambment, as the opening monologue of the <u>final rescue drama</u>, for it describes the despair of the one who is to be its isolated principal.

The last drama of the *Heracles* is formally a rescue action in which a desolate hero is found by his champion in a place of death and removed by him to a place of life. The role of the helpless exile, the Philoctetes role, is taken here by the world's strongest man; the champion is one whom this victim has only now saved from hell, and the physical threat is one that comes not from outside, but from the victim's own guilt and his desire for suicide. The rescue in this case is ostensibly achieved by persuasion (like that of the Euripidean *Philoctetes*, perhaps), but in fact Heracles rejects all the arguments that his champion proposes and finds his way alone to a decision to return to the world. It is his rhetoric that catches the ear, and as he argues with himself, he returns to the subjects that occupied Megara and Amphitryon in the opening section of this tripartite play. At first he sees the petty and vicious god of his foster-father's blasphemy, and with this vision before him he chooses, like Amphitryon, to die. (Compare his, 'Who could worship a god like that?' of Hera at 1307–8, with Amphitryon's, 'Either you are stupid or you are unjust' to Zeus at 347, and note that this frame of mind causes him to claim Amphitryon for his father, 1265.) Theseus unwittingly provokes a realignment in Heracles' thought, however, by seeming to agree with him. In his desolation Heracles had imagined Hera as a kind of monster, but when Theseus seconds him, and continues with an expression of the vulgar notion that gods are not merely anthropomorphic but morally anthropoid (1314 ff.), Heracles revolts.

Theseus had fallen into a version of the argument of Phaedra's nurse, and had hoped to show that the existence of suffering among the gods makes it hubris in a man to try to do anything but suffer himself. As examples of divine suffering he mentioned two that have epic associations, adultery and the chaining of parents by sons, thinking evidently of the anguish of Hephaestus over Aphrodite's infidelity, of the impatience of Hera on her magic throne, and of Cronus' experience at the hands of Zeus. Heracles answers reasonably enough that conditions in heaven are not relevant to human behaviour (1340 ff.). From this premise he concludes that in his own case he must act according to his own secular sense of honour and good fame, which means that he must give up the anodyne of suicide because death would be cowardice. Between premise and conclusion, however, he pauses to say that anyway his friend is mistaken about the nature of heaven. Gods do not suffer, for there are neither crimes nor punishments among them; divinity is perfect and complete, its actions all are *themis*. He too refers to the semi-comic Olympus of Homer when he says:

> I do not think that gods desire unsanctioned marriages
> or try to fetter one another; this I never have
> and never will believe, nor do I think
> that one is master of another, for a god who is God
> wants nothing. It is the poets who invent
> the wretched tales you tell.

(1340–5)

These lines about the gods have struck many critics as being seriously at odds with the rest of the play. They are an attack upon mythology, it is said, in the mouth of a mythic figure and therefore they must either stand clean outside the play (as the musing of the poet) or they must have been planted here to indicate that everything just witnessed, including the speaker himself, is an impossible fiction.[23] It is not necessary, however, to take either of these positions. The lines themselves belong to a recognized class of ancient passages in which a speaker decides not to attack but to select and to censor his mythic truths; they are like Pindar's lines on Heracles at *Olympia* ix. 41–2; they are like his version of the feast of Tantalus in *Olympia* i, and like the

---

[23] Grube and Conacher, among recent writers, take the lines to be extra-dramatic, an aside made by Euripides himself; Greenwood (op. cit., p. 64), after Verrall, insists that they are the poet's way of saying that the entire Heracles story is an absurd impossibility.

Euripidean Iphigeneia's imitation of that latter passage (*IT* 386 ff.). Only a mythic fundamentalist would construe them as a rejection of all mythology, and the relevant question to ask here is what effect their qualifications have upon the particular myth of this particular tragedy.

The minimal myth in this case is as follows: Zeus chose to engender a half-mortal son, and made Alcmene his mother; Hera set labours for that son that were difficult but beneficial to man and honourable for Heracles (labours which can also be described as fated, 828); Heracles was successful, and then when the labours were finished Hera, with the consent of Zeus, sent Iris and Lyssa against him; he was driven mad and forced to become an agent of death for his own wife and family. Athena put a stop to Heracles' madness in time to keep him from killing Amphitryon; Theseus, released from the underworld, appeared to interrupt Heracles' suicide and to lead him off to Athens.

This group of gods, as the play presents them, are easily reconciled with the Heraclean statement of faith. Nothing has suggested that they have experienced pain or anguish or humiliation in their mutual relations, that they have revolted against one another, or have formed illicit alliances among themselves. On the contrary, there seems to be a well-oiled anthropomorphic polytheism here that works on the principle of enlightened self-interest, just as it should. We have been given no reason to suppose that the total effect of Heracles' success, Hera's wrath, Lyssa's unwillingness, Athena's intervention, and Hades' carelessness (or compliance) is not the general will of heaven; indeed, we are encouraged to think that Zeus has sanctioned everything (827–32; 1086–7; 1127; 1263).[24] There

---

[24] Like Theseus in the lines he is refuting, Heracles is here describing conditions in heaven, and so his words about divine marriages have no relevance to Zeus' union with Alcmene. Another point sometimes cited, Lyssa's οὐδ' ἥδομαι at 846, can hardly be said to indicate suffering or revolt among the immortals. Critics like to pretend that Heracles' announcement that gods do not put fetters upon one another means that all the polytheistic divinities must be forever in literal harmony, like some great angel chorus. They forget that each separate god will have his own function and will not simply move and speak in meaningless reduplication of all the other divinities. One will initiate, another terminate, but this is not evidence of strife in heaven. The ultimate cause of the modern failure to understand this play, however, is a pervasive Voltairianism; thus Greenwood can argue that Athena's failure to avert the slaughter of Megara and the children, as well as that of Amphitryon, is so outrageous that it must represent the poet's open satire upon the gods

is only one detail in the total fiction of the play that cannot be adjusted to Heracles' words, and this is the suggestion that Hera was jealous of a mortal rival for the favours of Zeus. Such an emotion would quite clearly be outside the ken of a 'god who is God'; the motif is plainly one that belongs among the poets' 'wretched tales', and if it were essential to the action here, then there would in truth be a conflict between that action and the beliefs of its principal. It must be noted, however, that jealousy of this sort is attributed to the goddess only once, by Heracles, when he is at his most faithless point of despair (1309–10).

Heracles announces that no one could worship a goddess who had destroyed the best of men just because of one of Zeus' infidelities, but nothing in the tragedy as it is written suggests that anyone is expected to do so. Iris is the voice of Hera in this play; she speaks directly from the machine and she gives the lie to this bit of worldly gossip when she describes Hera's emotion. It is not mortal jealousy of a female, but pure anger against a male that the goddess is said to feel, and the word used (χόλος, 840), has nothing of sexual vindictiveness in it. This is the magnificent, almost personified wrath that sometimes came upon a Homeric warrior from outside himself. The Aeschylean Zeus could feel it, or the Demeter of the Homeric Hymn (*PV* 376; *Hom. h. Cer.* 350); here it belongs also to Iris (841) and is felt in behalf of all the gods (841).

Heracles' statement does not concern itself with the relations of gods and men; it is an attempt to rid the concept of the divine of apparent flaws in power, while maintaining the doctrine of polytheism. There is no reason to suppose that gods such as he describes would not be as jealous of their power, in respect to an encroaching mortality, as the Greek gods always were. Thus the words of this famous passage do not contradict or even correct any part of the present mythic fiction; they only remove one peculiarly sordid interpretation of the divine impulse behind it. In a moment of terrible bitterness Heracles was tempted by the 'jealous Hera' theory, but he knows that heaven does not house such divinities, and he saves himself, turning from suicide to a

(op. cit., p. 87). He may find it outrageous himself, but it is surely a mistake in method to attribute this Lisbon earthquake style of thinking to a poet who has never for a moment shown that he found the existence of evil on earth incompatible with the the idea of the existence of god in heaven.

desire to live, as he repudiates his father's theological error.[25] Heracles accepts the totality of his life as an expression of the will of the self-sufficient heaven he has described, and he moves off stage in final resignation, feeling himself to have been honoured, tortured, and at last deserted by a multiple, incomprehensible divine power that included Hera (1393).

The spectator, however, needs to feel some comprehension, as well as a simple submission to the disasters the playwright has portrayed. If Hera's wrath was not caused by a Homeric jealousy of Alcmene, he will inevitably ask after its true cause. Hera's persecution of Heracles was one of the great facts of Greek religion, and the ancient audience presumably felt much less need of instruction about it than the modern one does, but the poet himself has forced the problem of the cause of Heracles' punishment into the foreground of this play. He showed first the killing of Lycus—a crime against the suppliant plot and an excessive gesture touched with verbal impiety, but an action that was, in a primitive sense, just (732–3). He then made a parody of that deed, with all its violence and unreason highly exaggerated, in the 'Mycenaean killing' of Eurytheus and his sons, but this is at best only a symbolic crime and it is plainly the effect, not the cause, of the heavenly intervention. No specific deed has been mentioned or shown that can be identified as the crime that caught the eye of a punitive heaven, and yet we have been told that Lyssa's driving him mad was a means of 'exacting retribution' (842) from this son of Zeus.

Since divine punishments, especially those described by tragedians, tend to fit the crime, the sensible thing is to look closely at the stated purpose and at the execution of this one. Iris explains that Hera's general intention is to defend the grandeur of the gods by defeating an attempt at grandeur on the part of man (841–2); her specific programme is to defile Heracles with kin-blood (reading Wakefield's κοινόν at 831). The fit of madness is her means, and her total achievement is to change one who was himself a refuge into one who must take refuge with a friend. Such a punishment presumes a Heracles whose consistent

---

[25] The ideas that Zeus could be guilty of disloyalty or could be inadequate in his *arete*, that the gods could be lacking in mother-wit (as the chorus charges, not quite seriously, at 655), are like the notion of Hera's jealousy, and like it are made impossible by Heracles' confession of faith.

good fortune and freedom from stain constituted a kind of conspiracy against Olympus. The threat he offers is, however, both very minor and very great, for it can be checked mechanically with a temporary miasma (note 1324, where he is promised purification in the near future), though it must be punished with the extremest suffering that a man can know.

What Hera achieves in her punishment is the destruction of Heracles' peculiar superiority, that invincible success (*eutychia*) that had made him the most blessed of men (1300; cf. 1306). This is the quality that had brought him his title, *kallinikos* (582), and it was, like his bow, the special gift of heaven. Heracles' inevitable ability to succeed was in fact the sign of his half-portion of divinity, and like all divine gifts, it had been misunderstood, not so much by himself as by others. The hero's double nature[26] has been in question throughout the play; it is a fact that no mortal among the characters has been able to hold comfortably in mind. Both his own family and the old men of Thebes tended in the beginning to believe that Heracles was wholly mortal and yet (here is the danger) they began to treat this 'mortal' as if he were a god. Even when they remembered to call him *Dios pais* they were likely to go on to assert that his own *arete* was far more responsible than his paternity was for the benefactions he had brought to men (696–700; cf. 407, where they make him hold up heaven simply by his εὐανορία; and cf. 475, where Megara says that he made his conquests μέγα φρονῶν εὐανδρίᾳ). Conversely, when Heracles' opportune return from Hades had inspired in the citizens a rush of faith (802–3), they were seen to go too far in the opposite direction and to forget Alcmene's share in the making of this hero. As a result a bloody

---

[26] The mystery of the double nature of Heracles is one of those subtleties of theology that Greek mythology almost accidentally produced. It was of course a commonplace of Greek thought, the everyday way of expressing what the Orphics expressed with their myth of the Titan god-eaters. The only Euripidean innovation here is the alteration of the traditional chronology so as to sharpen the paradox. The poet has moved both Heracles' greatest triumph (the descent to hell) and his greatest humiliation and crime (the madness and kin-slaughter) to the end of his life, so that they will stand as close as possible, both to one another and to his translation to heaven. Another innovation, or at least a deliberate choice of a comparatively recent mythic variant, is the association of Theseus with the descent, so that Heracles' threat to heaven will be increased, and so that he will be saved here by one to whom he had given life. (Note H. Lloyd-Jones, 'Heracles at Eleusis', *Maia* 3, xix [1967], 226, where it is assumed that this association was first made in a 6th cent. Athenian poem about the Nekyia of Heracles.)

act of private vengeance became for them the occasion for a hymn, and so for an ignorant slander upon the true nature of god.

Heracles enters this play having just transgressed the most jealously guarded boundary between gods and men, that of death. He has mirrored the crime of Tantalus, at the opposite end of the cosmic geography, by descending to hell and bringing back not only Cerberus but an incidental hero as well. His whole career has come to its climax in his initiation[27] and his harrowing of hell; he has robbed Death and played *soter* to other mortals; he looks much like another Asclepius, and having now in a sense conferred life, he cannot be left at large. His deeds, his aspect, and his singular good-fortune constitute a threat in themselves, for if they are thought to have been attributes of his mortal part, he will inspire, as Megara's example shows, a Pelagian worship of man and a spread of the godless doctrine of Necessity. And so Heracles had to pay a penalty (cf. μὴ δόντος δίκην, 842); he was forced to make restitution and to render up all that was god in himself.[28] He had to undergo suffering as great as his good fortune had been (1252); he had to return to Hades to be led out by another; he had to appear, naked of all divinity, sinful, weak and even mad—wholly man—before he could be allowed to disappear. In this condition he bears witness (against his wife) to gods who are masters of necessity and chance (1393), and measures the part of himself that was Zeus' by showing us Alcmene's share.

When the *Heracles* closes any mortal pretension to autonomy, knowledge and grandeur that is exclusive of the gods has been destroyed. This, the only Olympian heresy, was expounded by Megara and embodied in the purely mortal Heracles of men's imagination; the first of these figures has been cut down and the second has been stripped of his glory. The play does,

---

[27] The reference to his initiation at 613 is on the surface wholly gratuitous and very probably therefore has some point that we miss through our ignorance of the mysteries. Given the importance of the notion of Heracles' *eutychia*, the presence of the verb εὐτύχησα here seems hardly accidental, and at least it can be said that the hero's recent initiation is made to cap the extreme height of blessedness from which he is brought down.

[28] I find an ironic statement of this necessity at 1232 where Theseus reminds Heracles: '*As a mortal* you do not (have the power to) soil heaven.' Note how all the ironies of 574–82 have prepared for this effect of stripping Heracles of his deeds.

however, in the end work a kind of restoration for humanity, showing a form of self-salvation in which the chastened Heracles is sufficient to himself. There is no monster here but his own momentary cowardice and his own mistaken view of Hera; there is a friend, but he is one who walks the earth now only because Heracles had earlier played the saviour role for him. (Note how Theseus dwells on this fact; 1170; 1221; 1336.) In the final rescue Heracles takes over all three of the conventional parts, playing monster, saviour, and saved in an inner drama in which he wrestles with himself in order to rescue himself. This is why his final scene has been read as a monumental affirmation of Euripides' faith in heroic humanism, and why we must look closely at what the poet has allowed this self-rescuer to salvage of himself.

Heracles escapes paradoxically from his own chosen means of escape, the death that he longs for, but he seems to move only from one part of his wasteland into another. He will travel from Thebes to Athens, and yet remain forever in his ubiquitous Hades of guilt and remorse (see 1397, with its reference to memory; first his crime, then his consciousness of it have been described as a new sort of hell, at 870; 1101; 1119; 1336; 1415). He escapes death and moves into a new life, but that life, with all its outward honours, will be a reduction of what he has known for in his new existence he, the symbol of strength, can shed tears (1355; 1395), he can be called womanish (1411), can feel himself to be like an old man (1401) and can be compared to a child (1424, with its echo to 631). He has been reduced to the level of those he used to champion and he finds that all his great deeds, the glories that made the chorus greet him with song-forms borrowed from Apollo (678), have been capped by his present evil (1280; cf. 575). His bow and his club are hateful to Heracles now (1377 ff.; cf. 570). He has salvaged life and avoided his own charges of cowardice, but he is apparently condemned to wretchedness, for he can forget neither his past grandeurs nor his crime.

The *Madness of Heracles* thus resembles a tetralogy that has lost its satyr play. An opening tragedy is concerned with men who believe that they, along with chance, control the pattern of events, and when they, the faithless, are given an upward reversal and granted the rewards of faith, the suggestion is strong that their principles are right. The universe seems to be ruled by chance or by gods who take no interest in the world. The second play undoes the pragmatic outcome of the first and also destroys its apparent premises, for it is the portrait of an act of worldly intervention made by gods who are powerful and interested in their own prerogatives. This second action shows heaven's exploitation of a single human event for a double purpose, for the vindication of Zeus Soter is combined with the satisfaction of Hera's wrath. The Heracles who must be stripped of his partial divinity before he can become wholly god is used as the agent of destruction in the deaths of those who denied Zeus. As they are destroyed, the faithless suppliants become the substance of their destroyer's punishment, and so their lesser fates are made to serve Zeus in one of his grandest designs, the elevation of his son. The final tragedy works a reconciliation in secular terms and it also repeats and corrects the pattern of the first one.[29] Heracles reverses Megara's direction by moving from death to life; he abandons the palace she was so eager to enter, and he gives himself to his friend instead of to an enemy. The suppliants' escape had led to an anomalous violence, but this second escape allows Heracles to leave the dead behind and to begin a journey that will presumably end in Athenian quietude. The remorse and the misery remain, however, and Heracles' self-salvation proves to be an admirable but an imperfect thing.

A tragic action of rescue ordinarily ended with the translation of the principal to a new state of blessedness; the virgin became a bride, the exile returned home, the imprisoned queen ascended a throne. In this case, however, nothing romantic or satyresque, nothing even of the sombre glare of divinity and fame that marks the end of Philoctetes' exile, has been allowed to touch the hero's departure from Thebes. This is Heracles' second escape from the mouth of hell, but for him it seems that he is about to enter a lower, not a higher phase in his existence. The usual consummation in love, wine, and home is painfully absent here, and this failure of a familiar motif is technically responsible for the

---

[29] Megara's errors about *elpis* were corrected in the first action itself, her errors about god in the second, and those about humans in the third, where Amphitryon's theological errors are also corrected. There are critics who believe that the unifying motif of the play is *philia*, the whole being a correction of Megara's statements about friendship; see J. T. Sheppard, 'The Formal Beauty of the Heracles', *CQ* x (1916), 72 ff. and H. H. O. Chalk, 'ΑΡΕΤΗ and ΒΙΑ in Euripides' *Heracles*', *JHS* lxxxii (1962), 7–18.

desolate effect of the final exit of the principal. An ultimate
fourth action of divine salvation, one that will rescue him even
from his remorse and set him banqueting among the gods, will
soon be produced for Heracles, but of this he knows nothing at
all.[30] The hero is gone, the chorus marches away, Amphitryon
withdraws with the corpses, and then the spectator begins to
recall once more all that he knows about Heracles' life on
Olympus. He remembers Hesiod's joyous lines, and the heavenly
satyr play begins at last, though only on the inner stage of his
imagination.

> Now indeed he is a god; he has escaped from every bane
> and where the Olympians have their homes, there does he live too!
> He will not die, he will not age, for he has lovely Hebe as his own
> and she is child of Zeus and daughter to the golden-sandalled one!
> Whom she once loathed, Queen Hera, goddess of the round white
>   arms,
> hating him beyond all blessed gods or fateful men,
> him she now loves! She honours him far above the rest—
> more than any blessed one, excepting Zeus himself!
>   (*Eoiai*, fragment 25. 26–33, Merkelbach-West)

[30] Any specific reminder of the future would undermine the effect of the hero's
present agony. The poet does, however, occasionally catch the light of the coming
miracle in the facet of a phrase, as when Heracles says that he would like to burn his
body and with it his mortal shame (1151), when he says that his woes stretch up
and touch heaven itself (1240), or when he supposes that in the end a voice will
announce that neither earth nor sea is to receive him and that he will be taken up
to heaven to spin there like another Ixion (1295–8). The apotheosis has been represented symbolically by tableaux in which Heracles was shown as the sleeper awakened, the bound creature unbound, the prostrate one raised (1226; 1395), while the
notion of miraculous youth has been broached in the ode at 637–700, which could
not fail to remind its hearers of the eternal second youth in store for Heracles as
the husband of Youth herself (cf. the reference to *hebe* in the last sung words of the
first stasimon, at 441). With all of these muffled hints compare the open instruction
of the *Heracleidae* (919 ff.):

> Your son, ancient Queen,
> has departed for heaven; the tale
> of his going to hell I can repudiate.
> His flesh was consumed
> by tongues of fire
> and now he lies, luxuriously,
> in a palace all of gold
> at lovely Hebe's side.
> O Hymeneus, thou hast made
> of each the other's best reward!

VIII

ORESTES

THE *Orestes* is perhaps Euripides' most difficult play, and its problems are compounded for the modern reader by the fact that the ancients thought it one of his best.[1] The action is complex, formally repetitious and increasingly sensational, so that terror soon gives way to wonder and then to a perverse pleasure as one exaggerated effect is piled upon another. No situation is allowed to resolve itself in the ordinary tragic way, no character behaves throughout quite as we feel he should, and meanwhile the dramatist seems to stand aside, refusing all aid. These characteristics, however, do not quite explain the unique effect of the play, since moral ambiguity has certainly not been absent from other tragedy, and melodrama likewise has been met before. The real reason why the *Orestes* produces for so many a sense not of pity but of profound revulsion

[1] Aristophanes of Byzantium, in the *Hypothesis*, says τῶν ἐπὶ σκηνῆς εὐδοκιμούντων, χείριστον δὲ τοῖς ἤθεσι, and most moderns agree with the latter phrase. There is, however, one group of critics who see in Orestes and his friends an example of the (positively evaluated) archaic sense of justice. This attempt to read the three central characters as representatives of virtue goes back to Jacob Burckhardt and has been restated more recently by W. Krieg, *De Euripidis Orestes* (diss. Halle, 1934), where it is argued (p. 22 f.) that those who cannot see the killing of Helen as a fine deed have been seduced by Christian principles from the true classical spirit. G. Méautis has gone a step further and found not only virtue but reason in the murderers: 'L'Oreste oppose la raison humaine et les caprices des dieux . . . jamais les hommes n'ont été, à ce point, présentés comme plus justes et plus raisonnables que les dieux' (*L'Oedipe à Colone* [Neuchatel, 1940], pp. 27–8). Other critics insist that the three principals, though perhaps not virtuous, are at least heroic because they are engaged in a despairing attempt to save their own lives (see Howald, *Die gr. Trag.* [Munich, 1930], pp. 167–71; A. Lesky, *WS* liii [1935], 41 ff. and *Die gr. Trag.* [Stuttgart, 1964], pp. 238–42). Another school is represented by Pohlenz, who insists that the desire for vengeance becomes in these characters so strong that it conquers the will to survive and so is a form of madness (*Die gr. Trag.* [Gottingen, 1954], pp. 412–21). For H. G. Mullens the play is a 'pathological study of criminality' which uses its impossible finale to show the audience 'what might have been' (*CQ* xxxiv [1940], 153–8). A. Scarcella (*Dioniso* xix [1956], 266–76) finds that the play is a description of 'folie morale et physique . . . dominée par un pessimisme sans solution', while H. D. F. Kitto avoids all moral evaluation and calls the *Orestes* 'melodrama based on character drawing and character imagined sensationally, not tragically' (*Greek Tragedy*, p. 344).

lies in its most abstract part, its praxis. Every other surviving tragedy is an imitation of an action that is in some sense a success—a divine punishment that reaches its object with terrible accuracy, a self-sacrifice that results in death, a vengeance that ends in blood, or a rescue that sends its principals into actual security and joy. The essential point about even the interrupted catastrophe is that it shall be, in its own terms, an absolute success right up to the penultimate moment when its normal effects are replaced by their successful opposites. Only the *Orestes* makes outright failure its subject, imitating it with a series of actions that one after another go astray or simply disintegrate. Euripides' long experimentation with distorted and aberrant stage forms culminates here in a fantastical plot machine that artfully sticks and jams, first in one part and then in another, until finally it begins to smoke and is replaced by a divine conveyance. The play contains a suppliant action, a rescue, and a mixed rescue and vengeance action, every one of which fails. These failures create a final situation in which those who have tried to escape, together with those who have pursued them, face a common holocaust, and then the holocaust fails too, for a rescue comes from the *machina*, operative for all.

This curious formal structure is built up with infinite care so that it never loses its similarity to genuine tragic plot. Each new peculiarity is insinuated with such skill that it is accepted before its eccentric nature has been recognized. The poet's understanding of the difficulty of the grotesque can be seen in the time he takes to approach his play, for he sets his piece upon an introductory base of 250 lines that postpone the beginning of the action proper until the second episode. This long *prooimion* describes a pair of principals threatened by death, and the first plot begins with the announcement that a champion is at hand who will rescue them. The situation is thus made to take the essential suppliant shape: a threat (from the *demos*) holds principals immobile (though not at an altar) while they await the coming of another power who can offer them a refuge.

Given the circumstances special to this fiction, an action made with one or more rhetorical contests is to be anticipated. The champion will have to be persuaded to take up the cause of the children of Agamemnon, and probably a representative of the 'pursuing' Argive people will try to dissuade him. When the champion is won over, he will either persuade the *demos*, or bully it with a show of public force, unless the plot is to resolve itself into a physical rescue, with the city somehow bamboozled as Electra and Orestes are smuggled away. These are an audience's formal expectations, as the extended prologue comes to its close and the arrival of the protector is announced.

A slight shock occurs at once, for the champion, when he enters, does not stride on like a competent Theseus, or even like a dubious Pelasgus. Instead, he minces forward, branded by costume and wig as a languishing and effete prince who has spent too long in softening Eastern climes. (His key word is ἁβροσύνη, 349, and his shoulder-length curls are confirmed at 1532.) Nevertheless, a traditional scene of decision is soon mounted with this same Menelaus at its centre, wielding the judicial power that belongs to the prince in a suppliant play. Orestes speaks for the persecuted and Tyndareus is brought on to give voice to the opposition. The debate is long and the conflict, as it should, grows more and more bitter. The effect of the confrontation of the two parties is to make the representative of the threat all the more determined, and he leaves the stage having resolved not only to visit his daughter's grave, but to attend the Assembly meeting and there urge a sentence of death for Orestes and his sister. Formally this is all very well, though the discerning listener has been troubled by the fact that Tyndareus, cast in the role of the man of violence, has spoken sensibly of law and the proper maintenance of the polity. Still, he has taken himself off with threats, as this character should, and we wait to see how the champion will act to ensure the old man's final defeat. Orestes frames a last appeal, and then, with victory and safety presumably his, he hears the prince pronounce himself too weak to be of any aid!

Menelaus makes a few windy promises as to moral support (no one is surprised to learn later that he did not begin to fulfil them), but he frankly refuses to do anything or risk anything for his brother's children. And that is the end of the 'suppliant' action. The helpless principals are as helpless as before; indeed they are faced now with a stronger threat, since Tyndareus has joined the death party, and they have lost their single hope. The monumental scene of confrontation and persuasion (it is 450 lines long, while the comparable scene in the *Children of*

Heracles is 287 lines, the comparable pair of scenes in the Euripidean *Suppliants* only 277) has ended in total failure. Its rhetoric
has not simply gone wrong, it has gone for nothing, for the
champion has refused to be a champion, not out of regard for
the counter-arguments of Tyndareus, but simply because he is
greedy for power and sees that his own advantage will best be
served by complete inaction. He does not mean to enter into the
case of his relatives on either side; he means to see Orestes and
Electra put to death by the city's command, and then he means
to take the palace, the throne, and the land for himself (1058–9).

Menelaus leaves the stage and the educated play-goer expects
a choral ode that will direct his reflections upon what he has just
seen. The music, however, does not begin. Instead, a new
character runs (726) down the parodos and into the playing area,
labelled by his breathlessness as Menelaus was by his languid
approach. It is Pylades, and he is presented as being everything
that Menelaus was not; he is young and strong and masculine,
and though he is not related to Orestes he is apparently a true
example of *philia*. Thus the audience is led to assume that
Pylades will now do what Menelaus would not, that he will play
the champion and rescue his friends from the death that
threatens them. He is not a ruler, of course, and he cannot effect
the almost ritualistic rescue that raises suppliants and leads them
into the safety of the city's succour. He will have to operate in
some other way, and his arrival thus serves notice that a rescue
intrigue will now be substituted for the suppliant action that has
so elaborately collapsed. The dramatist, however, is using his
plot as a means to force Orestes' sense of confusion upon the
audience, and he therefore builds this new expectation as he
did the old, in order that it may be baffled. The scene that
follows Pylades' entrance is indeed a version of the traditional
one in which escape is plotted, but from the beginning it refuses
to follow the usual pattern. Pylades in no way takes command;
instead he remains wholly subordinate as a new plan is made,
and he seems far more interested in the arrival of Helen than in
the departure of his friends. It is Orestes, the weak, mad, bloodstained suppliant *manqué* who now attempts to save himself.
He decides to confront his enemy, the *demos*, in a kind of single
combat in the Assembly; he means to put himself into the monster's jaws and there defend himself so well that he will be freely

released and sent off with new power and an enhanced reputation. According to his scheme Pylades is not, after all, to be a champion, he is merely a secondary figure who will lead Orestes to the scene of battle.

Only when this new survival plan has replaced the one that collapsed with Menelaus' exit does the poet stop to write an ode for his chorus to sing. It is performed during the time that Orestes and Pylades are attending the Assembly, and it is composed so as to maintain an unconscious expectation of good news at its end.[2] When the song is finished, however, Electra appears to receive a messenger who will, unlike any other of his breed, describe the hero in a completely abortive offstage action. A second *agon* of persuasion has been attempted and this time the victim, instead of failing to persuade his champion, has failed to persuade his enemies, those who would pursue him and put him to death.

The messenger speech is not long, and it has none of the visual or epic embellishments that usually bring delight to such a performance. There are no leavetakings by the shore, no battles at sea, and above all, there are no miracles—no foam-spawned bulls, no hair-raising voices that fill mountain glens, no flights of doves or sudden gusts of wind. In quick succession the messenger mimics five speakers at a public meeting and records the popular response. He then reports the passage of a decree with an amendment, and he is finished. What he has described is a new failure which, like the earlier one, is complete and yet unsatisfactory even as a disaster. Orestes' speech in the assembly was apparently neither good nor bad; it was not marked by any drama—the hero did not, as he had feared, suffer a fit of madness while he stood on the *bema*, and he was neither attacked nor acclaimed. His address, in fact was redundant, since its argument had already been made by the old independent from the Hill.

---

[2] As a general rule a moment of hope, if it is to be deceived, is acclaimed by a joyous chorus (e.g., the chorus that follows Oedipus' Son of Tyche speech at *OT* 1086 ff. or the chorus at *Helen* 1107 ff.). The short song at *Orestes* 807 ff. is on the contrary filled with dark Aeschylean reminders (note especially the echoes of 819–24 to *Eum.* 459-61, *Agam.* 1493, the close of the *Choephoroi*, and to the Binding Song of the *Eumenides*) about the pedigree of Orestes' guilt. The overt instruction of the song is that Orestes' present attempt to save himself by altering his fame is doomed to failure and this fact causes a hyper-sophisticated audience to think that this lesson in pessimism is only the dramatists' trick to make his subsequent joy more extreme.

The only thing accomplished was an alteration in the form of the death sentence, and so we reach a point well past mid-play (at line 959 in a play of 1693 lines) to find that the threatened principals have, after a double exertion, succeeded only in substituting their own swords for the people's stones. They are still condemned to die.

At line 960, then, the play begins afresh. Electra laments and then a third attempt at escape from the catastrophe is inaugurated. The new episode at first strikes the onlooker as being a bit shopworn, but he soon notices a curious understatement in it, and then something more seriously negative. This is overtly a 'let's live and die together' scene, the ordinary function of which is to prolong a recognition scene's depiction of the emotion of love but to touch it now with terror (as at *Helen* 835 ff. or *IT* 1002 ff.). Here, however, there has been no preceding miracle of recognition with its inevitable intimations of success and of the love of god, and it is notable that there is also no one here who offers to die for anyone else. Electra, instead of making an offer makes a demand, saying not, 'Let me die for you' (as Iphigenia did) but 'Won't you relieve me of the task of killing myself?' (1037–8). And Orestes somewhat impatiently responds that his mother's blood will suffice his hands and she must do away with herself (1039–40). A little later Pylades interrupts: Orestes is wrong if he thinks that his friend means to survive him (1070). This sounds like the motif we have been expecting, and indeed a pair of fine speeches are exchanged, ostensibly on the subject of Pylades' death,[3] but when they are finished they prove to have been a mere exercise. Pylades in his final line reveals the pressing thought that had made him preface all this by shouting, 'But wait!' (ἐπίσχες, 1069, the formula for interruption). 'Let me die with you', was really 'Let's find a way to pay off Menelaus before we die' (1099), which was another way of saying 'Let's make Helen die with us' (1105), and that has led directly to 'Let's make Helen die and we will live!' Pylades does not propose a love sacrifice at all; what he has in mind is a vengeance killing (1131).

---

[3] On the anomalies in this scene, see Strohm, *Euripides*, p. 123. The tragic quality of the exchange between the friends is to a degree undermined by the fact that Pylades, as an exile, would not be sacrificing by his death all the things that Orestes here urges him to keep.

At this point Pylades does for a moment take the lead. He has the details of an intrigue worked out and it proves to be a bloody variant of the programme Orestes has already failed at, for Pylades also means to convert the threat—the hatred of the *demos*—into its opposite, praise. He means to do this, however, not by words but by action; he will not defend the murder of Clytemnestra, he will repeat it, hoping to obliterate the old unpopular crime with a new and better one, the murder of Helen.

> Kill *her*, and a new title will be yours—
> no longer 'Orestes who murdered his mother'
> but 'Killer of Helen, the Murderess'.
>
> (1140–2)

Pylades seems to look forward to a final scene in which he and Orestes will come wheeling out on the *eccyclema*, the body of Helen at their feet, to be met by a cheering crowd of citizens. He does, however, have a premonition of failure, too, for he finishes his proposal by saying, 'Unless I can draw a black sword on Helen, I do not wish to live, so if we fail to kill her, we set fire to the palace and we perish in the flames! This way, whether we live or die, we will do it gloriously and will earn our portion of fame' (1147–52).

The admixture of vengeance blood in an escape intrigue is an anomaly, for escape gained by means of vengeful murder can no longer evoke the simple pity and terror proper to the ancient release from demonic evil.[4] Electra almost makes this point, for she implies that Pylades' plan, though good as vengeance, is bad as a form of rescue. She has a sounder sense of political reality than her future husband does; she does not believe in the new popularity that is to release them from the threat of death, and she sees that Menelaus is apt to continue to be a significant

---

[4] When escapes were from monsters, as in *Andromeda*, a killing was sometimes (though not always, viz. *Cyclops*) necessary, but this agonistic deed was like Heracles' wrestling with Thanatos and had nothing in common with vengeance murder as it is portrayed in tragedy. The mortal opponent, if there was one in the normal rescue action, was properly fooled or persuaded or bullied, like the fathers of Andromeda and Hesione, or like Thoas and Theoclymenus, but he was not killed. It is notable that in the *Antiope*, Dirce's death was explicitly separated from the boys, being wrought not by them but by the gods, while divine intervention prevented what would have been a vengeance killing of Lycus.

enemy. And so she separates the two parts of the programme, retaining the killing of Helen as their vengeance act, but adding the seizure of Hermione, and the blackmail of Menelaus by a threat to her life, as the proper mechanism of release.

Electra believes that, with a sword at Hermione's throat, they can yet force the man whose wife they will have killed to be their saviour from the mob. The plan is cruel and psychologically uncertain, but it is based on a presumption of success, and in its formal outline it is not unlike Iphigeneia's use of the image of Artemis to force aid from Thoas for her escape. At any rate, this idea of taking his cousin hostage seems so genial to Orestes that he breaks out in praise of Electra's masculine wit, and in congratulatory admiration of the friend who may, if all goes well, have such a woman for his wife (1204–8). The double rescue-vengeance intrigue is now complete, and the scene ends with a prayer to Agamemnon, after which the young men enter the palace and Electra and the chorus mount guard.

A standard vengeance-play lyric interlude follows, as the chorus and one character wait in suspense outside a palace where a murder is to take place. Helen's cries from within are made after the pattern of the Sophoclean Clytemnestra, and they produce an exaggerated echo of Electra's response in the older play. The single Sophoclean imperative, 'Strike again!' (Soph. *El.* 1415) becomes here a frenzied 'Kill! Cut! Thrust! Ply the two-edged double-jawed sword!' (1033–4). Just at this point, however, the scene takes a new turn, for it is interrupted as Hermione comes stepping gently into the trap that is waiting for her. She is young, and being Helen's daughter, she must be beautiful; this is the first and last time that her voice sounds in the play (in the prologue she was mute), and it is a voice unlike any other to be heard. Innocence, sympathy, duty and concern make up its melody, an almost shocking sound, coming hard upon Electra's murderous screams. Hermione willingly, naturally, offers herself to her unfortunate cousins, wishing to help in any way she can, and the final meaning of her candid promise is pointed up by Electra's irony, ugly in its intent but beautiful in effect. 'You and you alone can confer on us salvation's prize', she purrs as she thrusts the hostage through the door (1343). 'Take such salvation as resides in me', answers the girl (1345). and Orestes, deceived by his own irony, repeats the idea a third time from within the palace, saying 'It is we who are to be saved, not you!' (1348).

As soon as the door shuts behind Hermione, a terrible confusion breaks out, for the chorus decides to cover the noise of the conspirators by shouting and wailing as they wait for evidence that Helen is truly dead. The stage action recently has been so nearly that of the traditional vengeance plot that the audience waits with the women, sharing their certainty that they are about to see a bloody body on display (1357–8).[5] 'Look, the door is opening', the chorus calls, and the audience cranes its neck in order not to miss the familiar shudder, but then the anti-climax comes: 'Be quiet, it is one of the Phrygian slaves, from whom we can learn all that has happened inside' (1366–8).[6] The spectator sinks back, still anticipating the eventual glimpse of gore, only to be confronted with something far more sensational than the corpse he was looking for.

A singing, dancing, trembling eunuch bursts out from the palace. He is one of Helen's fan-bearers, got up to represent all the supposed depravity and effeminacy of the East. Slippered and plump and sweating with fear, he is the only tragic messenger we know who has lost the power to speak in ordinary iambics. Indeed, his parody of the late Euripidean lyric monody is so exaggerated that his gestures, if they matched his music, must have been the most outrageous ever seen on the classic stage. At first it seems that the poet is amusing himself by having an action that was swift and sinister prolonged and dissipated by the delaying speech habits of the narrator, but gradually we realize that the events related by this bizarre messenger are themselves all wrong. The actions described are neither swift nor sinister, and they have not produced a victory for the vengeance heroes. The Phrygian's style proves to be no more confused than is the situation within the palace, for we learn that

---

[5] It might be argued that the ἐν δόμοις κείμενον of 1358 supports the notion (strongly urged recently by Hourmouziades, *Production and Imagination in Euripides* [Athens, 1965], pp. 93 ff.) that the *eccyclema* brings a piece of interior space outside.

[6] The scholiast suggested that this speech was a later interpolation, added to cover the fact that the actor who played the Phrygian no longer wanted to make the required entrance by a leap from the eaves. Page follows him (*Actors' Interpolations*, p. 42) but A. M. Dale makes a strong argument in defence of the lines (*WS* lxix [1956], 103). There is no need to suppose that the Phrygian's 'leap' describes his entrance; it will describe an earlier act that he pantomimes now in his dance.

the murder of Helen has turned into an ill-contrived farce.
Heroes have wept false tears and prostrated themselves, fleeing
slaves have tripped over one another and have been locked into
closets only to burst out again just as the knife was at the victim's
throat. The slaves have been routed, but an inopportune
entrance by the hostage has interrupted the killing a second time.
The assassins evidently dropped their victim in order to seize
Hermione, and when they turned back for a third time to the
business of cutting her throat, they found that Helen had
disappeared. Where she went or where she is now the messenger
cannot say; all he knows is that if she fails to reappear, the Trojan
War will have been for all concerned a profitless affair (1500–1).

When the Phrygian finishes his 133-line song we are already
257 lines beyond the moment when the assassins entered the
palace to do their deed of vengeance, and nothing has been
accomplished. (The double murder in the *Choephoroi* is finished
in 137 lines, which include a chorus that reflects upon the deed,
and the whole murder section of the Sophoclean *Electra* is 132
lines long.) Orestes now bounds out of the palace (ἐπτοημένῳ ποδί,
1505) and he neither bears a corpse nor shows a bloody hand as
his namesake does in the Sophoclean play (*El.* 1422). He has
been, for the fourth time, distracted from the killing of Helen,
for he is fearful that an alert might go out. He is in pursuit of the
Phrygian and when he finds him he toys with him briefly, then
sends him indoors, and announces that he has, after all, no reason
to be afraid of Menelaus. He has remembered that the possession of Hermoine gives him power and so at last he reminds
himself of the job left undone within the palace, and hurries
back inside, talking now of two corpses, though he has not yet
slaughtered even one.

Soon smoke appears from within and the spectator, remembering Pylades' words at 1149–50, is forced to conclude that the
murder of Helen has once more been frustrated. A quick
search has apparently produced no sign of her, and the longed-
for vengeance has dissolved into thin air. The conspirators,
knowing their time is short, are prepared now to destroy the
palace, but they have taken the one weapon they still can use—
Hermione—and they appear next, grouped in readiness on the
roof. Orestes is at the centre, holding his sword to Hermione's
throat, and Electra and Pylades flank him, each with a torch

and ready to consume their defeat in fire, if Electra's blackmail, their last salvation plan, should fail.

The news of the young people's exploits has of course reached Menelaus by now, and he returns to the stage. He has been told that Helen is dead, and this misconception ought to play into the hands of the principals, for it should make their threat to Hermione seem the more actual. Cruel as they have shown themselves to be, they have not, however, guessed at the depraved cruelty of their adversary, and so they fail once more. Electra's astute plan goes wrong because Menelaus will not give up his chance at the Argive throne, just to purchase his daughter's life. Orestes makes the mistake of announcing that he means not only to live but to rule (1600), and Menelaus, who is waiting for reinforcements from the city, plays for time. He contradicts himself and leads Orestes on to hope that he will capitulate. He provokes the boy to angry taunts and so postpones the decision a little longer, but at last Orestes realizes that Menelaus is quite ready to sacrifice Hermione if he must. At the same time he sees a band of armed Argives crowding into the orchestra, and he knows that for a second time a hope of salvation built upon his uncle has collapsed. 'You coward, you have ruined yourself!' (1617) he shouts, and gripping his sword ready for the slaughter of the girl he turns to his accomplices with the command, 'Fire the house!' In this moment Menelaus too becomes aware of the presence of the soldiers behind him and he calls out to them, ordering an attack upon the palace and demanding the death of one who, as long as he is alive, will be a blot upon the fame of this noble city (1624).[7] Menelaus' strategy has proved to be magnificent; his kinsmen will be removed, the throne will be empty, and he will be able to pose as the saviour of Argos. If his supporters are preternaturally quick, he may even get his daughter back almost unharmed.

[7] Lloyd-Jones' change of ζῆν to ζῶν in 1624 brings sense to this line and makes it what it obviously is, Menelaus' call for the death of Orestes at the hand of someone other than himself (CR N.S. vii [1957], 97–8). Apollo's words at 1625 prove that Menelaus is in an attitude of defiance when the god interrupts, and this fact is borne out by the Hypothesis, ἐπεβάλλετο τὰ βασίλεια πορθεῖν (16-17); cf. Pap. Oxy. xxvii (1962), 2455, fr. 4, Col. iv and p. 55. This means that there is no reason to quarrel, as most critics do, with Orestes' command to fire the palace. Menelaus' arriving reinforcements are visible to the men on the roof, and as far as they can see the game is lost. Menelaus' continuing resistance means that his initial response to the threat of Hermoine was his genuine one: 'Go ahead. You will suffer for it!' (1597). When he next says,

The orchestra fills with soldiers; Menelaus' gesticulations are silhouetted against the palace front while on the roof the sword gleams and the torches swoop towards the architecture's flammable parts. Then a golden chariot swings through the sky and in it a radiant pair is seen to sit—Apollo and the Helen who had so strangely disappeared.[8] The god first countermands Menelaus' attack, then turns to Orestes, who still holds his sword but is frozen in an attitude of amazement. Apollo explains that he has rescued Helen by the order of Zeus and that, on the strength of a divine pun (1635), she is to live from this day on among the immortals, a saviour god like her brothers. Heaven now takes her back, after having made use of her to diminish the numbers of mankind, and Menelaus is to find another wife. Enough of Helen; as for Orestes, he is to leave the Argive land and begin his traditional exile, which will take him in due time to Athens and the Areopagus where he will be acquitted by the gods. He is to marry Hermione, and Pylades is to have Electra; Menelaus will leave the rule of Argos to Orestes and go himself to Sparta, where he will be exceedingly rich. The emnity of the

'No, never that!' (1598), he is stalling, as he is later when, by crying out irrelevantly to Helen, he avoids making the promise that would save his daughter but lose him the throne (1613). What then of his ἔχεις με at 1617, which has been taken as the proof of his cowardly surrender? It may be a feint, one further attempt to preserve the palace and the girl, made by a man who does not realize that his reinforcements have at this moment arrived. It may mean not 'I give in', but 'You have me in a difficult spot' (so Strohm, op. cit., p. 88, note 2). A third possibility is that it refers only to the immediately preceding remark. In this case the exchange goes as follows: 'How I have suffered!' 'And all for nothing, too!' 'You have me there!' (1616–17). Menelaus complains, Orestes taunts him with Helen's disappearance (echoing the eunuch at 1500–2), and then goes on in good stichomythic style to twist his opponent's bitter admission ἔχεις με into σαυτὸν σύ γ' ἔλαβες, 'You have defeated yourself' (i.e. 'You are the cause of your loss'). A full summary of the difficulties to be found in this passage, and of the solutions proposed, is given by G. A. Seeck (*Hermes*, xcvii [1969], pp. 9 ff.); the conclusion there urged is that the entire motif of firing the palace (and therefore lines 1149–52, 1541–4; 1593–6, 1618–20) should be deleted as interpolated matter.

[8] Murray deleted 1631–2 and so removed Helen from the finale, but the excuse for excising the lines lay only in their repetition of the phrase ἐν αἰθέρος πτυχαῖς which appears also at 1636; Page (op. cit., pp. 41–2) believes the lines to be late, but still can in conscience only classify them as a 'highly probable instance of interpolation for the sake of spectacle'. There is in fact no reason why Euripides should not have put Helen in the *mechane*, and no reason why he could not have repeated the phrase; see the comments of di Benedetto ad loc. and also A. Spira (*Untersuch. zum Deus ex Machina* [Kallmünz, 1960], p. 144). For other views on staging see M. Bieber, *Gnomon* viii (1932), 480 ff.; A. Frickenhaus, *Die altgr. Bühne* (Strassburg, 1917), p. 15; H. Bulle, *Untersuch. an gr. Theatern* (Munich, 1928), p. 225.

Argives, which has been the overt problem of this play, Apollo promises to put right, since the murder of Clytemnestra was done by his command. When the god's speech is done, the four mortals on the roof regroup as two bridal pairs while from the ground Menelaus sends his goddess-wife a final salute. The chorus cries out to Victory and the aerial chariot swings out of sight, as the most complicated finale of classical tragedy comes to its end.

Such is the plot of the *Orestes*. In its three actions, Orestes has failed as a 'suppliant', failed as a rescue hero, failed as a vengeance killer, and failed as a destroyer of himself and his house. Menelaus has failed twice over as a rescuer, Helen has failed as a vengeance victim, and Hermione has offered herself as a saviour but has been taken instead as a victim of those she meant to aid. Tyndareus has failed as a representative of force, and the *demos* likewise has refused to take on its role as villain. Arguments have failed to persuade and swords have been unable to draw blood; all this bootless turmoil culminates in civil-war, kin-murder, self-immolation, and the destruction of state property, and then every one of these disasters fails. Apollo comes, the wedding march begins, and catastrophe becomes blessedness in the twinkling of an eye. The effect is perverse to the point of absurdity, but after a moment's rebellion the spectator realizes that this final reversal is no more unreasonable than everything else he has seen. The entire play has been an assault upon his educated expectation, and the question is: What did the dramatist mean by indulging in such behaviour? In order to answer this question we must return to the symbolic spectacle, the opinionated speech, and the poetic echoes and images that have accompanied this extraordinary conflation of plots.

The opening scenes are of course always of primary import-ance in fixing the ethical and emotional tone of a play, but the unusually long *prooimion* of the *Orestes* is peculiarly worthy of study. It consists of a prologue closely linked to the first episode by a dramatic parodos, so that the effect is of one long whole. This extended introduction is mechanically superfluous to the move-ment of the plot[9] but magnificent in itself, and quite unlike

---

[9] The only element of these two scenes necessary to the bare plot is the removal of Hermione from the palace, and this is a manoeuvre which could have been achieved in a very few lines. It certainly does not require Helen's presence on stage,

anything else in extant tragedy. Helen interrupts, Hermione interrupts, the chorus interrupts, but this is in essence one long, intense exchange between Electra and Orestes. The two are isolated by their guilt and by the destruction of their house; there are no children, no parents, no brothers and sisters,[10] no city, and no duty to dissipate the concentration of their fraternal love. It is strong, reciprocal, and dreadfully intimate, and it has been brought to this pitch of expression by illness and by crime.

In these paired opening scenes the dramatist expresses the peculiar situation of his principals with a series of visual surprises. Brother and sister are seen to take up postures that are private and unguarded, and they make gestures that have nothing of the hieratic or ceremonial about them. They are brought down and forced upon the audience's sympathies in a way that no other tragic characters are, and this fact is given material embodiment in the décor, for the stage movements here do not take as their focus an altar, tomb, or palace door. Instead it is a low cot that fixes the choreography of the whole sequence, an unpretentious bed (κλινίδιον, *Hypoth.* 11) at the foot of which there is a stool (ibid. 12). During part of the time the audience spies upon the hero as he sleeps, and watches his sister sit at his side in a posture that is in fact much more astonishing than his. Heracles and Philoctetes do likewise sleep on stage, though not thus comfortably stretched out upon an every-day piece of furniture; Phaedra and Alcestis have litters, though they do not sleep, but who besides old Oedipus simply finds a convenient place to sit on the tragic stage? Yet here sits Electra on her stool.

During roughly half the opening sequence the prince remains asleep, occasionally tossing, and his visual presence affects all the sounds that come from the stage. Electra will presumably rise to deliver her prologue speech, but she will pitch her voice to an unusually low tone and the entire straining audience will become her accomplice in her loving concern for silence. Helen's speech will likewise take on a special note in recognition of the sleeper's prerogative, while the whole of the parodos is

---

as the Sophoclean *Electra* demonstrates, for the movements of Chrysothemis are there exactly the same as Hermoine's here.

[10] Chrysothemis must be presumed to be alive, but for the purposes of the dramatist she does not exist.

built upon the choreographic and musical conceit of the chorus that tiptoes and whispers. Here the poet has amused himself by giving Electra's friends a song that must conventionally be sung at a very high pitch and therefore ordinarily as loudly as women can sing. His chorus must maintain this pitch, in great contrast to Electra's low tones, but yet sing so as barely to be heard.[11] By the time Orestes is ready to awaken, then, the whole theatre is in a conspiracy to keep him asleep and so has been given an active share in Electra's tenderness.

In the exchange that follows the waking of the sleeper, the two figures on the stage touch one another again and again and their speech is full of affection. Electra lifts Orestes, pressing her side to his (223), and then she puts him back; she smooths his hair and perhaps wipes his face (225); she helps him to his feet and then, when the madness comes, she seizes him and tries to force him back upon the couch (258). Her brother strikes her, since she appears to him as one of his pursuing furies, and she moves away and covers her head, but she is drawn back when the frenzy is gone. Orestes now repays his sister's tenderness with a like return. He is ashamed of being always the receiver of her benefactions, and he makes himself feel her suffering instead of his own as he urges upon her all the physical indulgences that he himself most needs—rest, a bath, and food (301 ff.). She protests his concern, promises to live and die with him, but then with true self-abnegation agrees to take care of herself as well as of him and goes inside the palace. He, reassured, falls back upon his couch as the opening scenes come to an end.

This long sick-bed tableau is an evocation of mutual physical tenderness that has no parallel in surviving Attic tragedy. Love is the subject of the traditional recognition scene and of some scenes of self-sacrifice, but recognition is usually made to melt very quickly into intrigue or resolution of some other type, and scenes of sacrifice tend to produce a contest.[12] The final scene

[11] The Scholiast B at 176 says: 'This song is sung to the strings called the "furthest" and is of the highest possible pitch. This high tone is contrary to Electra's commands, and so she rebukes the chorus.'

[12] There are brief moments evocative of a similar emotion in some of the exchanges between Antigone and the old Oedipus in *OC*; cf. also Phaedra and her nurse and the scene between Pylades and Orestes described by the first messenger of the *IT*. No one of these passages has anything like the extent of the present scene, nor do they portray a reciprocity of love, as this one does.

between Theseus and Hippolytus might be cited in comparison with the present one, but there a retrospective question of justice deflects the expression of emotion, and much the same can be said of Alcestis' farewell to Admetus, where her tenderness is obscured by her concern for the future. The brother and sister of the *Orestes* have nothing to settle between them. They have nothing to *do* at this moment, they only mutually *feel* his illness, her dedication, their danger and their hope, and they effectively force the spectator to feel these things too. The sequence meanwhile is made so as to measure the effect of their love, for Orestes returns, as it ends, to a sleep that is far healthier than his earlier tormented tossing. He has learned that his saviour is almost in sight, he has survived one more attack of the Furies and has rediscovered his sister at its end, as faithful as before. He has in fact gained enough strength to play nurse to her for a moment. Love and sleep mix together in this opening movement of the play; they are cause and effect, but also somehow like to one another. Both are said to bring an escape from present evils, a forgetfulness that is like the visitation of a kindly god.[13] Together they hold out a symbolic promise of healing and renewal that makes a deep impression on the spectator in his unthinking heart.

The brother and sister are, however, not the only actors in this close-knit pair of scenes. One post-classical director actually opened his play not with the vision of Electra at the cot of Orestes but with the pre-dawn pageant of Helen's return with the spoils of Troy. This enviable piece of showmanship cannot be defended by any line of the play, but it is hard to think that the poet would have been offended by it. Helen's presence in the palace is central to the play, and her arrival in the beginning would offer a fine counterweight to her departure at the end. Be this as it may, it is a fact that Helen has just arrived and is inside when Electra begins her prologue speech. She has come surreptitiously under the cover of darkness and fearful of the Argives, but she has come with a full parade of Asiatic slaves and oriental luxuries. And just as Electra gets to the subject of salvation (having named Menelaus and then digressed to speak of his wife) the fabled Helen hurries out.

[13] Hermione is to Helen an ἀλγέων παραψυχή (62); through her Helen can ἐπιλήθεσθαι κακῶν (66); sleep is the work of πότνια Λήθη κακῶν (213), and Lethe is σοφὴ καὶ εὐκταία θεός (214).

Helen's entrance is unheralded, and her whole manner is surprisingly informal. She has an almost vernacular naturalness[14] in this unnatural situation; she asks after the health of her nephew and niece, mentions her conviction that Apollo is to blame for what they suffer, and refers without embarrassment to the long-ago day when she left this place for Troy. She is home again now and she is happy in her reunion with Hermione (62; 66); indeed, Electra calls her 'blessed' (86). She is however grieved by the death of her sister and she would like to make the proper funeral gifts; this is what has brought her out. Helen has come in fact to make the extraordinary suggestion that Electra should carry her offerings to the tomb of Clytemnestra, since she herself would rather not face the Argive public. When Electra says that she could not go to her mother's grave, Helen accedes to her suggestion that Hermione should be sent instead, calls the girl and charges her with a libation, a lock of hair and a prayer, and herself goes back inside the palace.

This is Helen's only appearance previous to her final assumption, though her voice is heard, deceptively, in the 'murder scene'. Her essence therefore, as far as this drama is concerned, must be contained in the few lines that she speaks now. The point to which our attention is drawn is her gesture towards Clytemnestra; here she has made a decision and therefore it is here that her ethos is to be observed. Is she being shown as morally insensitive to the point of depravity, or is she being shown in quite an opposite light, as a further exemplar, after the brother and sister, of uncritical *philia*? The poet has made her deputation to the tomb remind us of Clytemnestra's actions at the beginning of the *Choephoroi* or of the Sophoclean *Electra*, but the result of his comparison is to establish significant differences rather than any real likeness between the two queens of this house. In the older plays a murderess tried to placate her own victim whom she feared, while she prayed that she might continue to enjoy in private the fruits of her crime against him. Here, on the other hand, one who has not done her sister any harm[15] would send

---

[14] I would follow Kirchhoff, Paley, Wecklein and di Benedetto in rejecting line 74, which leaves Helen with a rather breezy πῶς at 73; this seems quite in keeping with the rest of her speech and with her entrance, which is unannounced and informal.

[15] The sacrifice of Iphigeneia, for example, is never charged against Helen in this play; both Helen and Hermione are instead associated with Iphigeneia as being likewise innocent victims, for the poet calls them *skumnoi* (1387; 1493; cf. *Agam.*

untainted gifts to the dead woman accompanied by a prayer
that is not for herself but for the re-establishment of good-will in
all the family. Helen prays for reconciliation, on the grounds
that Electra and Orestes have acted under a divine command
(121), and in doing so she asks no more than what heaven intends.
She herself will help Apollo to produce just such a reconciliation,
before this day is done.

When Helen's ritual instructions are finished, she selects the
least evident of her abundant curls and cuts from its very end an
infinitesimal strand as her personal offering at Clytemnestra's
grave. Her gesture makes Electra burst out with expressions of
anger and contempt, but no audience could view it without a
strong desire to laugh. This lock so grudgingly given is in fact full
of the poet's instruction, for Helen's grave offering marks her
permanently as a silly and charming creature who can only be
innocuous, since vanity like hers will keep a woman from the
dishevelment of crime. This Helen can never have shaped events
by any weight of her own; she would never dry up the entire
sea of family wealth to get an enemy into her hands, nor would
she ruin her clothes and her coiffure by standing in the bloody
rain that came from a husband's wound. She is no Clytemnestra,
she is rather exactly what Apollo describes at the end of the play,
a piece of surpassing loveliness (καλλίστευμα, 1639) cast in the
form of human flesh, a kind of toy that might be used by the gods
to lure men into war. The quality she needed in order to do the
gods' bidding was an ability to love without discrimination, and
this is the quality that she brings with her into the *Orestes*.

Helen is thus the exact opposite of her father, Tyndareus,
who argues, like Creon, that principles must override the ties of
blood. Her first words are an explicit refusal to shun Orestes
and Electra, though they are under ban (75), and she soon asks
of others that they should treat her, not according to a strict

141–3 of Artemis and her love of young animals, i.e., Iphigeneia). Electra blames
Helen generally for all the deaths at Troy (1306), the chorus accuses her of filling
Greece with tears, but then moves on to find in Paris a causal figure that stands
behind that of Helen (1361–5). The charge most frequently made against her in
this play is that she was loose, not *sophron* (1132), though Pylades calls her ἡ πολύκτονος
at 1142. On Helen's character, see F. Will, *CJ* lv (1960), 338–44, where it is argued
that she is being labelled as 'worthless'. A. M. Dale, *Euripides. Helen*, viii, calls her
'a lightweight, almost trivial character whose deliverance and apotheosis make as
it were a casual mockery of the realities of human desperation around her'.

sense of rectitude, but according to love (100). Later in the play she is able to give a full demonstration of what she stands for in the scene described by the Phrygian slave. There again she is first given the attributes of extreme luxury, of sisterly devotion, and of thoughtless familial sympathy, for she is weaving a further offering for Clytemnestra's grave. She does only one thing in this late and invisible scene, but her action is the result of a decision and her decision is one of love for her kin. When she is approached by her nephew and his friend, she is asked to move to the household hearth, ostensibly that they may bind her solemnly to intercede in their behalf, and to this request Helen immediately yields. Like her daughter she graciously agrees to what she hears as a plea for aid, and like Hermione she does unwittingly become, in the end, an instrument in the paradoxical salvation of these false suppliants who would contrive her death.

The Helen of the prologue is a figure that repeats that of Orestes. Both are tools the gods seem to have laid aside, and both in consequence are unpopular among mortals. Both have as their chief personal qualities a kind of weakness (vanity with her, madness with him) and an ability to love. And so it is that even here, at the beginning, Helen, in her happy return from war and wandering and in her reunion with her adored child, seems to hold out the promise of a like end for her sister's wretched son. The curl she cuts is incompatible with any final disaster; it suggests rather an outcome somehow satyresque, an ultimate phase of rejoicing in a world that can afford the embellishments of charm and vanity.

One last thing must be said about the opening of the *Orestes*, and that is that Apollo is tangibly present in these scenes. There is an instant, a moment or so in the spectator's experience, when Orestes is displayed in the grip of madness, and in this instant he takes into his hands a gift that had been the possession of the god. As the frenzy comes on, Orestes' eye begins to roll (253); he speaks of evil women and commands his sister to keep her own heart pure, and then the full hallucination begins. Orestes sees his mother, as we all have seen her at the opening of the *Eumenides*, rousing her furies as if they were beasts and setting them on the victim's trail (255). The reference to the older play is so marked that it would threaten the dramatic illusion here if it did not serve as the foil for a very un-Aeschylean and highly theatrical detail in the stage business that follows at once. Faced with the Erinyes, Orestes calls to Apollo for help, throws off the sister whom he takes for a fury, and demands the bow that Loxias had given him for his defence. Electra produces the weapon and with it in his hands Orestes does a wild brief pantomime of shooting down his enemies while he screams at them to leave him and to attack Apollo's shrine instead.[16] Then he falls back exhausted but once more perfectly sane.

This god-given bow has been borrowed from the simpler world of Stesichorus, a world where Apollo's command was indubitably just, and where his support of his servant was immediate.[17] A fairy-tale Orestes who knew no guilt and was troubled simply by a set of bothersome female monsters could be saved once and for all if he shot the furies down with Apollo's magic bow. These conditions do not hold in tragedy, but Euripides has nevertheless ostentatiously chosen to make his Apollo give Orestes the bow, before the murder of his mother, and he has chosen to bring the bow on stage so that all the assembled audience may see it. He has chosen to make Orestes' seizure end when the boy takes the bow in his hands, and he has chosen to let him drop the weapon as the madness leaves him. The bow is never mentioned again; apparently it lies on the ground, unnoticed, until whatever time the cot is removed (if it ever is). It matters very little what becomes of this now useless property, for Apollo's bow has joined Helen's lock of hair and Electra's stool to become the third emblematic sign produced by the poet for the opening of his tragedy.

The bow is a visible proof of Apollo's presence and of his readiness to aid this miserable Orestes. The boy, however, remembers Apollo only as the author of his crime while he forgets him as a possible author of salvation, and with this borrowed weapon the error of his despair is made palpable. Electra asks, 'With heaven ill-disposed, what ally shall I find?'

---

[16] The Scholiast's note testifies to the use of a physical, visible bow, remarking that later actors gave it up and performed the dance with an imaginary weapon.

[17] See Page, *PMG*, No. 217; on the Stesichorean *Oresteia*, see L. Radermacher, *Jenseits*, pp. 125 ff.; W. Ferrari, 'L'Orestea di Stesicoro', *Athenaeum*, xvi (1938), 1–37, and note Wilamowitz' argument (*Aisch. Interp.* 189 ff.) that Stesichorus' poem was based upon a fuller epic source. It seems remotely possible that the dreams at *Or.* 618, communicated to Orestes by Electra before the murder of Clytemnestra, came also from Steischorus.

to which Orestes answers all unconscious of the appropriateness of his response, 'Give me the curved bow that Apollo gave to me!' (267–8). Then a few minutes later the irony is reversed when Orestes, having conquered his phantom attackers with the bow, drops the god's material gift and in blind faithlessness at once accuses Apollo of supporting him with words but not with deeds (287).

The verbal references to Apollo in this early section of the play have covered the traditional spectrum. The Delphic origin of the murder of Clytemnestra is indicated by a kind of Aeschylean shorthand, and is plainly meant to be taken as a fixed mythic fact. The murder was performed in obedience to Apollo's command (31); the essential responsibility for the crime lies with the god (76); it is the god who has brought Orestes and Electra to their present pass (121), for he has sacrificed them to the principle of blood exacted for blood (191). And so the Delphic injunction was a piece of unlovely (194–5) and unjust justice (163 ff.).[18] Neither the murder nor Apollo's part in it is here offered as a key point of concern. What interests Orestes is the question of Apollo's future support, and here his deviation from the Aeschylean precedent is very plainly marked.

At the end of the *Choephoroi*, as soon as the murders are done, the Aeschylean Orestes puts on his suppliant rig. He is attacked by the furies (the sequence of two-line exchanges there have provided the pattern for Euripides' similar scene here) but his madness only sends him off the faster towards Delphi and lustration. He never expresses a hint of doubt as to Apollo's support, and the chorus confidently prays for his good fortune and the protection of his kindly overseeing god (*Choeph.* 1063–4). The Euripidean Orestes seems to have received much the same initial assurance from Apollo as did the Aeschylean prince (τοῖς μὲν λόγοις ηὔφρανε, 287); he also seems to have been given instructions about his lustration after the crime (597–9), but this murderer does not become a genuine suppliant and he makes no move towards the Pythian shrine. The play opens on

---

[18] Note how these formations echo the Aeschylean ἀδόλως δόλια at *Choeph.* 955 (the paradox is surely to be respected though the passage is corrupt), his χάριν ἀχάριτον (*Choeph.* 43), and the ἄζηλα νίκης μιάσματα at *Choeph.* 1017. Note also Orestes' later play with ἀνόσιος and ὅσιος at 546–7, reflected at 563, and on this whole point see A. Lesky, *WS* liii (1935), 39.

the fifth day after the killing of Clytemnestra. Orestes has not set off for Delphi, perhaps because he is ill and a prisoner, but neither has he taken up the suppliant boughs, tufted himself with wool and sought refuge at any local shrine—an omission he himself insists upon when he describes himself as ἱκέτης, ἀφύλλου στόματος ἐξάπτων λιτάς (383). His father's tomb is close at hand (796) but he has not prostrated himself there. And when he begs for support from his uncle, it is for political support in moving onto his father's throne; he is never heard to ask for aid in leaving Argos or in getting himself to Delphi for his purification. On the other hand, he and Pylades are quite ready to become false suppliants who use the consecrated gestures with cynical hypocrisy, as a part of their vengeance plot (1332: 1337; 1414–15). This Orestes will not seek supernatural aid but he will, like old Amphitryon, reproach his god with the absence of that aid. Apparently he expects to have divine assistance forced upon him, and so it is, in the end, when he has done his worst without it.

In sum, this long prelude has seemed to promise Orestes a healing sleep and a fate that will include forgetfulness and love, homecoming and the kindly touch of god. It has defined the hero as one who is weak and sometimes mad, as one who loves and is loved with mortal tenderness, and finally as one who is closely allied with Apollo, but forgetful of that god. The audience is thus told to expect a play built on the deeds of one who has lost his faith, and here at least it is not disappointed. Orestes' despair soon becomes a total doubt that god has ever entered into his life, and this is what he confesses to Apollo at the end (1666–9). One final piece of instruction from the prologue seems to be that we should read this play always with its Aeschylean predecessors in our minds, and this exercise will provide the second step in the present attempt to understand the play.

ORESTES (continued)

In the prelude to his play, Euripides' Orestes drops Apollo's bow and clings to his sister and his cot as his only sanctuary. In the course of the actions that follow he experiments with a series of further substitutes for Apollo and his Delphic purification. He looks to a kinsman for salvation, and Menelaus betrays him; he goes to the *ecclesia* for absolution, and finds that the city wishes only to keep itself safe; he decides to die, still tainted, then resolves to live and to increase his blood guilt; then at last when he finds himself on what appears to be his funeral pyre, he decides to honour himself with the slaughter of a helpless victim. It is this irreligious sacrifice that is finally interrupted and transformed by the god. The blood of a pig, to be shed at Delphi, will presumably replace Hermione's blood and it will ensure life and purity instead of the death and miasma that Orestes meant to create with his impious private ritual.

The sequence of Orestes' adventures reflects his attempt to remove Apollo from his past as well as from his future, and it also allows the poet to make a commentary upon the *Oresteia*. Aeschylus had based the successful resolution of his trilogy upon a pair of related premises, arguing that political institutions could reflect divine Dike in an earthly administration of justice and that pious, innocent human beings do exist. Now Euripides, after half a century, uses his Orestean play to challenge both of these assumptions. He attacks the secular optimism of the *Eumenides* by showing a tyrant, a wise aristocrat, and a democratic polis, all equally unable to act justly in Orestes' case, and meanwhile he makes a fundamental criticism of the view of human nature that is found in the *Choephoroi*.

Orestes' first failure in this play is a rhetorical one, and he suffers it with Aeschylean words in his mouth. In the presence of Menelaus and Tyndareus he argues, after the fashion of the Apollo of the *Eumenides*, that he acted to honour his father and that a father is closer in blood than a mother is (546–63). He points out that he would have been tortured by the Erinyes of his father had he failed to perform the crime (582 ff.), this time echoing his own namesake in the *Choephoroi*. Most important, he reminds his listeners that he killed by Apollo's command and that the responsibility for dealing with him therefore lies with that god (591 ff.), just as it is felt to do at the end of the *Choephoroi*. Orestes gives his two kinsmen the benefit of the full Aeschylean interpretation of his situation, and he finds that, as a weapon of practical defence, this Aeschylean truth is useless. His claim to a guiltless guilt naturally fails to make any impression on Menelaus, for the Spartan king is here the unjust man, a politician in the worst sense of the word who has, with his opening questions (427; 431 ff.), discovered that Argos will welcome him as its new Aegisthus if he can only harm his friends without seeming to do so. (Aristotle's complaint that he is needlessly base is not fair, for Menelaus' opportunism is necessary to the full spectrum of political life that the poet is presenting here.) Tyndareus, however, has been brought forward as a sensible old aristocrat, the Argive equivalent of a good Athenian dicast. He ought to be able to appreciate Orestes' plea, if the world were as Aeschylus had pictured it, but in fact the Aeschylean arguments have with him the opposite of their intended effect.

Tyndareus had begun by saying that the proper private response to a murder was to demand recompense through established institutions, and then to let the murderer cleanse himself in exile (491 ff.). He accused Orestes of a lack of intelligence in not seeing the wisdom of this *nomos*, and presumably he was at first ready to let Orestes be treated as Clytemnestra was not (512–15). At any rate he arrived on the scene meaning to do no more than urge Menelaus not to help the boy.[1] However, once he has heard Orestes' Apolline defence, he decides to intervene actively, his response being the exact opposite of that requested of the dicasts in the *Eumenides*, for where Athena had urged acquittal he decides to ask for death. Indeed he speaks like one of the Aeschylean Furies. From his point of view the

---

[1] Lines 536–7 repeat Tyndareus' later lines at 625–6; the repetition alone does not condemn them, but whereas they make perfect sense in the latter position, in the former they are in contradiction to everything Tyndareus has been saying. I would therefore delete 536–7 and keep 625–6.

accused has nothing to do but plead guilty, and the mere fact that Orestes would defend himself constitutes a danger. Tyndareus is a reasonable man; he holds no brief for his daughter, whose death, he admits, was just (538), but he feels that men should live by law and that Orestes' defence of his action forbodes the death of law. Precisely because of his practical wisdom he is incapable of hearing the supernatural part of Orestes' Aeschylean defence, and so of being just in this peculiar case. Tyndareus is wholly rational and the crime and its origins are irrational; the old man sees before him only the Orestes of this play, not the innocent creature of the *Choephoroi*, and since he has no way of predicting the miracle the poet has in store for us, he sensibly concludes that this boy, left at large, will soon have spilled more blood.[2]

Orestes apparently judges the Aeschylean defence to have been discredited by Tyndareus' angry exit. When he makes his next appeal to Menelaus he ignores Apollo (he will never mention him again until the god appears) and argues with a dazzling sophistry from the aristocratic concept of repayment. 'The Trojan war was unjust', he says, 'and you received it as a gift at my father's hands; repay him now by fighting another "unjust" war for my acquittal. My father gave you the life of his daughter, Iphigeneia, and so by rights could ask for your daughter's life. That of course we do not ask' (he is sincere at the moment, but victim of the poet's irony); 'you can repay him instead with our two lives, Electra's and mine, rescued by your hand.' This argument is cleverly aimed at Menelaus' archaic self-respect, but since Helen's husband does not possess a single one of the heroic qualities, it fails. The demand for private repayment assumed a tribal rather than a truly political order, and so it had its suitability in a plea made to a kinsman; unfortunately Orestes continues in this primitivistic vein when he speaks before the Argive Assembly, and so he fails with them as well.

In his public harangue Orestes once again strikes an Aeschylean note, but now it is one borrowed from those who were his

---

[2] K. Reinhardt, *Tradition und Geist* (Göttingen, 1960), pp. 243 ff., believes that Tyndareus is a hypocrite, that he has been from the first behind the move to have the culprits stoned, and that he has only pretended to his initial moderation (why?); he comments that Tyndareus, at line 607, 'lässt . . . die Maske fallen'.

enemies in the *Eumenides*. He paraphrases the Furies' defence of
their primitive persecutions, like them presenting himself as a
necessary punitive force among men who are in a pre-political,
Hobbesian state of nature. 'In killing my mother', he says, 'I
acted in the public interest, for if women who shed masculine
blood were allowed to go unpunished, we men would soon be
either corpses or their slaves' (934–7; cf. the furies on their
function at *Eum.* 490 ff.). His failure to cite the Apolline command
leads him to turn to the argument Aeschylus had defined as
anti-Apolline; he cites the ancient *nomos* of blood-vengeance, and
the result is disastrous. He finds some support among the
reactionary faction, the party of the Hill personified by the
independent farmer, but his demand that popular justice be
abandoned in favour of a revival of tribal justice is heavily
defeated, and naturally so in a gathering of the people. He fails
before the *polis* because his aristocratic argument, put into
practice, would destroy the *polis*.

The report of the visit to the Assembly is an almost journalistic
exercise in political analysis, and yet this passage has a paradoxical air of unreality about it. The messenger's speech is
remarkably hard-headed, with its breakdown of parties and
opinions, but it seems, in the end irrelevant. And this is because
it is not just the report of a failure, it is the report of a mistaken
attempt on the part of the principal to leave the proper scene
of his play. In the Euripidean version, as in the Aeschylean, the
essential fact of the Orestean tragedy is the Apolline demand that
Clytemnestra should be killed, yet Apollo is absent from all
five speeches delivered to the people, and absent from their
decision in the end. Diomedes alone speaks even of *eusebeia*,
while the others, including Orestes, discuss in exclusively secular
terms what they frame as a very practical problem. They do not
ask, 'What did heaven intend?' or 'Is this man truly guilty?'
or even 'Where does justice lie?' Rather, each speaker gives
his own answer to the question, 'How, in this event, can we best
benefit the society that we know?' And the final answer is, not
unreasonably, 'By putting Orestes to death.' Euripides does not
mean that Orestes mistook his proper line of defence and should
have taught the people to recognize Apollo in his crime. Tyndareus' perfect deafness to the god's name in the earlier debate,
with Diomedes' avoidance of it here, is surely meant to show that

the argument from Apollo would have been as impossible in the democratic assembly as it was before the tyrant and the aristocrat. The Euripidean truth is that in going to the people Orestes has chosen the wrong arena in which to run his race with death (878). All reference to the Delphic command is missing from the Assembly scene because that command was not something that could be voted upon by any legislature or any court; it was a mystery. The god's unjust justice, his own innocent guilt, as Orestes himself had once understood (597–8, cf. 416), could only be taken back to the gods. Presented to a political body these paradoxes must be distorted to become questions to which a political answer can be given, and that answer, necessarily irrelevant, will be necessarily unjust.[3]

The failure in the Assembly marks the end of the first section of the *Orestes* and the end, too, of the rebuttal of the *Eumenides*. The accompanying challenge to the *Choephoroi*, made not on the basis of institutions but on the basis of human nature, speaks out from each of the play's developing scenes. The Orestes of the prologue and first episode seemed almost to come up to the Aeschylean standard, for he was characterized by love and that form of shame which is produced by a powerful respect, felt simultaneously for self, for family, and for the gods. 'I am ashamed', he said to Electra (281), because his uncleanness in the sight of the gods was touching her as well as himself, and 'I am ashamed', he said of Tyndareus, 'to have repaid his kindness as I have' (460; cf. 550). His final appeal to Menelaus is made in these same terms of kinship and archaic self-respect, but here the audience is made to feel a dubious ethical quality in the boy. Orestes begs Menelaus for help in the name of his love for Helen, then turns aside to murmur, 'See what a pass I have come to!' (672) and thus the poet brands him as a conscious hypocrite. In this moment Orestes is ready to use love, not to feel it. He has forgotten shame and no longer respects either his family or himself, and in the scene that follows he presents himself in an even worse light, for he goes into the Assembly to boast of his murder as if it were his own, and to try to use it for his own political advantage. The crime was one for which he had felt shame and remorse when he knew it as the execution of

---

[3] Kitto, without in any way supporting the interpretation suggested here, calls the appearance in the Assembly a piece of folly; *Greek Tragedy*, p. 347.

Apollo's will, but now, as his own, he is proud of it. He even suggests that it may provide a healthy precedent for the further private punishment of immoral women.

The vengeance action follows with a kind of ethical necessity upon the report of Orestes' shift to the rhetoric of secular opportunism in the Assembly. Now that he has achieved his altered sense of the old murder he is ready for new bloodshed, and the poet begins the third phase of his play with a passage that directly challenges the Aeschylean view of man's potential innocence. He writes a three-character scene of despair and decision, a scene in which an intrigue is laid, and as he does so he makes sure that no spectator shall fail to think of the *kommos* of the *Choephoroi*. Orestes, Electra and Pylades here trace a complex three-way pattern of emotion and influence, just as the brother and sister and chorus had done before, but while the Euripidean characters attempt to persuade one another that Helen is another Clytemnestra, the poet is at work to suggest that they themselves may be the Clytemnestras here. Like his Aeschylean mother, this Orestes feels no shame in speaking of his own dissimulation, and like her he will take pleasure in the shedding of kin blood (1122; cf. *Agam.* 1372 ff.). She chose to add an extra crime of vengeance, the killing of the girl Cassandra, to her duties as *alastor*; he chooses to add the killing of the girl Hermione to his private vengeance murder. Having earlier begged his sister to be unlike her mother (251–2), he now hails her for her masculine wit (1204, where the φρένες ἄρσενες of Electra are fearfully like the ἀνδρόβουλον κέαρ of Clytemnestra at *Agam.* 10), and she seems to accept the tribute as she plans to 'net' her prey (1315), and to hide her joy with her mother's pretence of grief (1319, σκυθρωποὺς ὀμμάτων ἔξω κόρας, cf. *Choeph.* 737–8 of Clytemnestra: πρὸς μὲν οἰκέτας θέτο σκυθρωπόν, ἐντὸς ὀμμάτων γέλων κεύθουσ').

Most damning of all, however, is the final prayer. It is divided, like that of the *Choephoroi*, into short responding phrases with an often repeated invocation, 'Father!' and it asks for Agamemnon's aid. Some of its sentiments exactly repeat those of the older prayer ('You will have honour,' *Choeph.* 483 ff. is echoed by the less extensive 'We will repay you in tears,' *Or.* 1239; 'Father, are you roused by these outrages?' *Choeph.* 495, by 'Having heard these outrages will you not save your children?' at *Or.* 1238); others are only subtly altered ('Remember your wrongs' has become 'remember our wrongs', and 'Do not die through us' becomes 'We are dying for you', though these children can no longer claim to be their father's saviour, as at *Choeph.* 505).[4] In this context of close similarity, the differences stand out with shocking clarity, and chief among them is a new lack of reticence. Orestes and Electra, in the *Choephoroi*, could not bring themselves to mention the crime they projected in any but the most general terms, and in their prayer, fearful of ill omens, Orestes speaks only of winning a fall from his father's ancient foes (*Choeph.* 498–9). It comes as a distressing surprise, then, to hear the Euripidean Orestes say in a matter of fact way: 'I am suffering unjustly and because of you, father, for though I did right I am betrayed by your brother; for this reason I want to seize his wife and kill her' (1227–30).[5] The crudely sinister quality of his intention is distilled for the listener in the final phrase added by the poet, for Orestes closes his address to Agamemnon with these words: 'Be my accomplice in this!' (1230). The word that Euripides has chosen here is not a common one, though it seems to have had a certain vogue in Socratic circles.[6] It is συλλήπτωρ and it is used in the *Agamemnon* in a moment of memorable intensity to describe the demonic assistance that Clytemnestra had in the accomplishment of her crime (*Agam.* 1507). Thus the Euripidean Orestes almost openly classes himself with his mother, and also betrays his moral confusion by saying in effect: 'Father, help me to murder Helen as Clytemnestra was helped when she murdered you!'

In the *Oresteia* the endless round of bloodshed was stopped and justice was institutionalized when the gods found, to do their will, an Orestes who was not like his mother. Euripides, in his Orestes play, has on the other hand shown a boy who looks uncomfortably like a Clytemnestra—one who has suffered in scale but one for whom a single blood bath will not suffice. The Aeschylean

---

[4] Reinhardt, op. cit., p. 253, finds the Aeschylean echoes to be no more than another sign of cynicism: 'Soll das Parodie sein? . . . Es ist die ad absurdum geführte Entartung des heroischen und religiösen Erbes.' Kitto, op. cit., p. 348, remarks that the prayer 'sounds positively blasphemous here'.

[5] Lines 1229–32 did not exist in all exemplars according to the scholiast, but this is no reason for deleting 1227–30, as is pointed out, ad loc., by di Benedetto.

[6] The Socratic usage suggests that in non-ironic speech the term had the strong negative connotations that caused Antiphon to use it of an accomplice in murder (*Tetral.* 2, 3, 10; cf. Plato, *Symp.* 218 D; *Laws* 968 B; Xen. *Mem.* 2.2.12). It is used in the light Socratic fashion at *IT* 95.

solution is thus absolutely denied, for Euripides depicts a world that is as incapable of dealing with this private frenzy as it was with the Delphic crime. The godless self-interest of the factions in the Argive *ecclesia* is a far cry from the silent subservience to Athena that marked the imaginary first Areopagus court; in truth this whole society is not unlike the new Orestes figure, and under these conditions murders far more selfish and senseless than that of Agamemnon, murders like those of Helen and Hermione, may be expected to spring up eternally. How then does Euripides end his play? Are those critics right who believe that the poet has purposely found a miraculous solution that is an ugly mockery and left his play without an end because he meant to announce man's inevitable return to an abandoned and ferocious savagery?[7]

Put crudely the question is this: How bad has Orestes been shown to be, and how good has Apollo been proven? Could this god by these means put a permanent stop to this sequence of violent acts and could he save this group of mortals, according to the play's own evidence? If he could, then the finale is meant as a fully functioning part of the drama and must be taken seriously. Apollo has been presented with perfect conventionality, though sparingly; he holds the tripod of Themis (164), he sits at the central navel of the earth and gives wise prophecy to men who do his bidding (591 ff.), and he can cleanse a mortal of miasma (597–8). This means that the answer to the question of Apollo's effectiveness here must be sought in the poet's presentation of the deeds of the principal, and even more in his presentation of the character of that principal, for here it does seem that, contrary to the Aristotelian rule, ethos has taken precedence over action. What we must determine first is whether Orestes' nature has been shown as a fixed and hardened ethical monolith or whether it has been described as open to influence and change; secondly

---

[7] Verrall in *Four Plays* (1905), p. 257, wrote of the finale: 'Of all the like scenes in Euripides it is perhaps the most prodigiously absurd, unreal, meaningless, impossible.' Lesky, *WS* liii (1935), 44, concludes: 'Der Dichter hat ... die Bewegung des Spieles hier bis an einen Grenzpunkt geführt, getan aber hat er es, um eine Szene zu gewinnen deren Effekte nicht zum letzten seinem Stücke den nachhaltigen Erfolg gesichert haben.' Reinhardt, op. cit., p. 256 finds that the last scene is simply meant to show that there is boundless confusion in heaven as well as on earth. N. A. Greenberg, however, concludes that the Apollo of the final scene represents a 'paradoxical equilibrium' (*HSCP* lxvi [1962], 157–92).

we must observe whether that nature, mutable or not, has already wrought things that cannot be undone. Are there causes here that cannot be erased, effects that cannot be reversed by the words of a *deus ex machina*?

In fact Orestes' character seems to alter radically in the course of this play, for the languishing boy of the first episode, the brother who tries to repay his sister's love in kind, becomes in the fourth a wild boar (1459) who plans to repay his uncle's desertion with the murder of his aunt. Whether such a change is to be viewed as necessary and irreversible, or whether it could with probability be undone, will depend upon the agency the poet has used to bring it about in the first place. And here, at least, the situation is clear, for the crude responsibility for Orestes' conversion to private vengeance and kin murder lies squarely with his old friend, Pylades. The arrival of a friend seems in this case to turn one who knows how to love into one who knows how to hate, and this paradox has struck many as the most cynical touch in a thoroughly disenchanted play.[8] However this may be, there can be no doubt that Pylades' presence is one of the central facts of the play. His role has the prominence that mechanical superfluity always gives, and his obtrusiveness has been emphasized by the poet. There was already at hand, in Electra, a figure who was the obvious and economical choice to fulfil the function of counsellor, and it is notable that the rescue part of the intrigue, though not the vengeance part, does originate with her. Pylades is not necessary to the plot, and though he is called for by tradition, a series of alterations in his usual history and behaviour prove that Euripides has, with this character, a new purpose in mind.

The old Pylades was Orestes' shadow, never absent from his side, but this one has already abandoned his friend. Immediately after the murder of Clytemnestra he went back home, and he returns now not primarily to aid Orestes but simply because his father has driven him from Phocis (765). His coming provokes a speech on 'friendship' from Orestes, but it, like his later

[8] The paradox is made the more extreme by those who read Pylades as the *preux chevalier*. The scholiast remarked that, among a cast of debased characters, Pylades was the only one of any real nobility, and many modern critics welcome him as a picture of true faithfulness and *philia*; Kitto, however, bluntly calls him 'foolish' (op. cit., p. 346).

apostrophe to his friend, is marked with an increasing, unconscious irony. In the first of these addresses, the prince apostrophizes Pylades as the outsider who is a thousand times a better friend than the kinsman is, but when the kinsman is Menelaus, no factor of multiplication will produce a positive quality of *philia*. This truth is borne out by the action, since Orestes is, in fact, only comparing one ineffective rescuer with another. Because his support is to end in disaster, the precise quality for which Pylades is praised becomes interesting, and we discover with amusement that Orestes hails him not for justice or virtue or love or loyalty, but for having a character that melts into his own (ἀνὴρ ὅστις τρόποισι συντακῇ, 805). The second speech, far more hyperbolic, is inspired by Pylades' assassination plan. Orestes can find nothing so suitable there, to greet the man who has just suggested killing the Spartan queen and setting fire to the Argive palace, as the old priamel of worth. 'Give me a true friend, and keep your wealth, your tyranny, and your popularity', he cries (1155 ff.) with great appropriateness, since this friend looks as if he will cost him all of this and more.

The old Pylades was the friend *par excellence* (e.g., *Pythia* xi) and, more important, the old Pylades was intimately associated with Apollo. He kept silent, or opened his mouth just once, to remind Orestes of his Delphic commission, whereas this new man speaks ceaselessly.[9] He urges a self-seeking vengeance, he embraces the chance of a little extra blood, and he counsels the destruction of property that is not his own. The old Pylades was disinterested, but this one takes an obsessive interest in the new murder. He cannot go on living, he says, unless his sword is black with Helen's blood (1148), and the poet, by repeating his phrase when Orestes has his sword at Helen's throat (1473), keeps Pylades closely present in the deed. This Pylades is not a follower but a leader in the vengeance, and his counsels urge a deliberate choice of all that is anti-Apolline; they create a riot of unreason, confusion, excess and violence. The old Pylades spoke with the voice of god, but this one uses the accents of that tragic bad counsellor who is so often a slave. His bad advice lightens the load of Orestes' responsibility and meanwhile he

---

[9] Grüninger observed Pylades' garrulity and thought it evidence that the part had been padded by interpolation, but see Page, *Actors' Interpolations*, pp. 48–50, for a defence of the authenticity of the role as it stands.

reminds us, with his mortal verbosity, that Apollo's command is silent in these new Atreid crimes.

The presence of Pylades marks the absence of Apollo, and it is to that absence that Orestes listens. He has moved into this vacuum of his own free will, for he has never become a suppliant and has ceased to think of himself as Apollo's creature. He has looked for his salvation exclusively among mortals, and so he cannot expect divine punishment for one who refuses to protect him. He has tried to make himself a secular creature like any other and so he must pay off his enemies for himself. It is thus natural that, once out of touch with the supernatural, he should welcome the idea of vengeance, but it is not natural that he should attack his enemy by proxy, try to kill a woman instead of a man, and remain unappalled by the notion of spilling family blood. His *aidos* has diminished as his forgetfulness of Apollo has increased, but the mere loss of this negative aristocratic restraint should not result in a positive lust for the blood of lady relatives in one who was not depraved before. Either Orestes' true nature has been all along that of Hesiod's man of iron in the hours before his destruction—in which case the early scenes were deceptive—or else there is some other force besides Pylades that is bending him to further crime.

There is in fact a second source of criminality specified for Orestes, and paradoxically it works, as Pylades' bad advice does, to ameliorate the burden of guilt that the hero has to bear. For a few moments at the beginning of the play Orestes is shown as raving mad, made so by the agency of the Erinyes, and the poet has contrived to keep a sense of his insanity alive throughout the play. Before he appears, Electra has described him in his frenzy as a colt who has escaped the yoke and runs wild,[10] and later, even in his so-called sanity, this hero runs and leaps. Running is likewise used to characterize the movements of Pylades, who makes his first entrance at a run (726; cf. 799 and 807 when the two friends exit in haste, awkwardly yoked together), and later Electra also runs (959). The whole erroneous appearance at the Assembly was a race run with death

[10] Electra's image strikes the ear with a morally disturbing sound because it is the reverse of the image used at *Choeph.* 794 ff., where the innocent Orestes in his obedience to heaven's will is seen as a yoked colt that pulls the chariot of Zeus with the disciplined pace of victory. The Euripidean phrase may, however, be more directly based on *Choeph.* 1021 ff.

(878), and lost. At the same time the furies who are causing Orestes to run in this mad way are seen as running too, like a hellish band of bacchantes (317; 411; 835). And finally the running prey join their pursuers in an ultimate image of madness, for Orestes and Pylades, when they rush upon Hermione, pounce like a pair of bacchic revellers who have never received the consecrated staff (1492).

This series of interlocking images suggests that the Erinyes have taken possession of their prey. Orestes spoke with their voice in the *ecclesia*; he suggested even there that he might take over the punitive function that had belonged to them, and it is this same idea that arouses him in Pylades' proposals. He is attracted by the notion of injuring Menelaus, but he is ecstatic before the vision of the death of Helen (1130),[11] and it is to be remembered that his first fit of madness came on him when he thought of her. Finally he freely decides to make of himself and his friends a band of human furies, in this sense outdoing Clytemnestra, who had the same function forced upon her. Like the Erinyes, he rejoices in his duty; like them he is full of righteousness, and like all divinities in their anger, he does not care if the innocent must occasionally go down with the sinner. The attempts upon Helen and Hermione are plainly the work of humans who would usurp a superhuman function, but these humans are in a sense possessed.

Orestes cannot tell his friends from his enemies, his victims from his saviours, or for that matter many another thing from its opposite.[12] His delusions all stem from his essential failure to

---

[11] Orestes cries μανθάνω τὸ σύμβολον (1130). His language may be borrowed from the world of business: 'I agree to that contract!' Or it may be a recognition token that has provided the image: 'Kill Helen! *There's* my own Pylades!' as if the plan had made his recognition of his friend complete. However, the usage with *manthano* suggests a religious point of departure (*LSJ* s.v. σύμβολον, iii 5 and 6): 'There's the kernel of our doctrine!' or 'There's the true revelation!' With this meaning the phrase suggests that their entrance into the palace is to be a kind of initiation, where after wandering through dangers they will finally penetrate to the chamber of the (goddess) queen. If this is true, the murder is seen as a kind of profanation of the mysteries, and this notion fits well with the description of the ungarlanded suppliant (383) and of the bacchantes without regalia (1492); there is also an non-Hephaestian fire at 621.

[12] Orestes thinks salvation is to kill without having to die (Apollo makes it to live without having to kill); he believes that when he takes refuge behind the body of a girl he will be a figure of manliness (1349-52); he calls it blessedness to have as a wife a woman who could hold a knife to her foster-sister's throat. To murder by

recognize the real cause of his suffering, and so he has persistently chosen the wrong champion, since he looks for rescue from the wrong pursuing villain. He has tried to escape Tyndareus' hatred, the people's stones, the necessity of suicide, and finally the attack of Menelaus and his party, because he has never been able to see that the real escape had to be from his mother's furies. He has on the contrary thrown himself into their arms, though they are the real villains of the piece. Here Euripides is in full agreement with Aeschylus, for it is the miasma of the old crime that has pursued Orestes throughout this new play. His poetic predecessors had fought the demons of defilement or fled to Delphi for release, but this Orestes has forgotten his magic bow and has never yet thought of sanctuary. He would rule Argos with Clytemnestra's blood still on his hands, and so in his search for secular power he surrenders to his supernatural opponents. They seem to show him the way to fulfilled ambition, but in fact they arrange for his self-destruction by giving him his mad taste for further familial crime.

To the degree that the furies have made Orestes over after their own image his madness is exalted, and yet when it is lodged in his ordinary flesh, it has the near-comic quality of Jacobean lunacy. The Phrygian, with his tale of rolling eyes and shrieking slaves, makes the palace at Argos seem more like a madhouse than a place where furies revel, and from that place Orestes is seen to leap in terrified confusion ($\dot{\epsilon}\pi\tau o\eta\mu\dot{\epsilon}\nu\omega$ $\pi o\delta\dot{\iota}$, 1505). His entrance marks the beginning of a brief scene of real insanity.

O. Where is the creature who fled past my sword? 1506
P. He grovels here before you sire, as we barbarians do.
O. Slave! This is no Trojan affair; we stand on Argive ground!
P. True, but wise men everywhere would rather live than die.
O. And have you called for aid from Menelaus yet? 1510
P. Not I. I mean to take your side, for you are worthier of me.
O. Then is it just or is it not, that Tyndareus' girl should die?
P. Juster than just, though your sword had three blades!
O. You fawn on me with cowardly tongue and hide your true opinion . . .?

deceit is what he calls freedom; to die by decree is for him slavishness (1170); murder at other times can be called piety (1137). What he sees as an evil woman turns out to be a goddess, what he thought of as her *nemesis* turns out to be her elevation among the gods, etc. On Orestes' madness, see W. D. Smith, 'Disease in Euripides' *Orestes*', *Hermes* xcv (1967), 291–307.

P. No, sir. That woman ruined Phrygians as well as your Greek
   host.   1515
O. Swear it—otherwise I'll kill you!—swear to your sincerity!
P. I swear it on . . . my life (and wish the oath were good)!
O. Do all you Phrygians cower so at the sight of steel?
P. Move the blade away; I see my death reflected in its glare.
O. You take it for a Gorgon, then, and fear you'll turn to stone?
                                                               1520
P. I fear I'll turn to carrion! (I never met this Gorgon's head . . . ?)
O. You, a slave, fear death, though it will bring release from ills?
P. Every mortal, slave or not, rejoices in his life.
O. Ha! that's well said—your wit has saved you! Go inside the
   house.
P. You will not kill me?
                 O. Go!
                                P. There's a truly splendid
                                        word!   1525
O. But I can change my mind!
                                P. Now his style degenerates!
                                (*Exit.*)
O. You fool, to think that I could bear to draw *your* blood!
   You are no woman . . . nor yet a man, so far as I can see!
   No, I came here to silence the alarm you meant to raise,
   for Argive men are quick to hear a call for help.   1530
   Of course I have no fear of Menelaus, if *he* gets within my
       range—
   just let him come, rejoicing in his dangling yellow curls!
   But if he calls upon the Argive host and urges an attack
   because of Helen's death—if he refuses safety to me,
   my sister, and my accomplice, Pylades—then he will find   1535
   two corpses at his feet, his daughter's and his wife's!
                                                     (*Exit.*)

As the Scholiast long ago said, this little scene is unworthy of
tragedy and unworthy of Orestes' own sufferings. There is an
almost Aristophanic use of standard comic tricks, most apparent
in the idiotic joke about the Gorgon, of which the Scholiast
remarked severely, 'comical and low' (cf. 1507; 1513; 1517).[13]
The whole thing is self-conscious and contrived, with its continuing discussion of its own verbal style and its sniping at the
play that contains it (note especially 1511 and 1527–8). Indeed,

[13] Grüninger thought the whole exchange was an interpolation, but Page
defends it, op. cit., pp. 45–8.

the lines are as ridiculous as Helen's lock of hair, and like that lock they have an emblematic function in this tragedy. Orestes' tribute to *synesis* (1524) is funny because the Phrygian's remark is not witty but terribly hackneyed; it is funny because it is Euripidean self-parody (cf. 396 and *Frogs* 893); [14] and finally it is funny because Orestes himself is quite out of his wits at the moment. He has come forth to make sure that his crime will not be interrupted from outside, [15] but he spends his time in begging his would-be victim's slave to tell him that her murder will be just. When the cowardly eunuch has sworn by his life, Orestes begins to taunt him so foolishly that he does indeed seem to be a worthy hero for this abject and silly slave. Orestes brandishes his sword and toys with the idea of making a new victim of the Phrygian, while he teases him with threadbare sophistries. He debases them both with threats that are idle, and then when the Phrygian has gone he still hangs about to remark that all he has just done is senseless since he really has no reason to be afraid of Menelaus. He rouses himself with a blustering challenge to the man he meant to avoid and then goes in to try once more to complete his incoherent crime.

The scene between the prince and the Phrygian has been useless from Orestes' point of view and it is just as useless in the development of the plot. A messenger ordinarily simply departs when his speech is finished, [16] and in this case there is no reason why the Phrygian should not have left by one of the *parodoi*, when his song was done. He does not have to be sent back into the palace, for he has said nothing about rousing the town. All he wants to do is hide, and this he could have done, on or off the stage. Orestes is not needed, but he has been plucked out of the

[14] On the various meanings of σύνεσις, see F. Zucker, *Conscientia* (Jena, 1928), and B. Snell's review in *Gnomon* vi (1930), 21–30; also H. Osborne, *CR* xlv (1931), 8–10.

[15] The dative in line 1510 is sometimes taken unnaturally to mean 'help *for* Menelaus, (most recently by di Benedetto, ad loc.), on the grounds that otherwise the line will contradict the sense of 1531. Orestes is not above self-contradiction, but in fact there is a kind of consistency here. He has rushed out because he fears an interruption from Menelaus or anyone else at this point; once Helen is killed, however, he thinks he will have little to fear, for he believes that he can appeal to the Argives as their benefactor and at the same time bully Menelaus with the threat to Hermione's life.

[16] The messenger who contradicts Lichas in the *Trachiniae* is a contradiction to this rule, as is the Corinthian in *OT*; both of these remain because they are of absolute necessity to the continuation of the plot.

palace because the poet must show him in a new and necessary light. Only by this means can the audience be allowed a glimpse of this 'bloodthirsty' criminal in mid-crime, and thus be enabled to judge whether or not he is in truth another Clytemnestra. And what it sees destroys any such identification, for here suddenly is no efficiency of net and sword but instead the grotesque wastefulness of bungling lunacy.

The Erinyes have gone to work in a creature who has turned his back on god and out of the void in his faith they have created Orestes' depravity. The depravity is real and its intentions are supremely ugly, but it is wholly ineffective. The weakness of Orestes and the strength of the rejected god have met in a strange collaboration to defeat the evil that the furies and their mortal allies have prepared. Orestes had criminal intentions that could be called insane, but there was also a mad mindlessness in his prosecution of them, and it is evident that though the god Apollo could make an effective murderer of this man, no other power could. If Helen's miraculous disappearance seems almost gratuitous it is because these assassins would probably never have been able to lay a hand upon her anyway. In the end, after all, it is not their success but the insane celebration of their total failure that the god must interrupt.

If then the changes in Orestes have been wrought by his old crime (the furies) and his new alienation from Apollo (Pylades), and if those changes have not produced irreversible effects (they have produced nothing!), then Apollo's bizarre solution to the final situation does have about it a certain probability. The old crime was his, and he can therefore arrange for the eviction of the Erinyes, the purging away of the blood, and the satisfaction of the Argives on the score of Clytemnestra's death. And since the doubts that produced the excesses of the present action came when Orestes lost sight of his god, the epiphany itself will be a most effective medicine (see 1666 ff., where this notion is put in aural, not ocular terms). Apollo's mere appearance can be expected to restore his servant's ailing faith, and with it his sanity, his *aidos*, and his normal pious lawfulness.

For the successful crime Apollo has almost the traditional prescription, lustration at Delphi and a trip to Athens; the unsuccessful crimes he simply obliterates. This Orestes is to appear before the Areopagus, but there he will be judged by gods alone, for only they can understand his divinely ordained crime. His reinstatement in the world, on the other hand, is to be accomplished not in any court of law, but in the bridal-bed, beneath which the furies of private enmity will be stowed. This is an astonishing solution, but it is one for which the audience has been subtly prepared. The spectator has seen the initial attack of the furies repulsed by Apollo's gift, the bow; he has seen Orestes' madness subside then, as it will now, into physical tenderness; he has seen the fond gentleness of Helen and of the daughter who becomes Apollo's second gift; he has seen this brother and sister in a fraternal imitation of lovers' domesticity, content with cot and stool. While the three would-be demons were without faith they were without shame and self respect and so they taught each other hatred, but they did continue to love one another throughout; Apollo now seizes upon that undiscriminating *philia* which is their only strength and makes of it the agency of their rehabilitation.[17]

If this Orestes is typical of men, then men are marked with guilt, but it is a guilt that heaven will help them to bear if they will act piously. The mortality of this play is characterized by love but also by weakness, madness, a touch of cowardice, and a tendency to fail in faith. The Orestean man has known god and has received benefactions from heaven but he has not known how to use them. When he forgets god, he tries to rival him and in this of course he fails, but since he is not the man described in the tragedy of divine punishment and does not have the force of these who go to war with god, he is not marked for a magnificent destruction. Mortals of this sort are instead allowed to fulminate, they are left to trip over their own swords and if necessary they are frustrated in small miraculous ways. Then in the end, if kindness is Olympus' current whim, they are brought back to faith and so to the patronage of heaven.

Neither the positive nor the negative forms of the conventional tragic action could imitate the deeds of such a man as this. Nor could the satyr genre quite serve the whole of the Euripidean intention with his Orestes, for the poet meant to portray a moral

[17] The mechanism of resolution by marriage may have been more frequent in tragedy than we think; it is paralleled by the similar command to marry that Heracles gives to Hyllus at the end of the *Trachiniae* and by the command that Thetis gives in connection with Andromache and Helenus at the close of the *Andromache*.

infirmity so serious that it would have put a Silenus to shame. And so he made his most brilliant use of the multiple plot, describing the men of his special vision with a contradictory sequence of actions each one of which is grotesque and deformed. The impotent tyrant, the non-violent pursuer and the suppliants who never seek a shrine meet together on this stage; they are followed by the unheard rhetorician and the unenforced decree, and then the unsilent friend comes forth to urge an intrigue that will produce an unavenged enemy, an unredeemed hostage and an unslaughtered corpse, as well as a final unignited fire.

Orestes is weak, ill and threatened, and these qualities are displayed by a 'suppliant' action; he is alienated from home and power and thus fits into a 'rescue' piece; he would destroy his kin, and so he plays the hero of a 'vengeance tragedy' with its catastrophe supernaturally interrupted. Each of these classic overturns, however, refuses to turn over as it should, for he and his friends are scaled for the cot and the stool, not for altar, tomb, or throne. Pylades in his bravura victory over emasculated slaves is likened in parody to an Ajax (1480), Helen is silly, and Orestes manifestly cowardly and confused enough to have danced beside Silenus; indeed he appears to do just that in his scene with the fat Phrygian slave.[18] And so, when the three 'tragic' actions have ended in conglomerate failure, these characters can gather to play a scene that caps this drama as a satyr play once capped the trilogy. Orestes, Electra, Pylades, Menelaus, Hermione and Helen are all incontinently rescued and like the undeserving chorus of cowardly beast-men they are rewarded with freedom and love and, in Helen's case, with immortality. If there is a hint of caricature in the speed and the perversity of this salvation scene, it is because Apollo's smile must stretch to a grimace to take these creatures in, for they would try the patience of a god.

[18] Hartung in 1849 classified both *Alcestis* and *Orestes* as satyr drama, and A. Olivieri, *Riv. di Fil. Cl.* xxviii (1900), pp. 228 ff. set out to discuss the satyr elements in *Orestes* but ended by talking of satire instead. L. Radermacher compared the scene with the Phrygian to the scene on the Busiris cup; he concluded, principally on the basis of the dissimulation practised by Orestes and Pylades in their approach to Helen, that likenesses to satyr drama were consciously contrived in *Orestes* and that the piece was, like *Alcestis*, played fourth (*Rh. Mus.* lvii [1902], 278 ff.).

INDEX